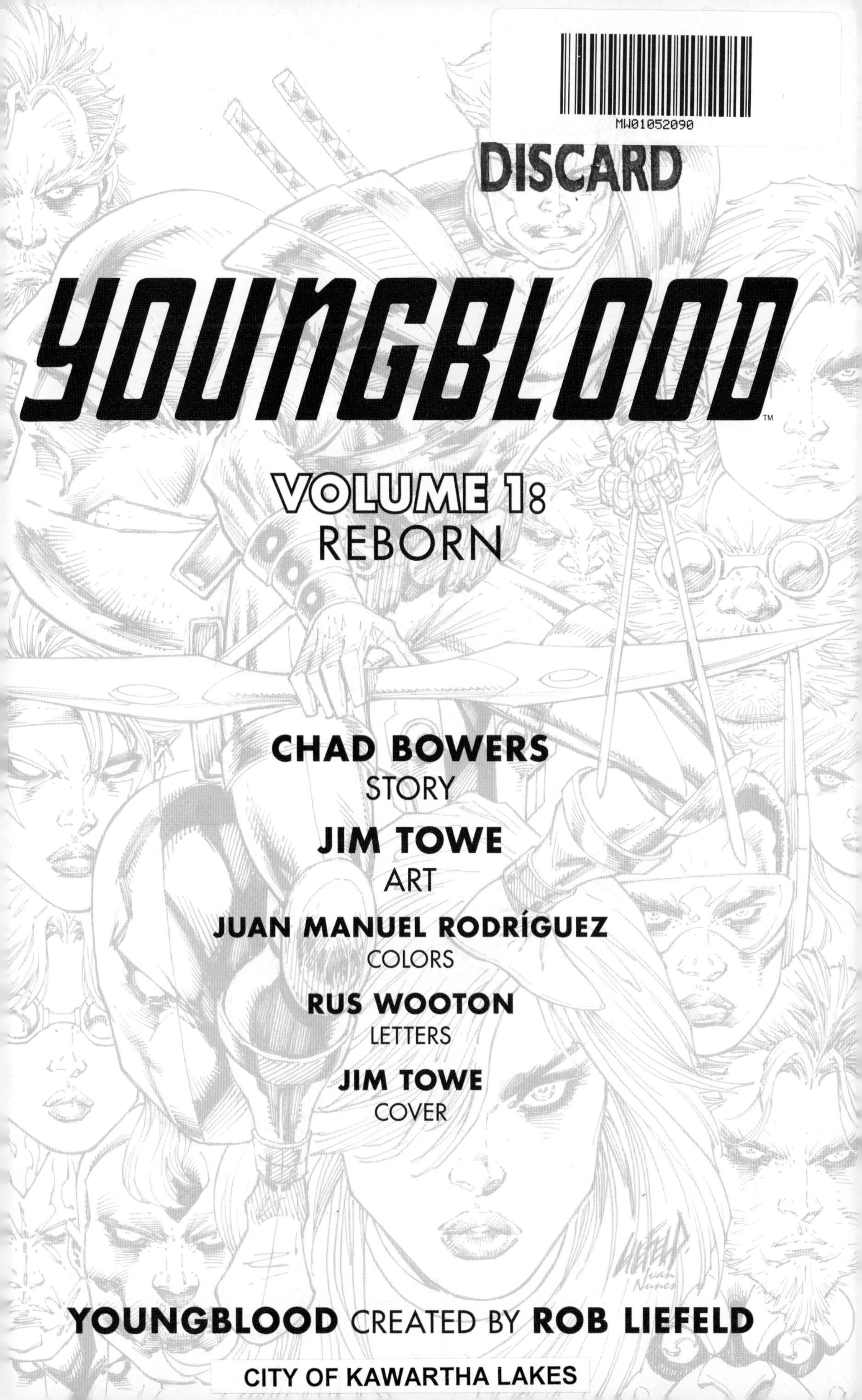

YOUNGBLOOD™

VOLUME 1: REBORN

CHAD BOWERS
STORY

JIM TOWE
ART

JUAN MANUEL RODRÍGUEZ
COLORS

RUS WOOTON
LETTERS

JIM TOWE
COVER

YOUNGBLOOD CREATED BY **ROB LIEFELD**

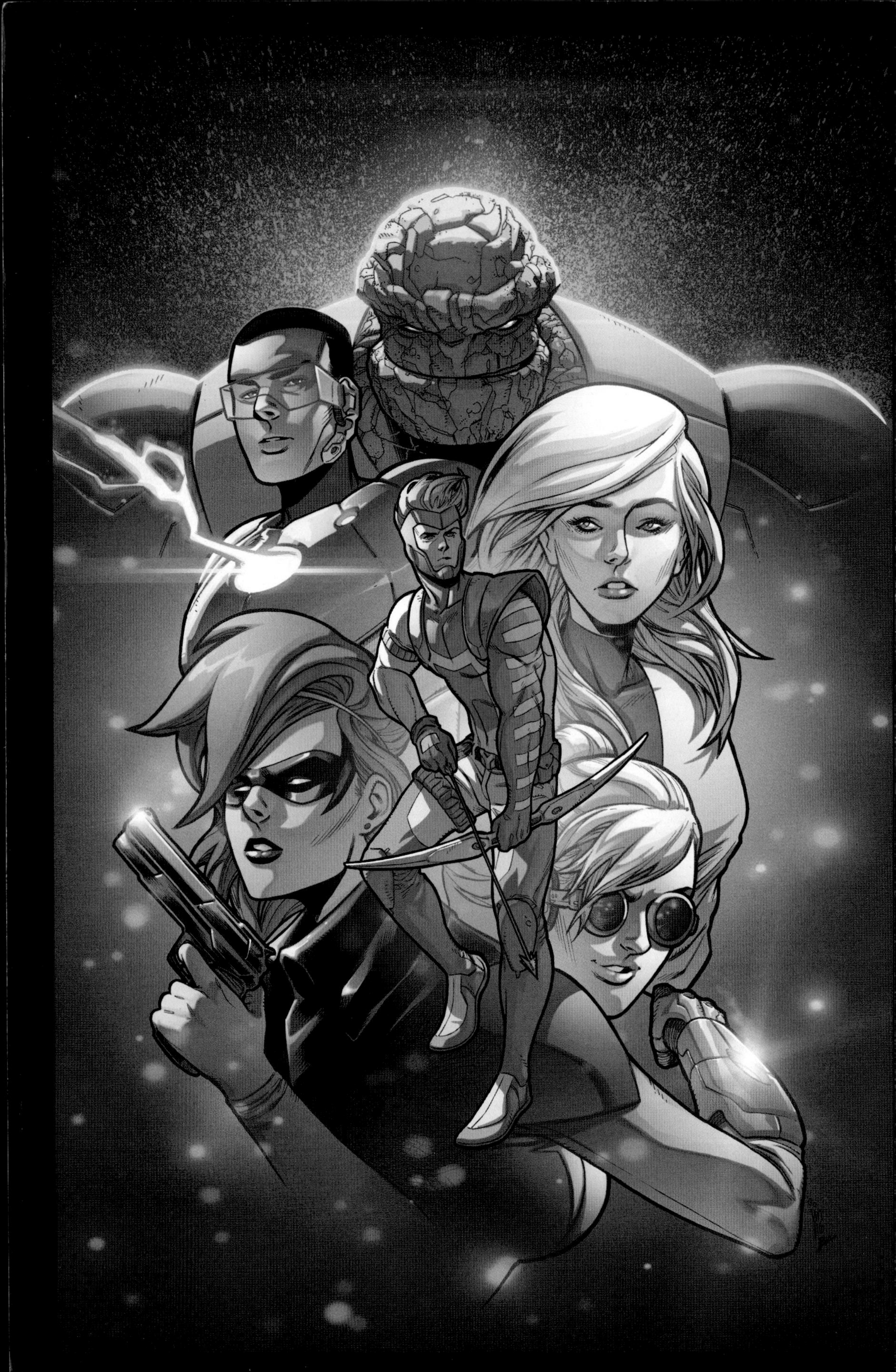

CHAPTER ONE: WHAT HAPPENED TO MAN-UP?

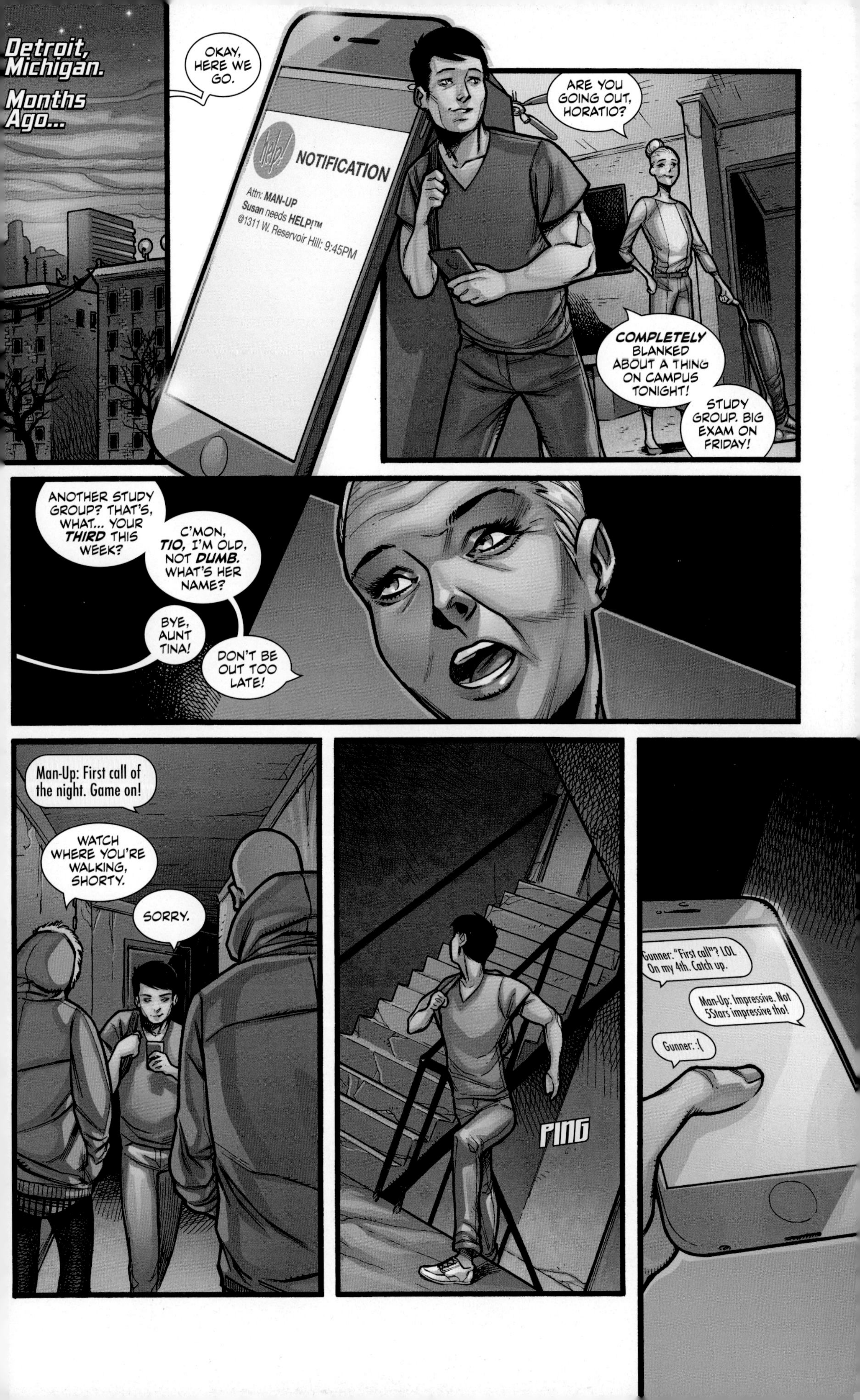
Detroit, Michigan.
Months Ago...
OKAY, HERE WE GO.
NOTIFICATION
Attn: MAN-UP
Susan needs HELP!™
@1311 W. Reservoir Hill: 9:45PM
ARE YOU GOING OUT, HORATIO?
COMPLETELY BLANKED ABOUT A THING ON CAMPUS TONIGHT!
STUDY GROUP. BIG EXAM ON FRIDAY!
ANOTHER STUDY GROUP? THAT'S, WHAT... YOUR THIRD THIS WEEK?
C'MON, TIO, I'M OLD, NOT DUMB. WHAT'S HER NAME?
BYE, AUNT TINA!
DON'T BE OUT TOO LATE!
Man-Up: First call of the night. Game on!
WATCH WHERE YOU'RE WALKING, SHORTY.
SORRY.
PING
Gunner: "First call"? LOL On my 4th. Catch up.
Man-Up: Impressive. Not 5Stars impressive tho!
Gunner: :\(

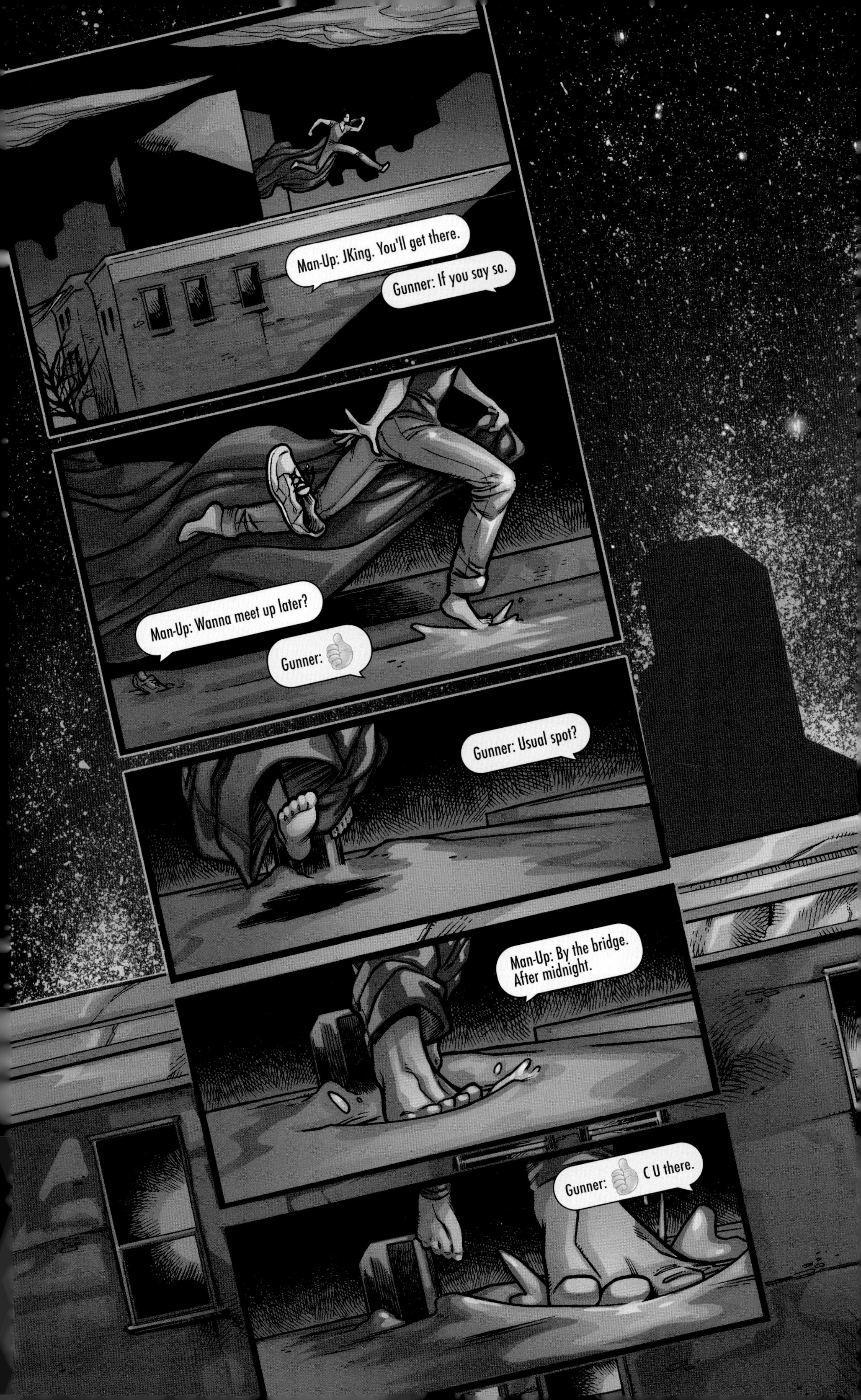
Man-Up: JKing. You'll get there.
Gunner: If you say so.
Man-Up: Wanna meet up later?
Gunner:
Gunner: Usual spot?
Man-Up: By the bridge. After midnight.
Gunner: C U there.

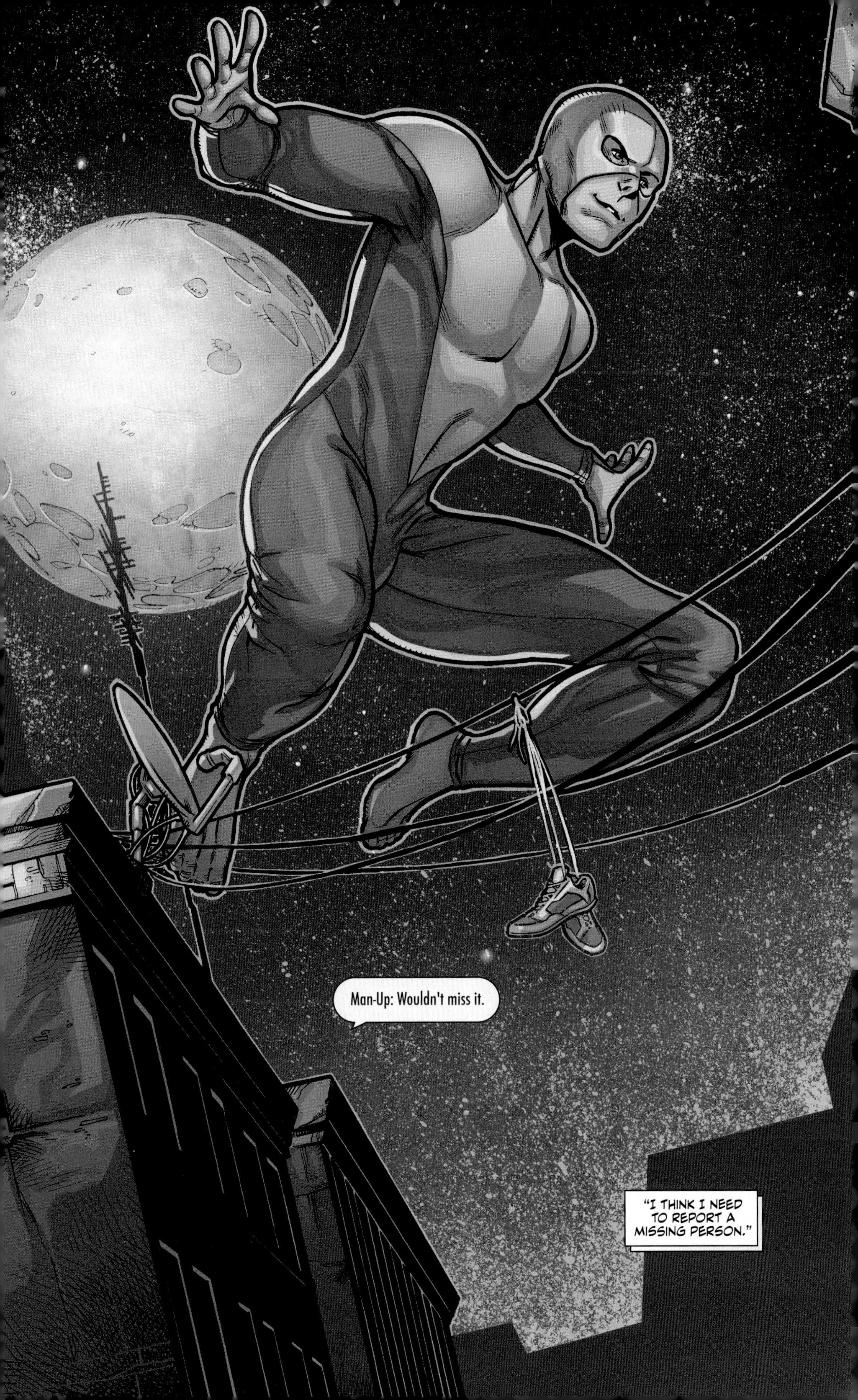
Man-Up: Wouldn't miss it.
"I THINK I NEED TO REPORT A MISSING PERSON."

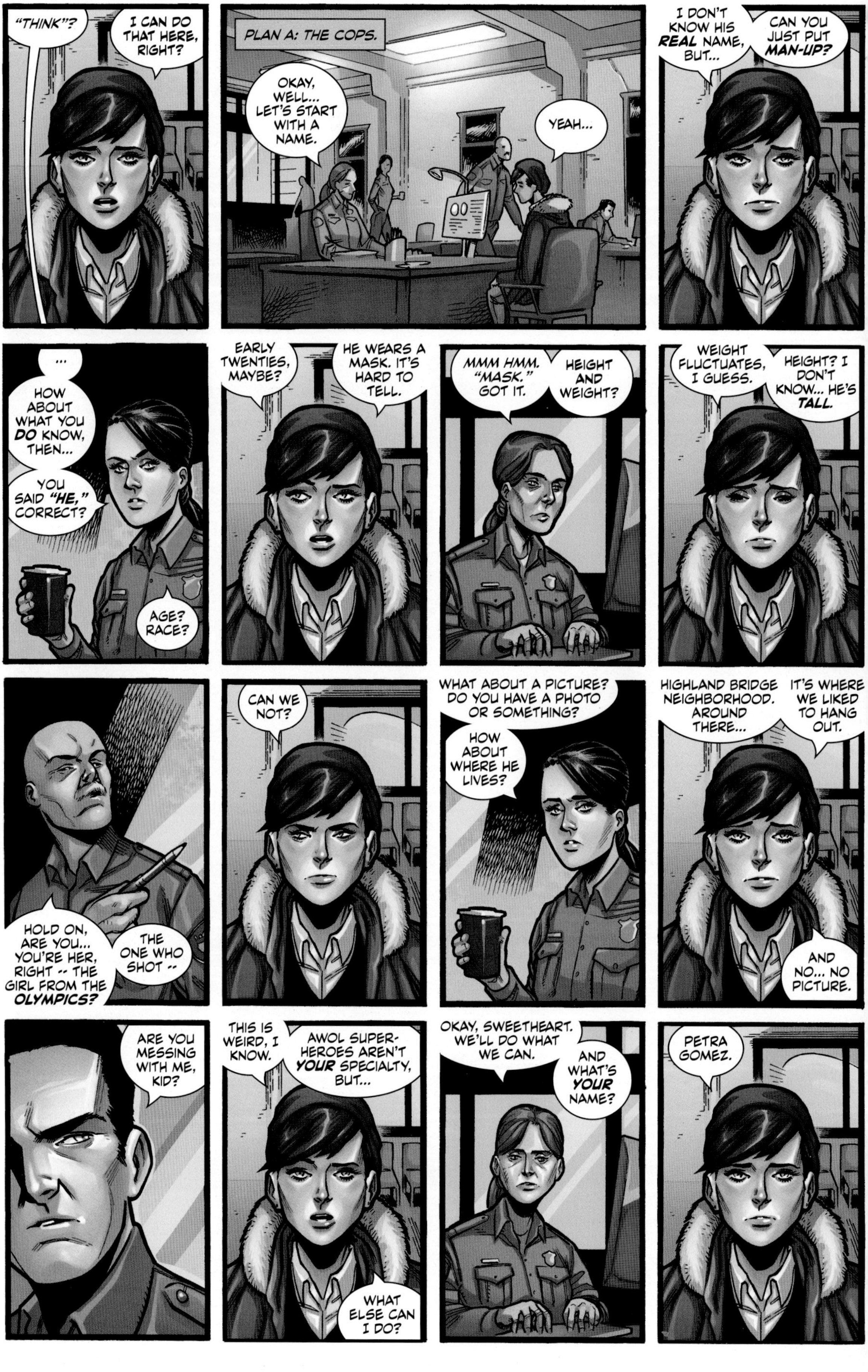
"THINK"?
I CAN DO THAT HERE, RIGHT?
PLAN A: THE COPS.
OKAY, WELL... LET'S START WITH A NAME.
YEAH...
I DON'T KNOW HIS REAL NAME, BUT...
CAN YOU JUST PUT MAN-UP?
...
HOW ABOUT WHAT YOU DO KNOW, THEN...
YOU SAID "HE," CORRECT?
AGE? RACE?
EARLY TWENTIES, MAYBE?
HE WEARS A MASK. IT'S HARD TO TELL.
MMM HMM. "MASK." GOT IT.
HEIGHT AND WEIGHT?
WEIGHT FLUCTUATES, I GUESS.
HEIGHT? I DON'T KNOW... HE'S TALL.
HOLD ON, ARE YOU... YOU'RE HER, RIGHT -- THE GIRL FROM THE OLYMPICS?
THE ONE WHO SHOT --
CAN WE NOT?
WHAT ABOUT A PICTURE? DO YOU HAVE A PHOTO OR SOMETHING?
HOW ABOUT WHERE HE LIVES?
HIGHLAND BRIDGE NEIGHBORHOOD. AROUND THERE...
IT'S WHERE WE LIKED TO HANG OUT.
AND NO... NO PICTURE.
ARE YOU MESSING WITH ME, KID?
THIS IS WEIRD, I KNOW.
AWOL SUPER-HEROES AREN'T YOUR SPECIALTY, BUT...
WHAT ELSE CAN I DO?
OKAY, SWEETHEART. WE'LL DO WHAT WE CAN.
AND WHAT'S YOUR NAME?
PETRA GOMEZ.

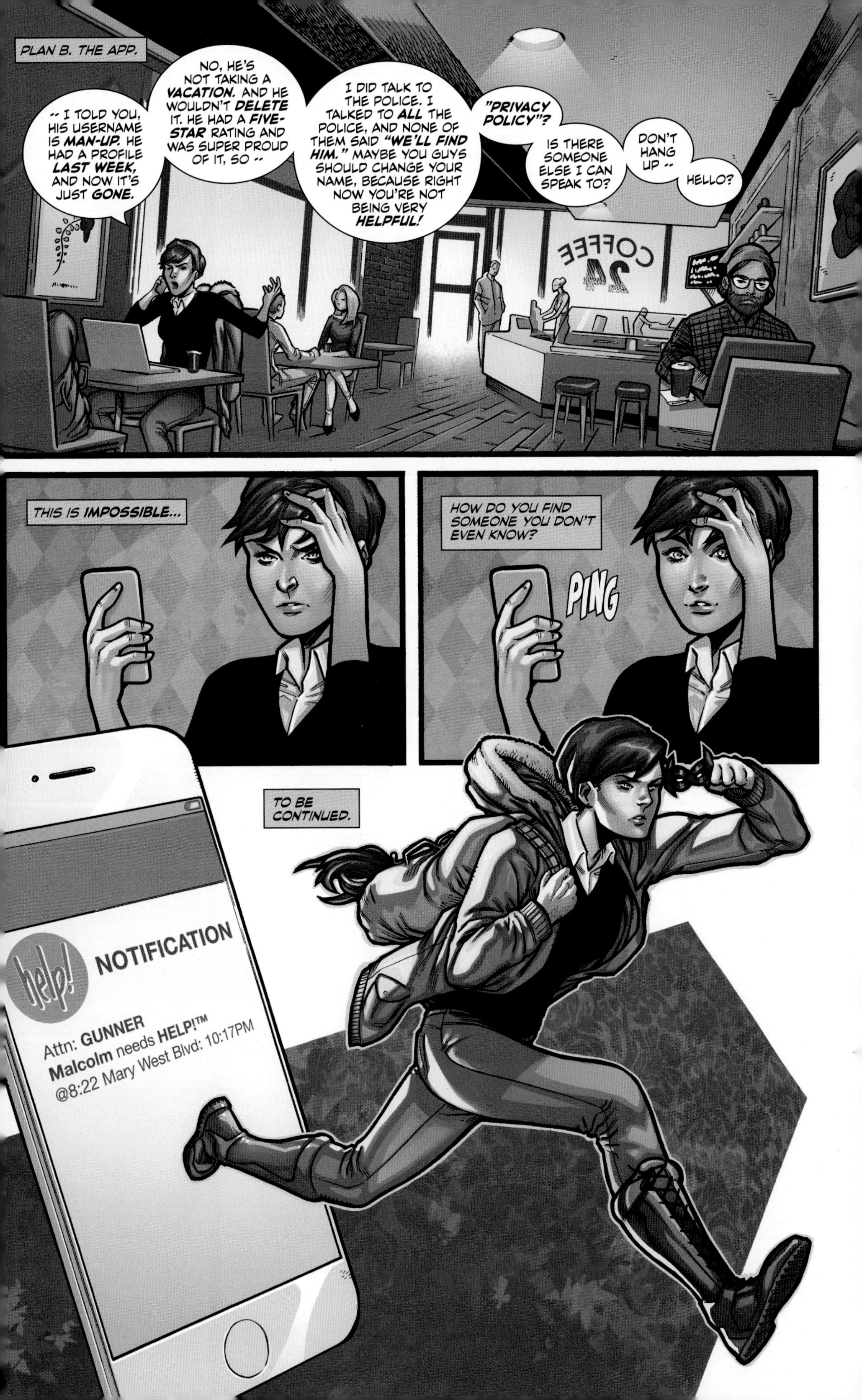
PLAN B. THE APP.
-- I TOLD YOU, HIS USERNAME IS MAN-UP. HE HAD A PROFILE LAST WEEK, AND NOW IT'S JUST GONE.
NO, HE'S NOT TAKING A VACATION. AND HE WOULDN'T DELETE IT. HE HAD A FIVE-STAR RATING AND WAS SUPER PROUD OF IT, SO --
I DID TALK TO THE POLICE. I TALKED TO ALL THE POLICE, AND NONE OF THEM SAID "WE'LL FIND HIM." MAYBE YOU GUYS SHOULD CHANGE YOUR NAME, BECAUSE RIGHT NOW YOU'RE NOT BEING VERY HELPFUL!
"PRIVACY POLICY"?
IS THERE SOMEONE ELSE I CAN SPEAK TO?
DON'T HANG UP --
HELLO?
COFFEE 24
THIS IS IMPOSSIBLE...
HOW DO YOU FIND SOMEONE YOU DON'T EVEN KNOW?
PING
TO BE CONTINUED.
help!
NOTIFICATION
Attn: GUNNER
Malcolm needs HELP!™
@8:22 Mary West Blvd: 10:17PM

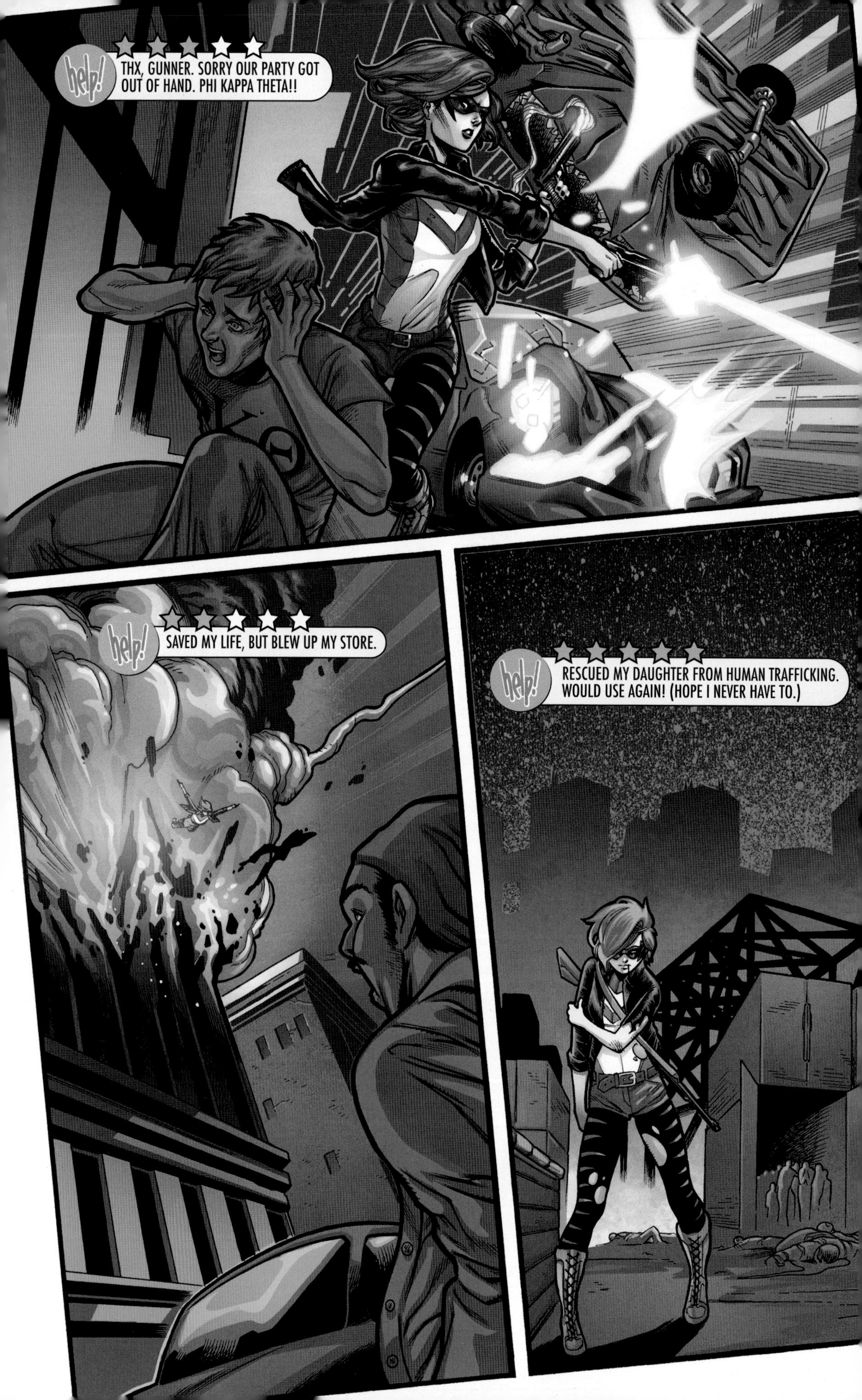
THX, GUNNER. SORRY OUR PARTY GOT OUT OF HAND. PHI KAPPA THETA!!
SAVED MY LIFE, BUT BLEW UP MY STORE.
RESCUED MY DAUGHTER FROM HUMAN TRAFFICKING. WOULD USE AGAIN! (HOPE I NEVER HAVE TO.)

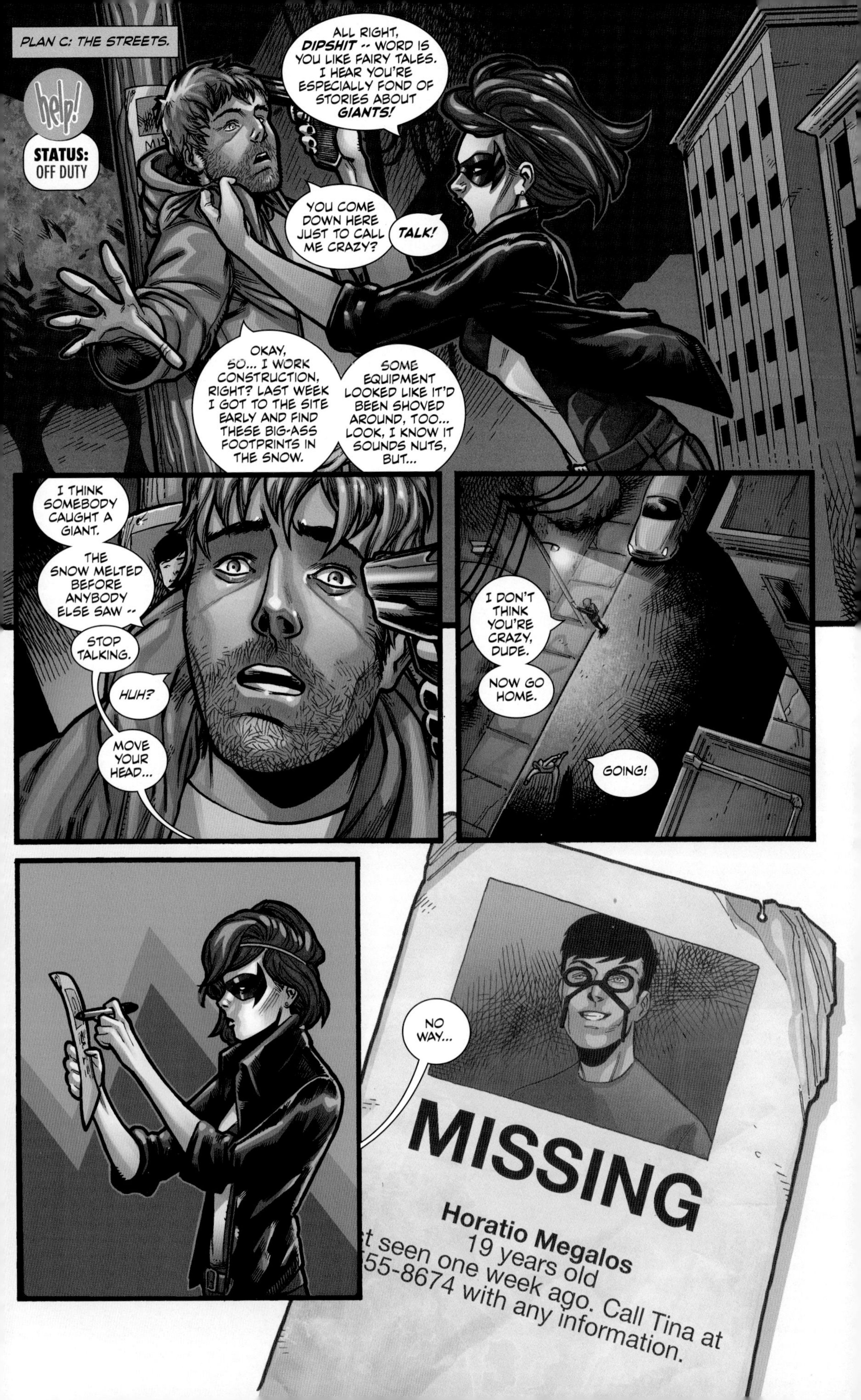
PLAN C: THE STREETS.
help!
STATUS: OFF DUTY
ALL RIGHT, DIPSHIT -- WORD IS YOU LIKE FAIRY TALES. I HEAR YOU'RE ESPECIALLY FOND OF STORIES ABOUT GIANTS!
YOU COME DOWN HERE JUST TO CALL ME CRAZY?
TALK!
OKAY, SO... I WORK CONSTRUCTION, RIGHT? LAST WEEK I GOT TO THE SITE EARLY AND FIND THESE BIG-ASS FOOTPRINTS IN THE SNOW.
SOME EQUIPMENT LOOKED LIKE IT'D BEEN SHOVED AROUND, TOO... LOOK, I KNOW IT SOUNDS NUTS, BUT...
I THINK SOMEBODY CAUGHT A GIANT.
THE SNOW MELTED BEFORE ANYBODY ELSE SAW --
STOP TALKING.
HUH?
MOVE YOUR HEAD...
I DON'T THINK YOU'RE CRAZY, DUDE.
NOW GO HOME.
GOING!
NO WAY...
MISSING
Horatio Megalos
19 years old
t seen one week ago. Call Tina at
55-8674 with any information.

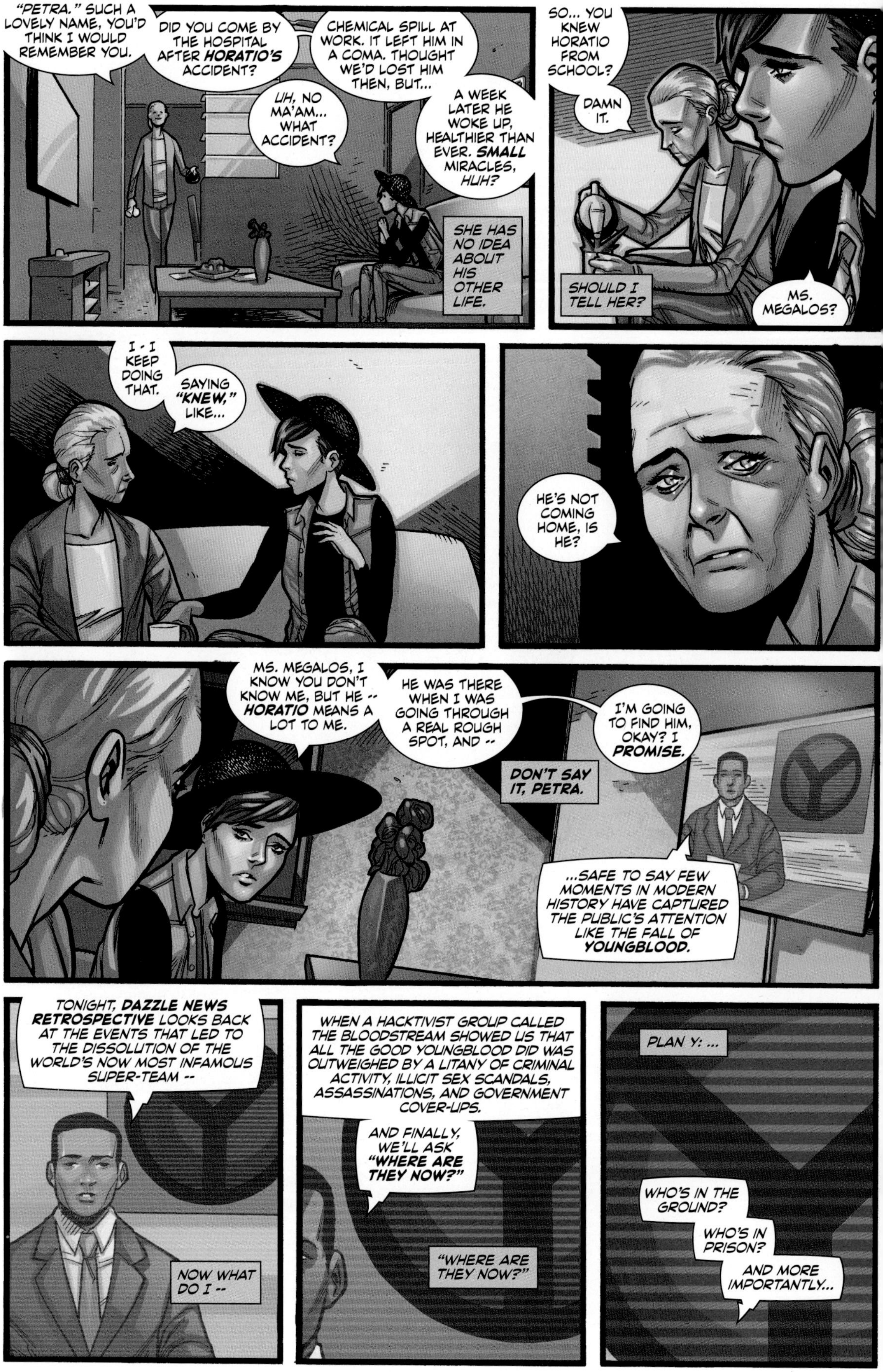
"PETRA." SUCH A LOVELY NAME, YOU'D THINK I WOULD REMEMBER YOU.
DID YOU COME BY THE HOSPITAL AFTER HORATIO'S ACCIDENT?
UH, NO MA'AM... WHAT ACCIDENT?
CHEMICAL SPILL AT WORK. IT LEFT HIM IN A COMA. THOUGHT WE'D LOST HIM THEN, BUT...
A WEEK LATER HE WOKE UP, HEALTHIER THAN EVER. SMALL MIRACLES, HUH?
SHE HAS NO IDEA ABOUT HIS OTHER LIFE.
SO... YOU KNEW HORATIO FROM SCHOOL?
DAMN IT.
SHOULD I TELL HER?
MS. MEGALOS?
I - I KEEP DOING THAT.
SAYING "KNEW," LIKE...
HE'S NOT COMING HOME, IS HE?
MS. MEGALOS, I KNOW YOU DON'T KNOW ME, BUT HE -- HORATIO MEANS A LOT TO ME.
HE WAS THERE WHEN I WAS GOING THROUGH A REAL ROUGH SPOT, AND --
I'M GOING TO FIND HIM, OKAY? I PROMISE.
DON'T SAY IT, PETRA.
...SAFE TO SAY FEW MOMENTS IN MODERN HISTORY HAVE CAPTURED THE PUBLIC'S ATTENTION LIKE THE FALL OF YOUNGBLOOD.
TONIGHT, DAZZLE NEWS RETROSPECTIVE LOOKS BACK AT THE EVENTS THAT LED TO THE DISSOLUTION OF THE WORLD'S NOW MOST INFAMOUS SUPER-TEAM --
NOW WHAT DO I --
WHEN A HACKTIVIST GROUP CALLED THE BLOODSTREAM SHOWED US THAT ALL THE GOOD YOUNGBLOOD DID WAS OUTWEIGHED BY A LITANY OF CRIMINAL ACTIVITY, ILLICIT SEX SCANDALS, ASSASSINATIONS, AND GOVERNMENT COVER-UPS.
AND FINALLY, WE'LL ASK "WHERE ARE THEY NOW?"
"WHERE ARE THEY NOW?"
PLAN Y: ...
WHO'S IN THE GROUND?
WHO'S IN PRISON?
AND MORE IMPORTANTLY...

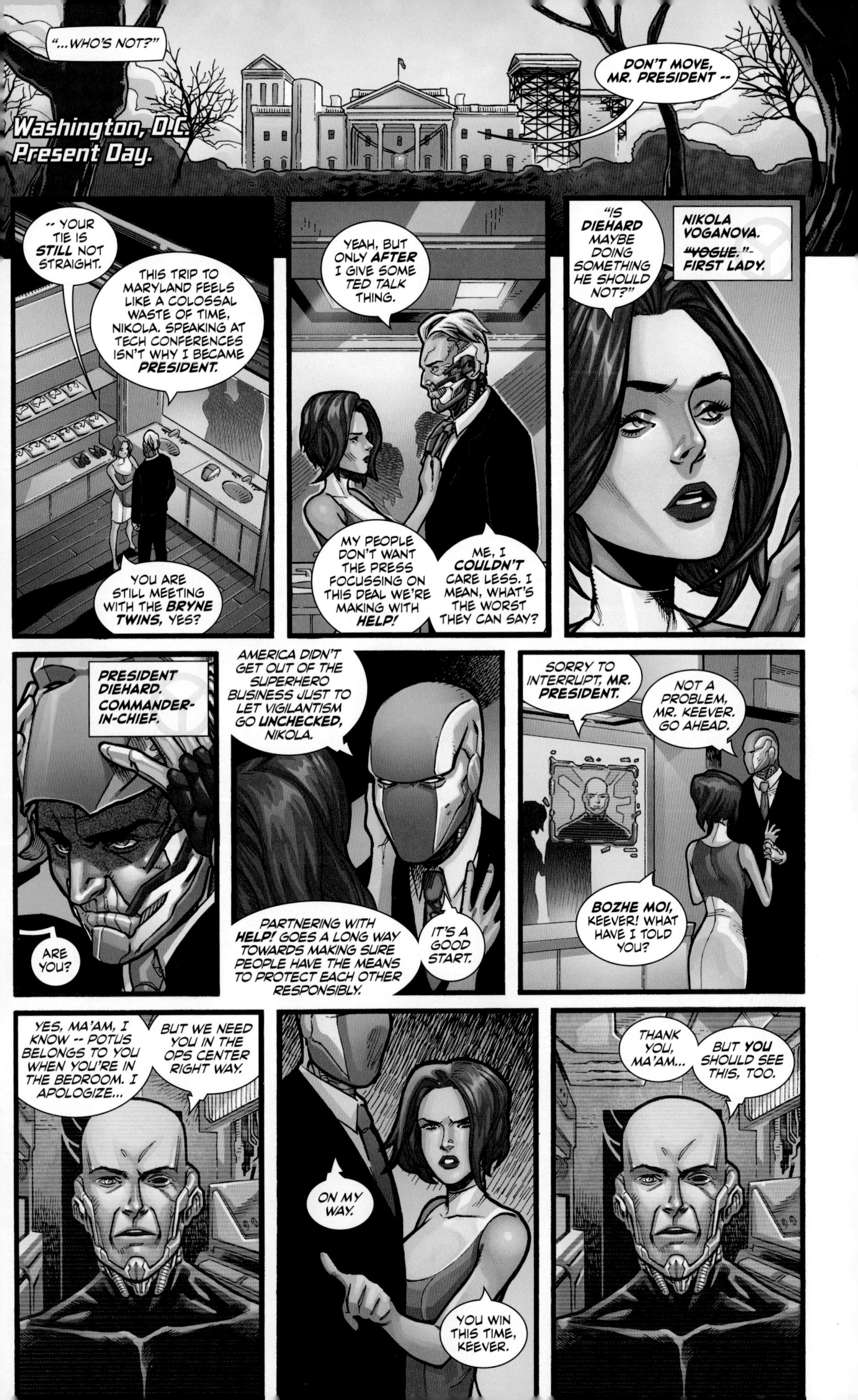
"...WHO'S NOT?"
DON'T MOVE, MR. PRESIDENT --
Washington, D.C. Present Day.
-- YOUR TIE IS STILL NOT STRAIGHT.
THIS TRIP TO MARYLAND FEELS LIKE A COLOSSAL WASTE OF TIME, NIKOLA. SPEAKING AT TECH CONFERENCES ISN'T WHY I BECAME PRESIDENT.
YOU ARE STILL MEETING WITH THE BRYNE TWINS, YES?
YEAH, BUT ONLY AFTER I GIVE SOME TED TALK THING.
MY PEOPLE DON'T WANT THE PRESS FOCUSSING ON THIS DEAL WE'RE MAKING WITH HELP!
ME, I COULDN'T CARE LESS. I MEAN, WHAT'S THE WORST THEY CAN SAY?
"IS DIEHARD MAYBE DOING SOMETHING HE SHOULD NOT?"
NIKOLA VOGANOVA. ~~"VOGUE."~~- FIRST LADY.
PRESIDENT DIEHARD. COMMANDER-IN-CHIEF.
ARE YOU?
AMERICA DIDN'T GET OUT OF THE SUPERHERO BUSINESS JUST TO LET VIGILANTISM GO UNCHECKED, NIKOLA.
PARTNERING WITH HELP! GOES A LONG WAY TOWARDS MAKING SURE PEOPLE HAVE THE MEANS TO PROTECT EACH OTHER RESPONSIBLY.
IT'S A GOOD START.
SORRY TO INTERRUPT, MR. PRESIDENT.
NOT A PROBLEM, MR. KEEVER. GO AHEAD.
BOZHE MOI, KEEVER! WHAT HAVE I TOLD YOU?
YES, MA'AM, I KNOW -- POTUS BELONGS TO YOU WHEN YOU'RE IN THE BEDROOM. I APOLOGIZE...
BUT WE NEED YOU IN THE OPS CENTER RIGHT WAY.
ON MY WAY.
YOU WIN THIS TIME, KEEVER.
THANK YOU, MA'AM...
BUT YOU SHOULD SEE THIS, TOO.

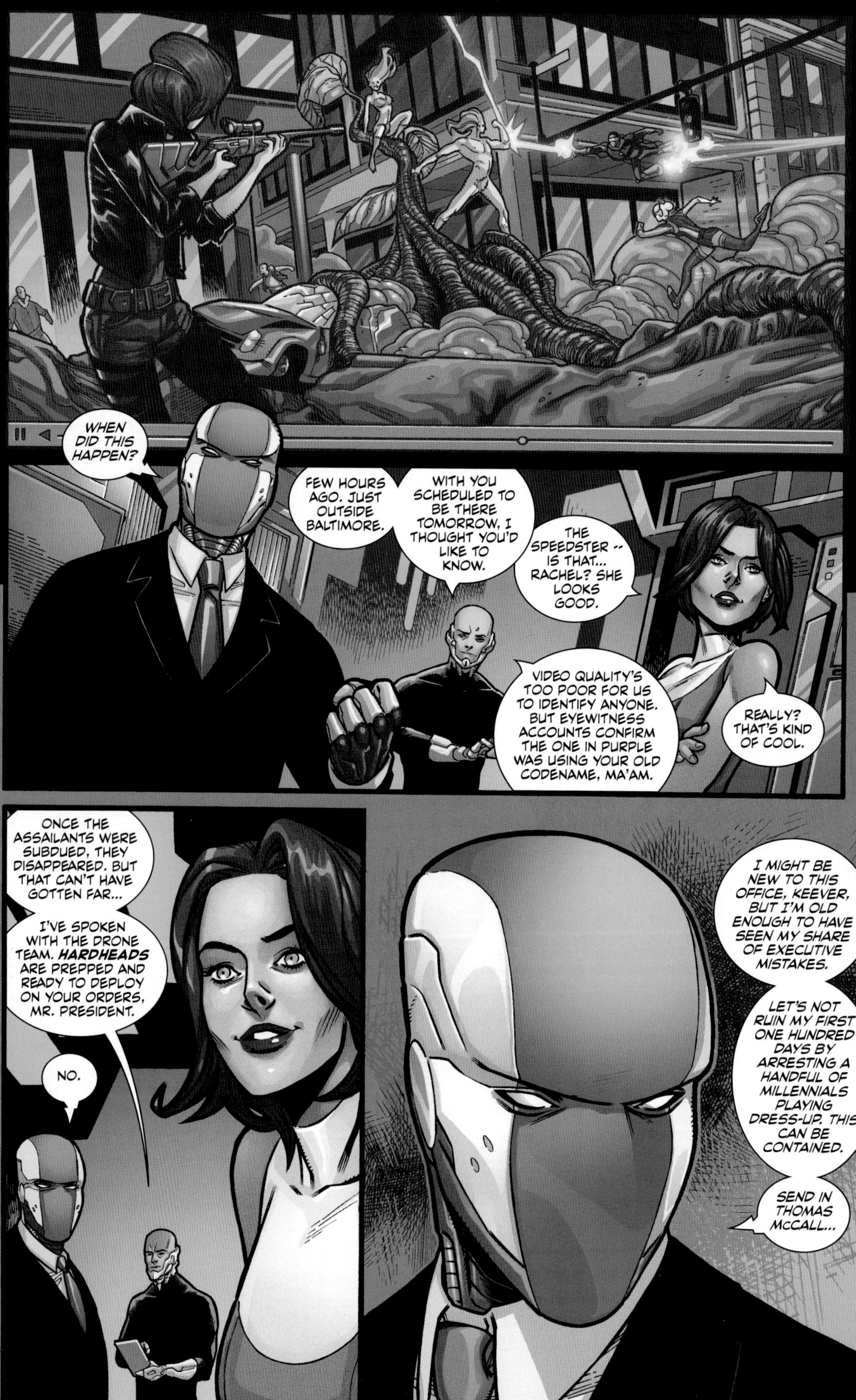
WHEN DID THIS HAPPEN?
FEW HOURS AGO. JUST OUTSIDE BALTIMORE.
WITH YOU SCHEDULED TO BE THERE TOMORROW, I THOUGHT YOU'D LIKE TO KNOW.
THE SPEEDSTER -- IS THAT... RACHEL? SHE LOOKS GOOD.
VIDEO QUALITY'S TOO POOR FOR US TO IDENTIFY ANYONE. BUT EYEWITNESS ACCOUNTS CONFIRM THE ONE IN PURPLE WAS USING YOUR OLD CODENAME, MA'AM.
REALLY? THAT'S KIND OF COOL.
ONCE THE ASSAILANTS WERE SUBDUED, THEY DISAPPEARED. BUT THAT CAN'T HAVE GOTTEN FAR...
I'VE SPOKEN WITH THE DRONE TEAM. HARDHEADS ARE PREPPED AND READY TO DEPLOY ON YOUR ORDERS, MR. PRESIDENT.
NO.
I MIGHT BE NEW TO THIS OFFICE, KEEVER, BUT I'M OLD ENOUGH TO HAVE SEEN MY SHARE OF EXECUTIVE MISTAKES.
LET'S NOT RUIN MY FIRST ONE HUNDRED DAYS BY ARRESTING A HANDFUL OF MILLENNIALS PLAYING DRESS-UP. THIS CAN BE CONTAINED.
SEND IN THOMAS McCALL...

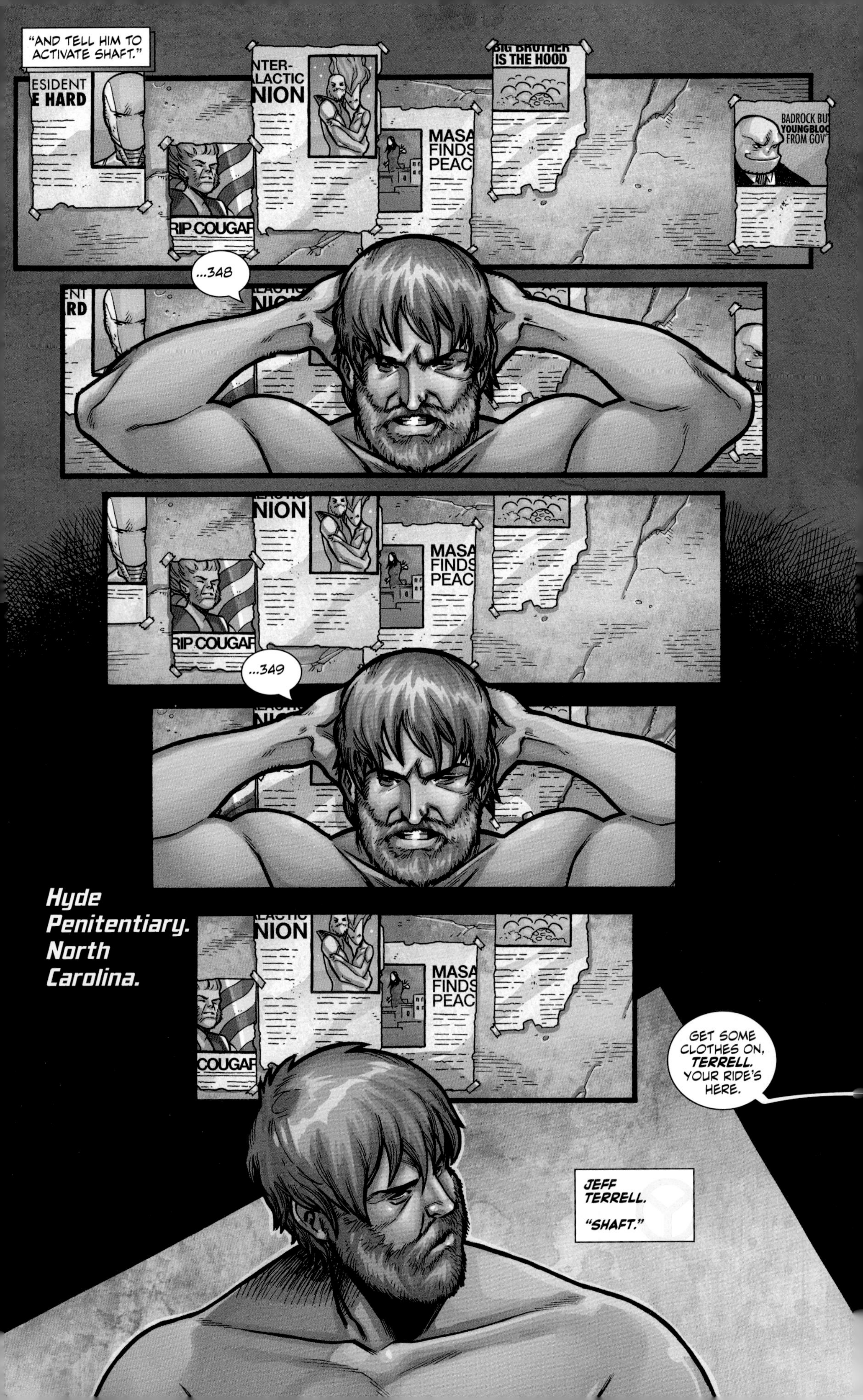
"AND TELL HIM TO ACTIVATE SHAFT."
...348
...349
Hyde Penitentiary. North Carolina.
GET SOME CLOTHES ON, TERRELL. YOUR RIDE'S HERE.
JEFF TERRELL.
"SHAFT."

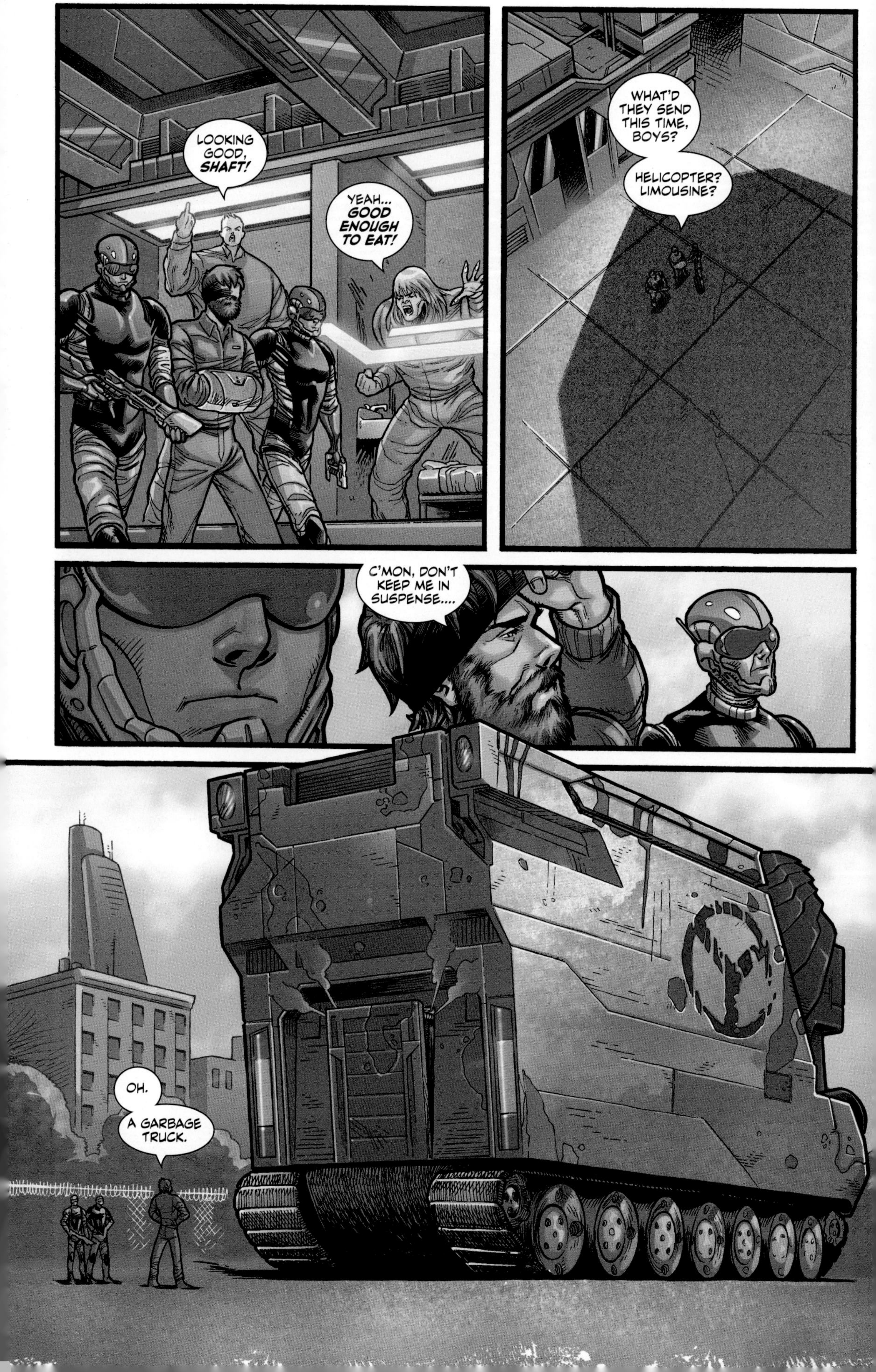
LOOKING GOOD, *SHAFT!*
YEAH... *GOOD ENOUGH TO EAT!*
WHAT'D THEY SEND THIS TIME, BOYS?
HELICOPTER? LIMOUSINE?
C'MON, DON'T KEEP ME IN SUSPENSE....
OH.
A GARBAGE TRUCK.

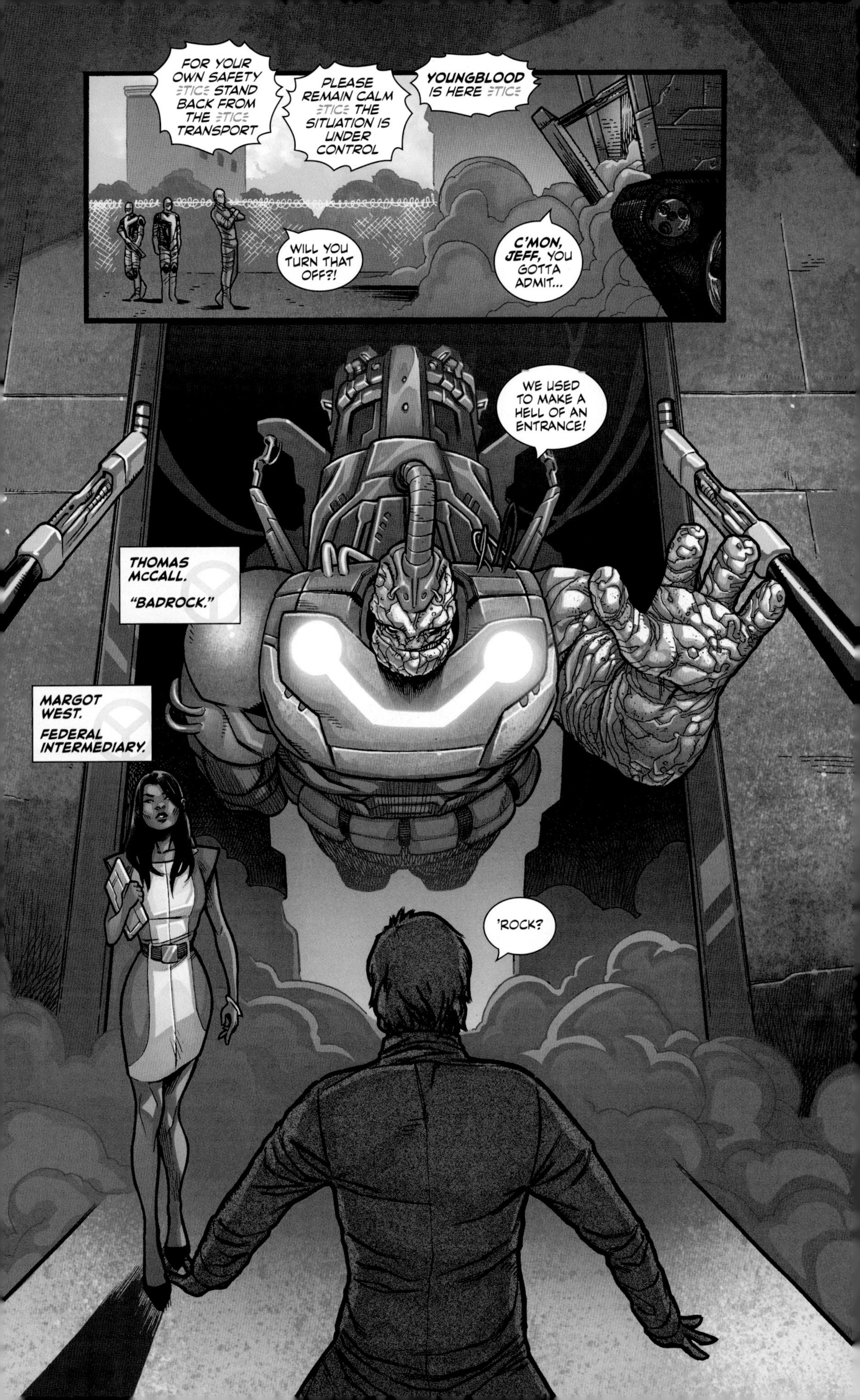
FOR YOUR OWN SAFETY TIC STAND BACK FROM THE TIC TRANSPORT
PLEASE REMAIN CALM TIC THE SITUATION IS UNDER CONTROL
YOUNGBLOOD IS HERE TIC
WILL YOU TURN THAT OFF?!
C'MON, JEFF, YOU GOTTA ADMIT...
WE USED TO MAKE A HELL OF AN ENTRANCE!
THOMAS McCALL.
"BADROCK."
MARGOT WEST.
FEDERAL INTERMEDIARY.
'ROCK?

THANK YOU, GENTLEMEN. WE CAN TAKE IT FROM HERE.

TOM, HEY... WHAT IS THIS? WHAT HAPPENED?

EH, IT'S JUST A THING I'M DEALING WITH.

DOCTORS ARE CALLING IT "MCCALL'S SYNDROME."

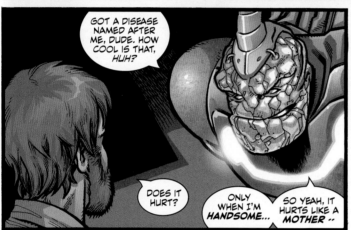

GOT A DISEASE NAMED AFTER ME, DUDE. HOW COOL IS THAT, HUH?

DOES IT HURT?

ONLY WHEN I'M HANDSOME...

SO YEAH, IT HURTS LIKE A MOTHER --

KAAFF KAAFF

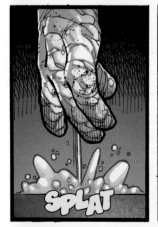

SPLAT

SO HE'S... COUGHING UP MUD?

I DON'T CARE WHERE WE'RE HEADED, MARGOT. HE SHOULDN'T BE GOING ON ANY MISSIONS.

SHARP-EYED AS EVER, MR. TERRELL.

UNFORTUNATELY, DUE TO THE TERMS OF YOUR PROVISIONAL RELEASE, MR. MCCALL HAS VERY LITTLE CHOICE IN THE MATTER.

YOU TWO ARE A PACKAGE DEAL.

WHAT SHE'S TRYING TO SAY IS, "GET YOUR ASS IN THE CRAWLER, BEARDO!"

WE'VE GOT PLACES TO BE.

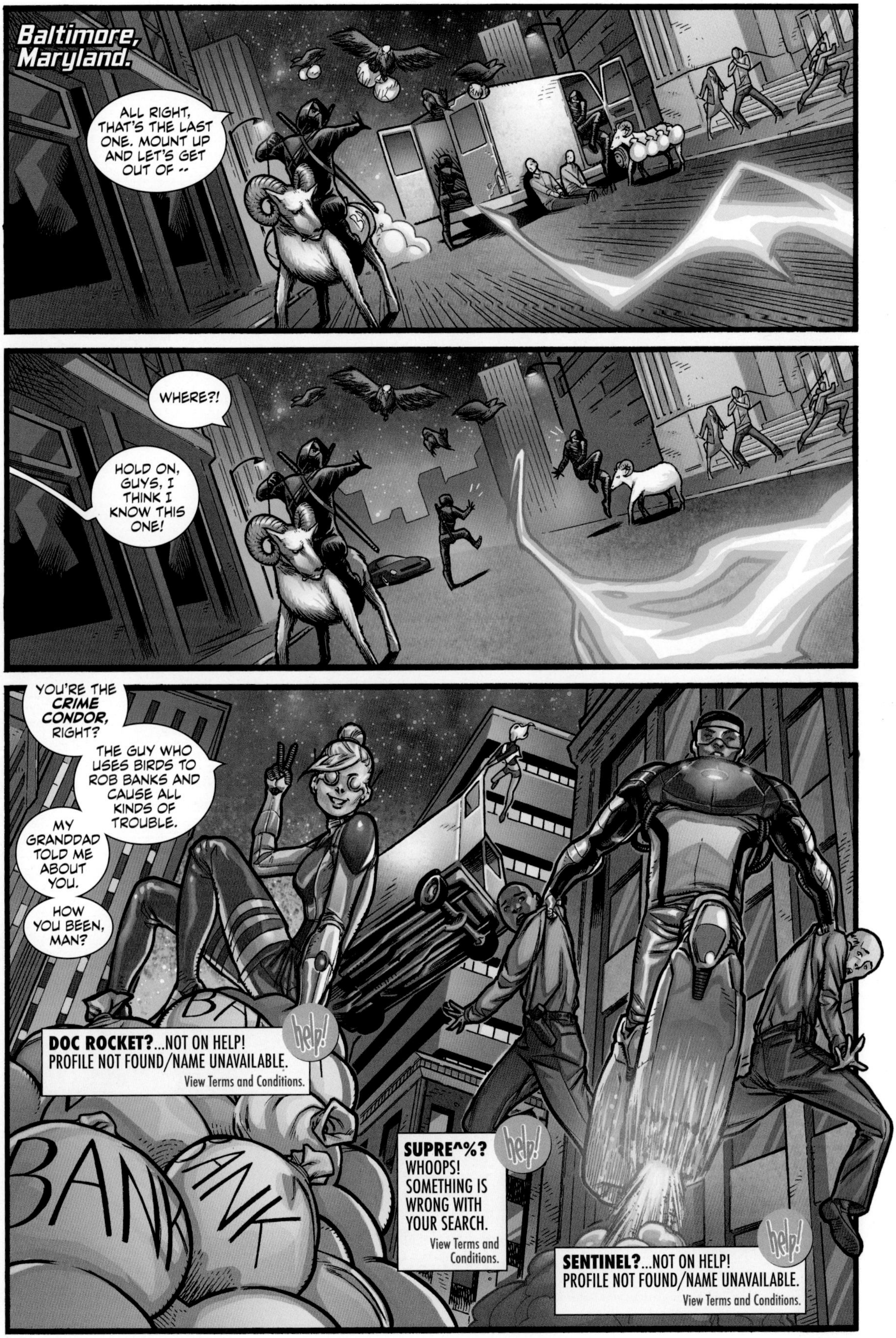
Baltimore, Maryland.
ALL RIGHT, THAT'S THE LAST ONE. MOUNT UP AND LET'S GET OUT OF --
WHERE?!
HOLD ON, GUYS, I THINK I KNOW THIS ONE!
YOU'RE THE ***CRIME CONDOR***, RIGHT?
THE GUY WHO USES BIRDS TO ROB BANKS AND CAUSE ALL KINDS OF TROUBLE.
MY GRANDDAD TOLD ME ABOUT YOU.
HOW YOU BEEN, MAN?
help!
DOC ROCKET?...NOT ON HELP! PROFILE NOT FOUND/NAME UNAVAILABLE.
View Terms and Conditions.
BANK
help!
SUPRE^%? WHOOPS! SOMETHING IS WRONG WITH YOUR SEARCH.
View Terms and Conditions.
help!
SENTINEL?...NOT ON HELP! PROFILE NOT FOUND/NAME UNAVAILABLE.
View Terms and Conditions.

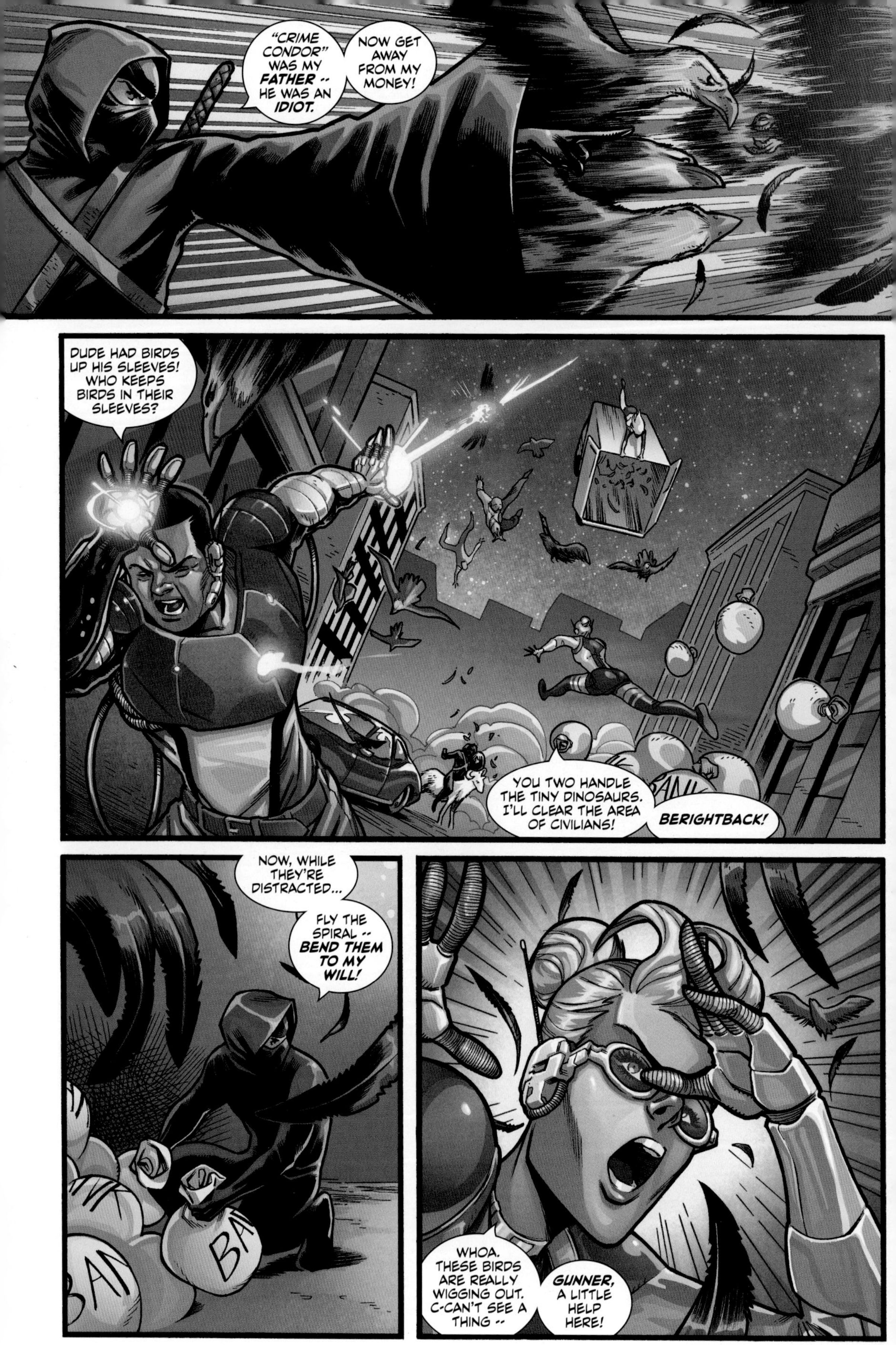
"CRIME CONDOR" WAS MY **FATHER** -- HE WAS AN **IDIOT.**
NOW GET AWAY FROM MY MONEY!
DUDE HAD BIRDS UP HIS SLEEVES! WHO KEEPS BIRDS IN THEIR SLEEVES?
YOU TWO HANDLE THE TINY DINOSAURS. I'LL CLEAR THE AREA OF CIVILIANS!
BERIGHTBACK!
NOW, WHILE THEY'RE DISTRACTED...
FLY THE SPIRAL -- **BEND THEM TO MY WILL!**
WHOA. THESE BIRDS ARE REALLY WIGGING OUT. C-CAN'T SEE A THING --
GUNNER, A LITTLE HELP HERE!

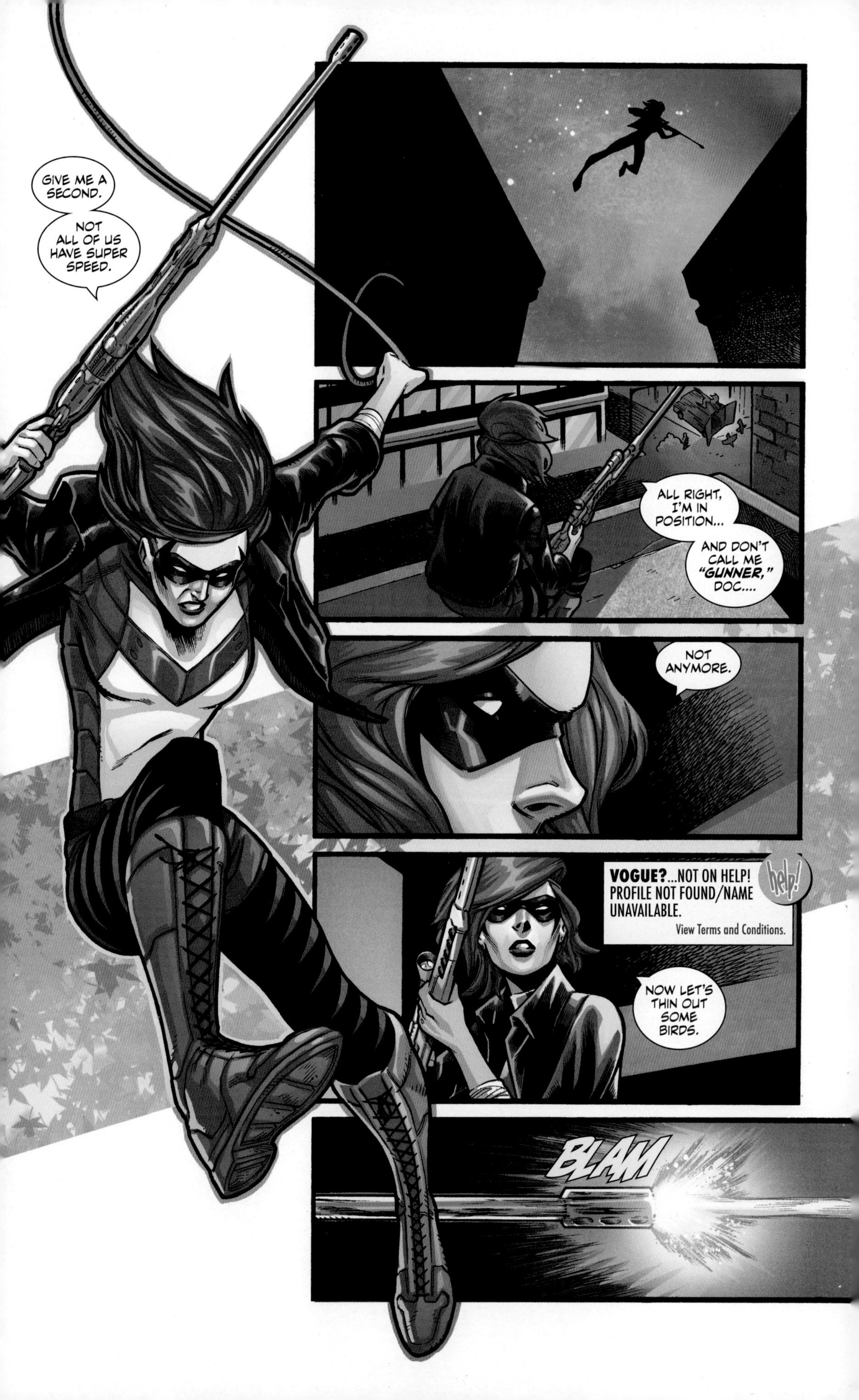
GIVE ME A SECOND.
NOT ALL OF US HAVE SUPER SPEED.
ALL RIGHT, I'M IN POSITION...
AND DON'T CALL ME "GUNNER," DOC....
NOT ANYMORE.
VOGUE?...NOT ON HELP! PROFILE NOT FOUND/NAME UNAVAILABLE.
View Terms and Conditions.
help!
NOW LET'S THIN OUT SOME BIRDS.
BLAM

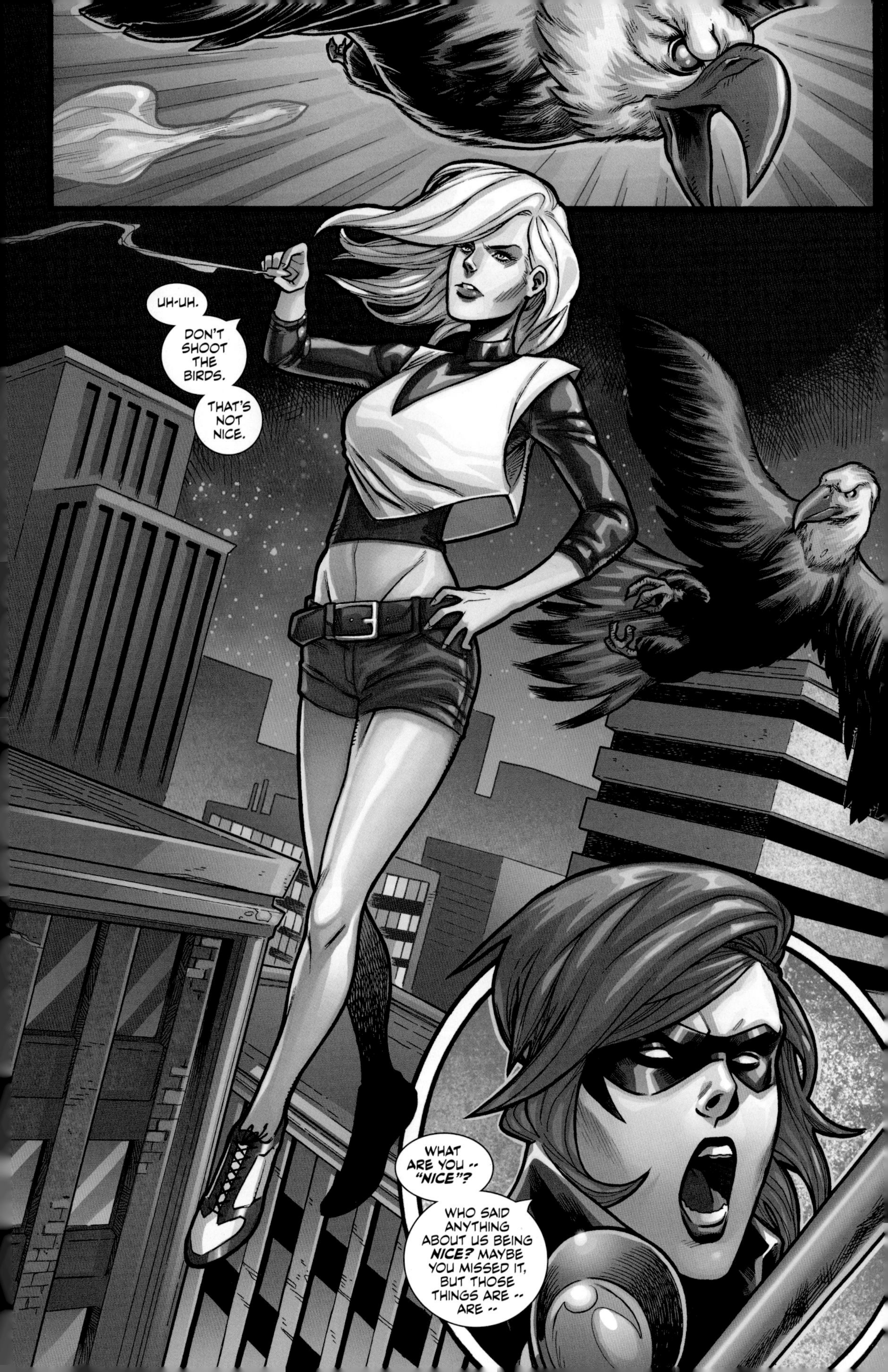
UH-UH.
DON'T SHOOT THE BIRDS.
THAT'S NOT NICE.
WHAT ARE YOU -- "NICE"?
WHO SAID ANYTHING ABOUT US BEING NICE? MAYBE YOU MISSED IT, BUT THOSE THINGS ARE -- ARE --

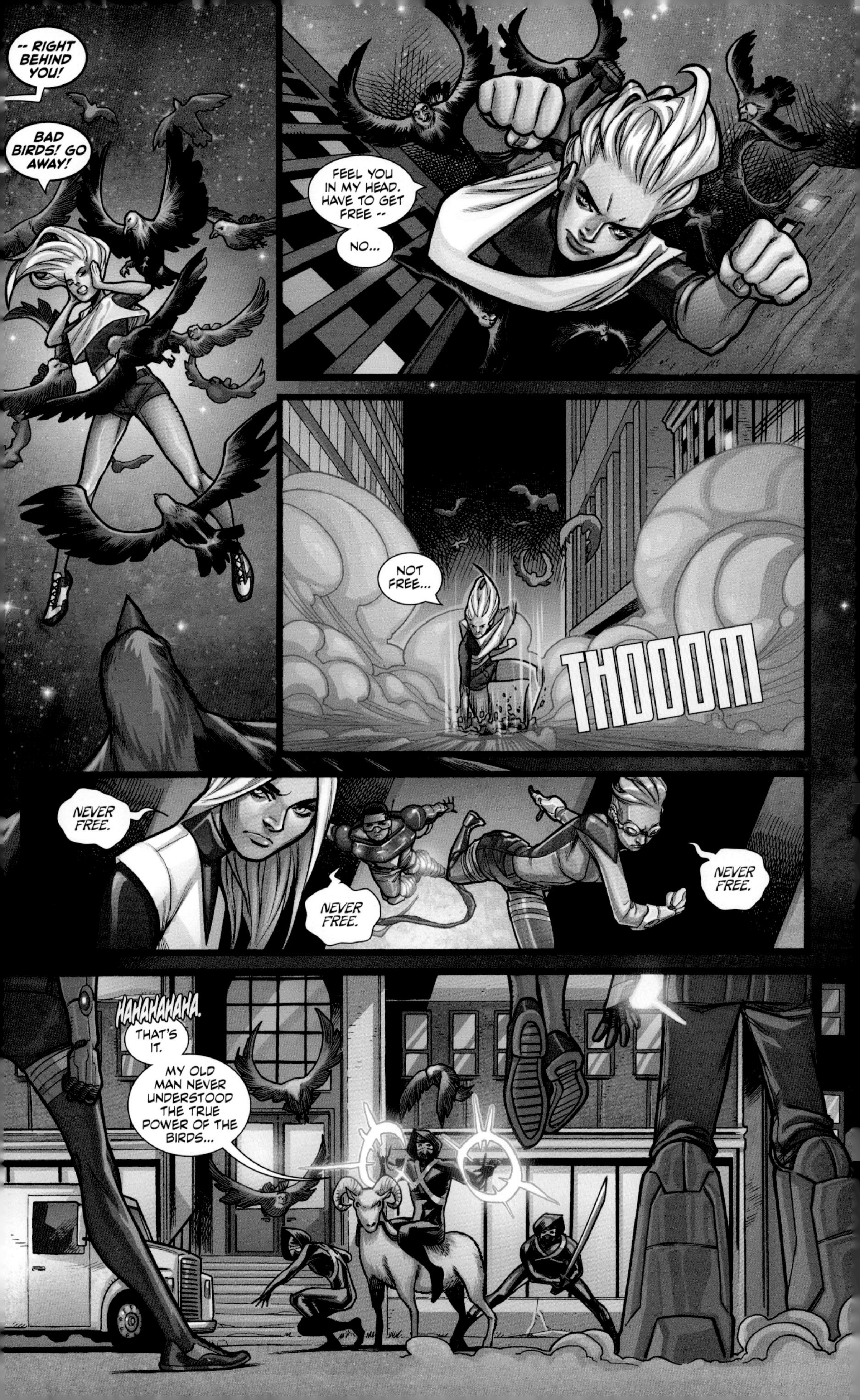
-- RIGHT BEHIND YOU!
BAD BIRDS! GO AWAY!
FEEL YOU IN MY HEAD. HAVE TO GET FREE --
NO...
NOT FREE...
THOOOM
NEVER FREE.
NEVER FREE.
NEVER FREE.
HAHAHAHAHA.
THAT'S IT.
MY OLD MAN NEVER UNDERSTOOD THE TRUE POWER OF THE BIRDS...

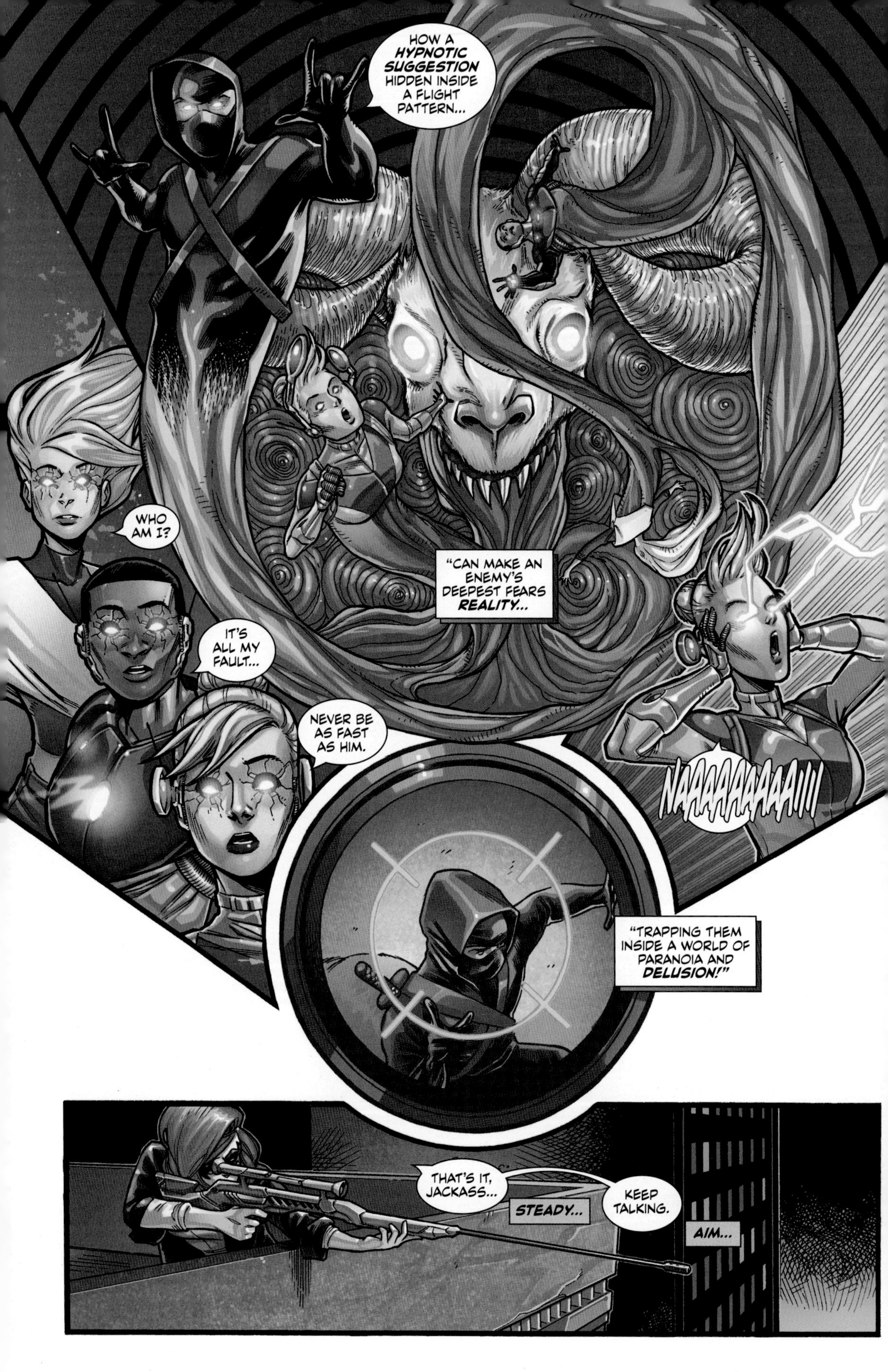
HOW A HYPNOTIC SUGGESTION HIDDEN INSIDE A FLIGHT PATTERN...
WHO AM I?
"CAN MAKE AN ENEMY'S DEEPEST FEARS REALITY...
IT'S ALL MY FAULT...
NEVER BE AS FAST AS HIM.
NAAAAAAAAAIIII
"TRAPPING THEM INSIDE A WORLD OF PARANOIA AND DELUSION!"
THAT'S IT, JACKASS...
STEADY...
KEEP TALKING.
AIM...

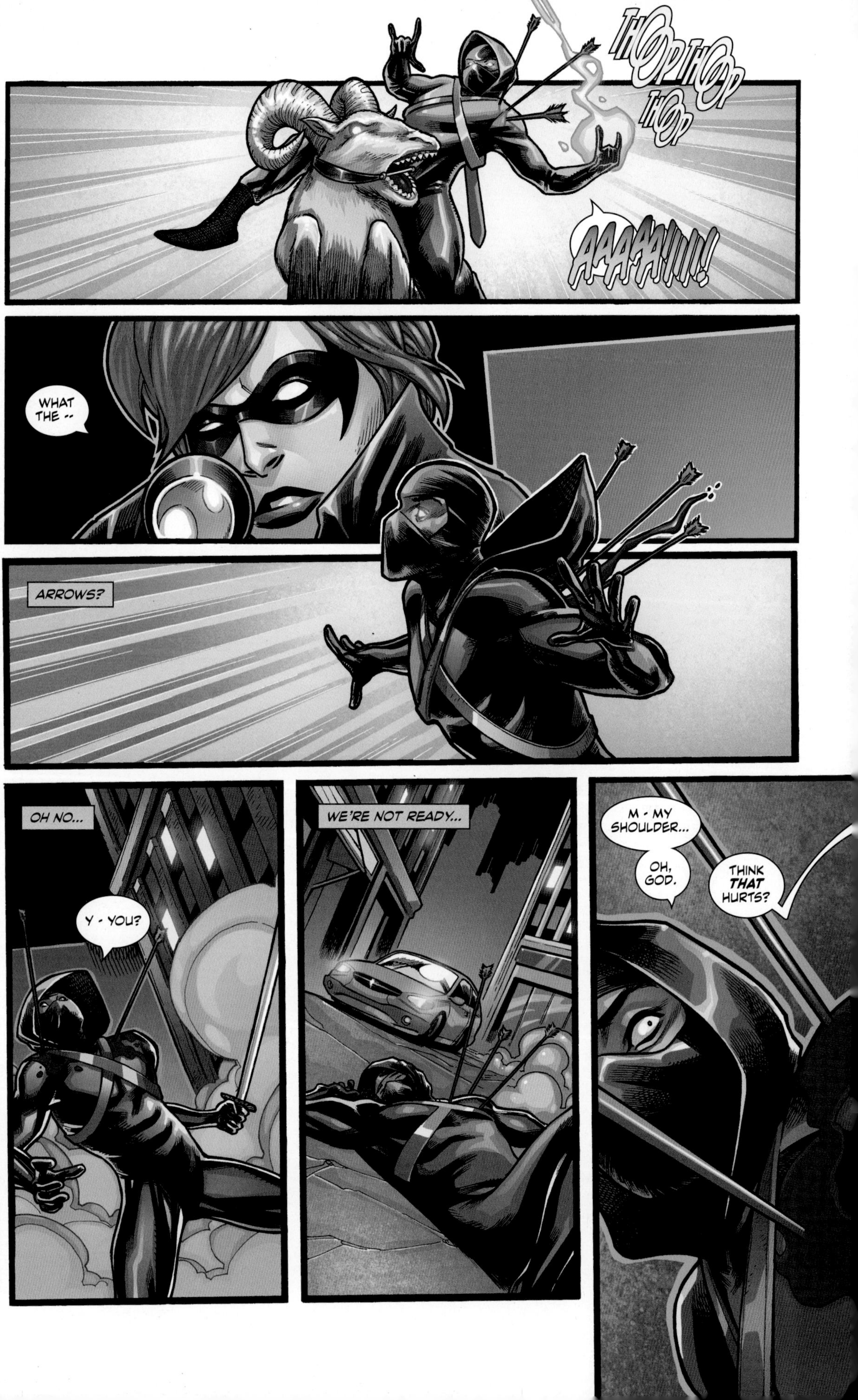
THOOP THOOP
THOOP
AAAAA!!!!!!
WHAT THE --
ARROWS?
OH NO...
Y - YOU?
WE'RE NOT READY...
M - MY SHOULDER...
OH, GOD.
THINK THAT HURTS?

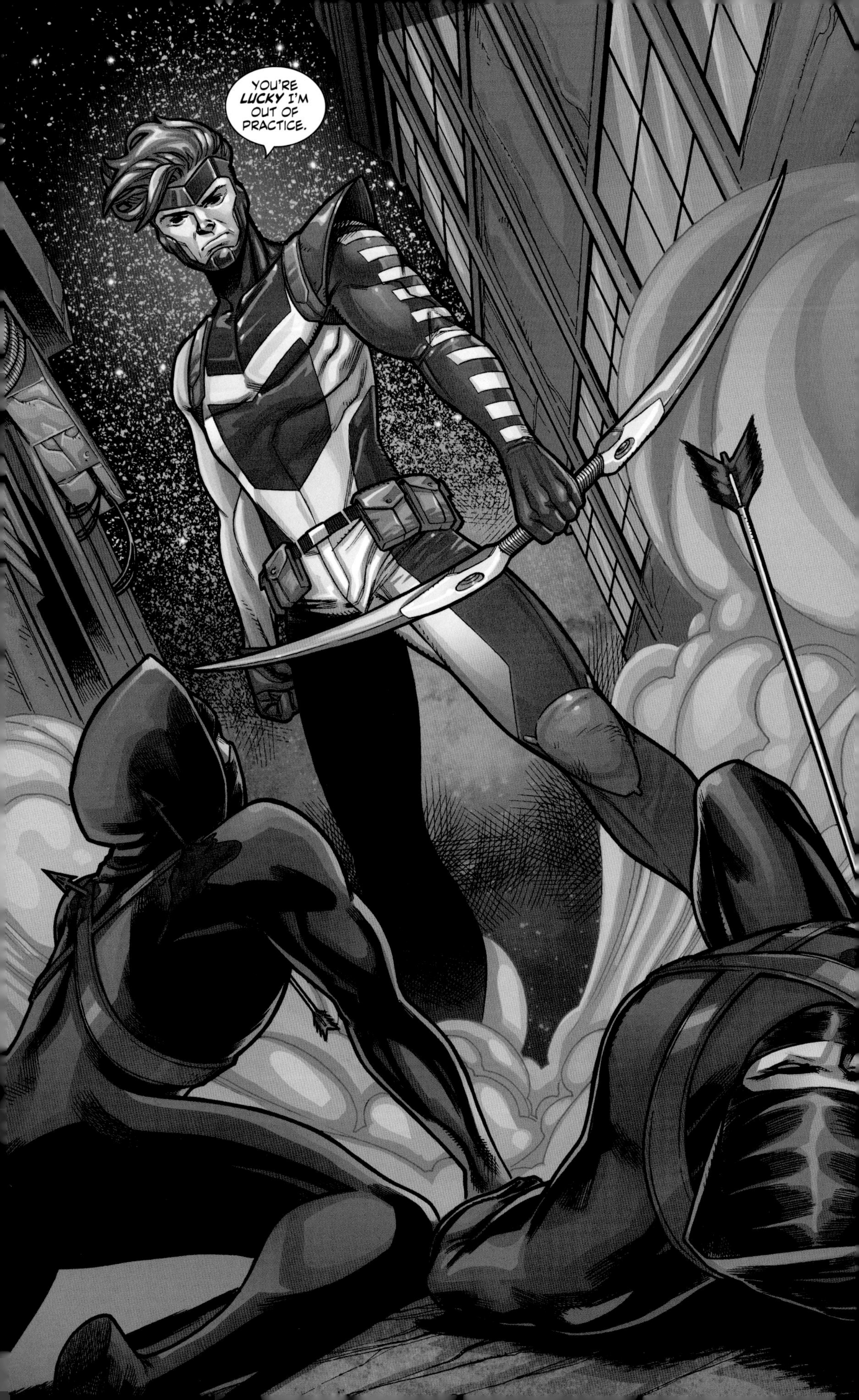
YOU'RE **LUCKY** I'M OUT OF PRACTICE.

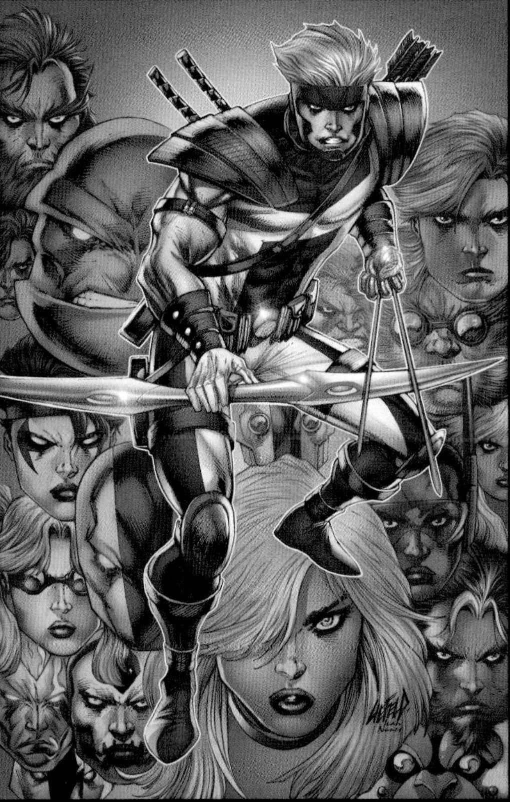

ART BY ROB LIEFELD

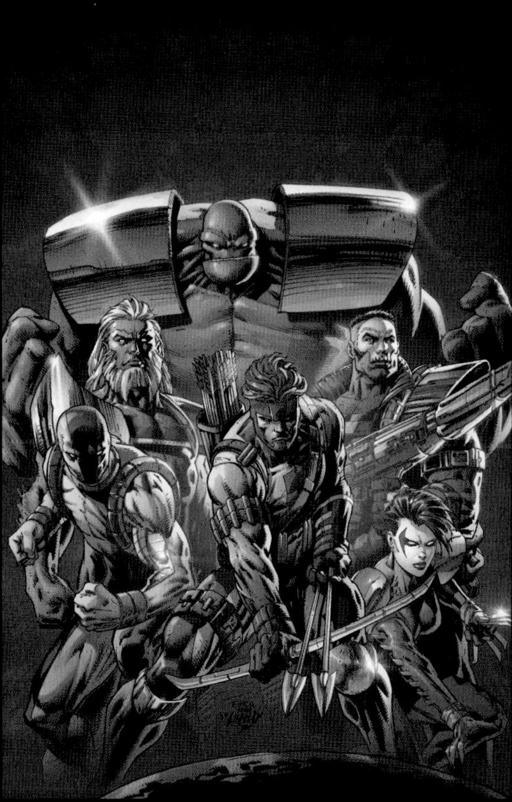

ART BY DAVID FINCH

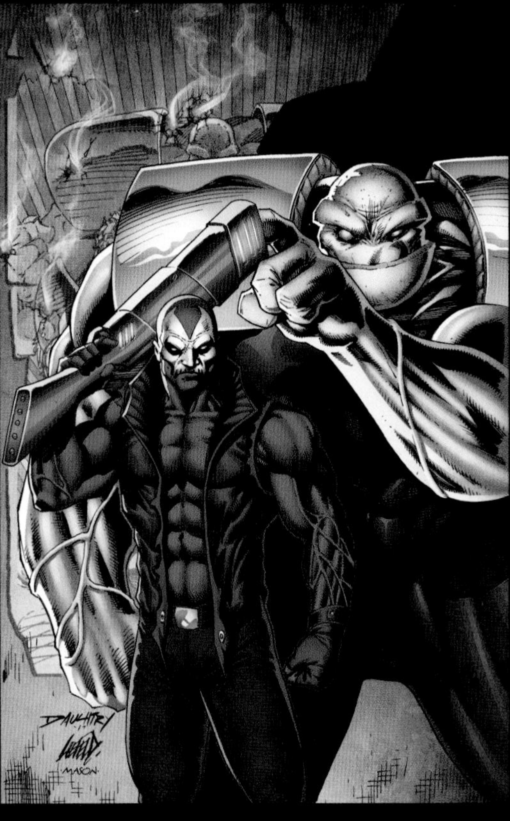
DAUGHTRY
MASON

ART BY CHRIS DAUGHTRY

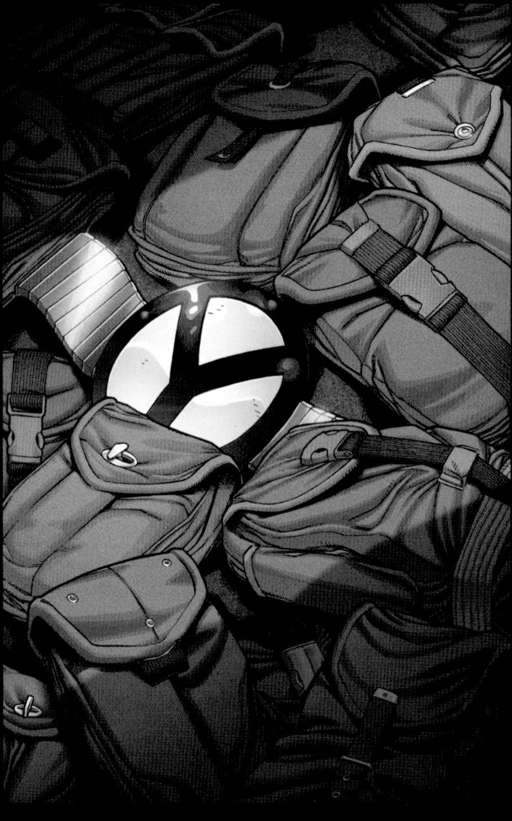

ART BY JIM TOWE

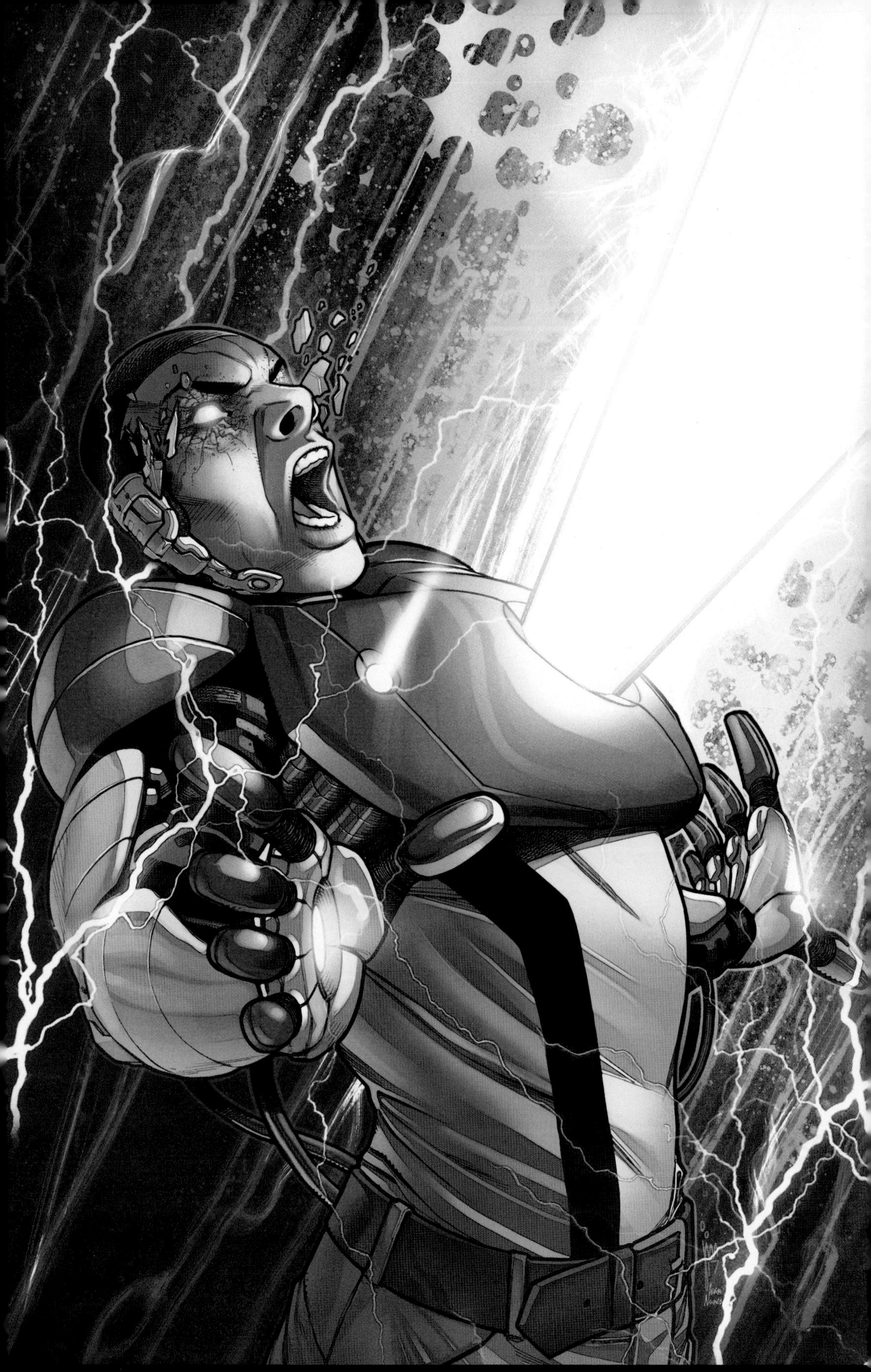

CHAPTER TWO: BADROCK & COMPANY

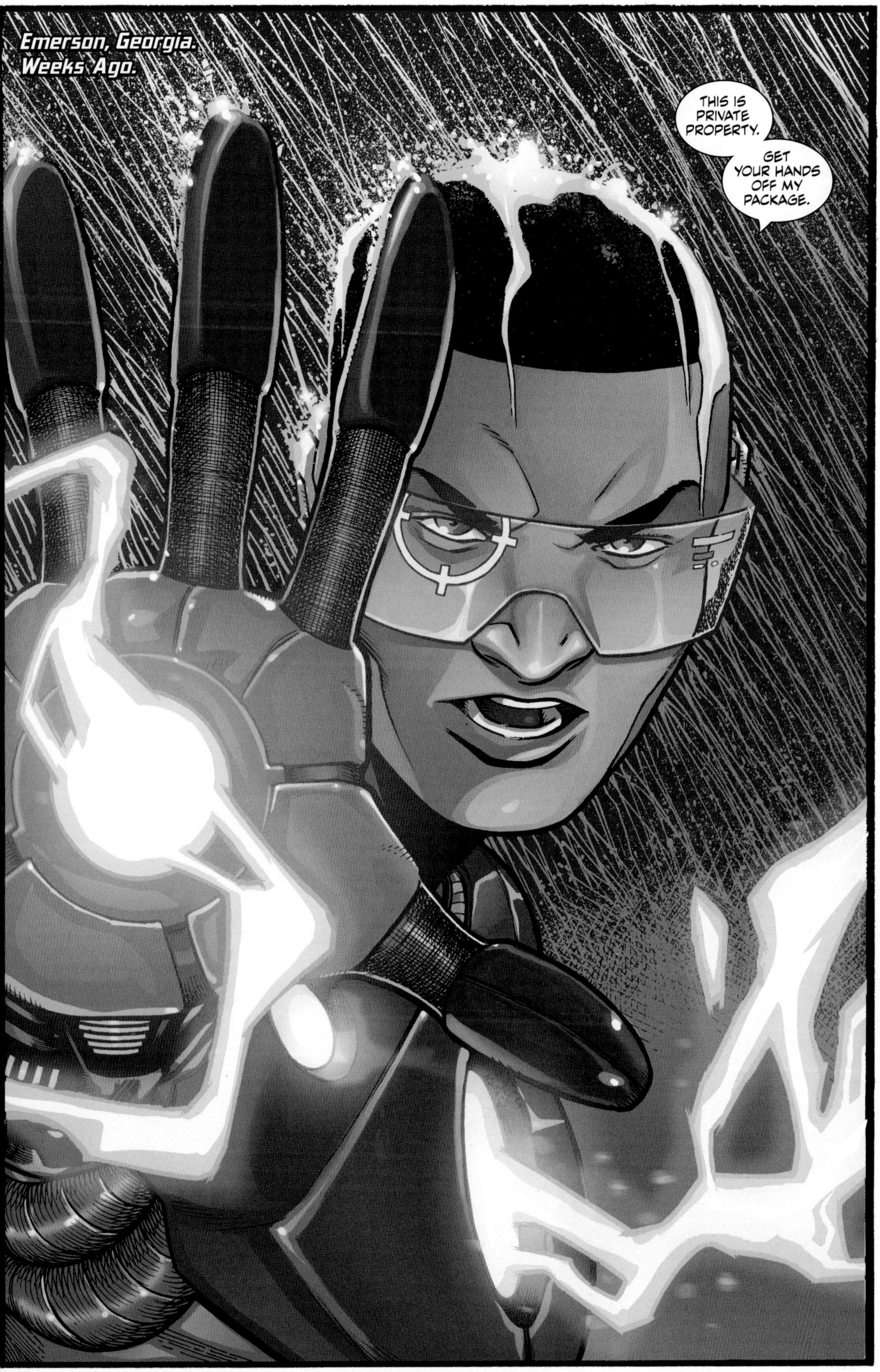
Emerson, Georgia.
Weeks Ago.
THIS IS PRIVATE PROPERTY.
GET YOUR HANDS OFF MY PACKAGE.

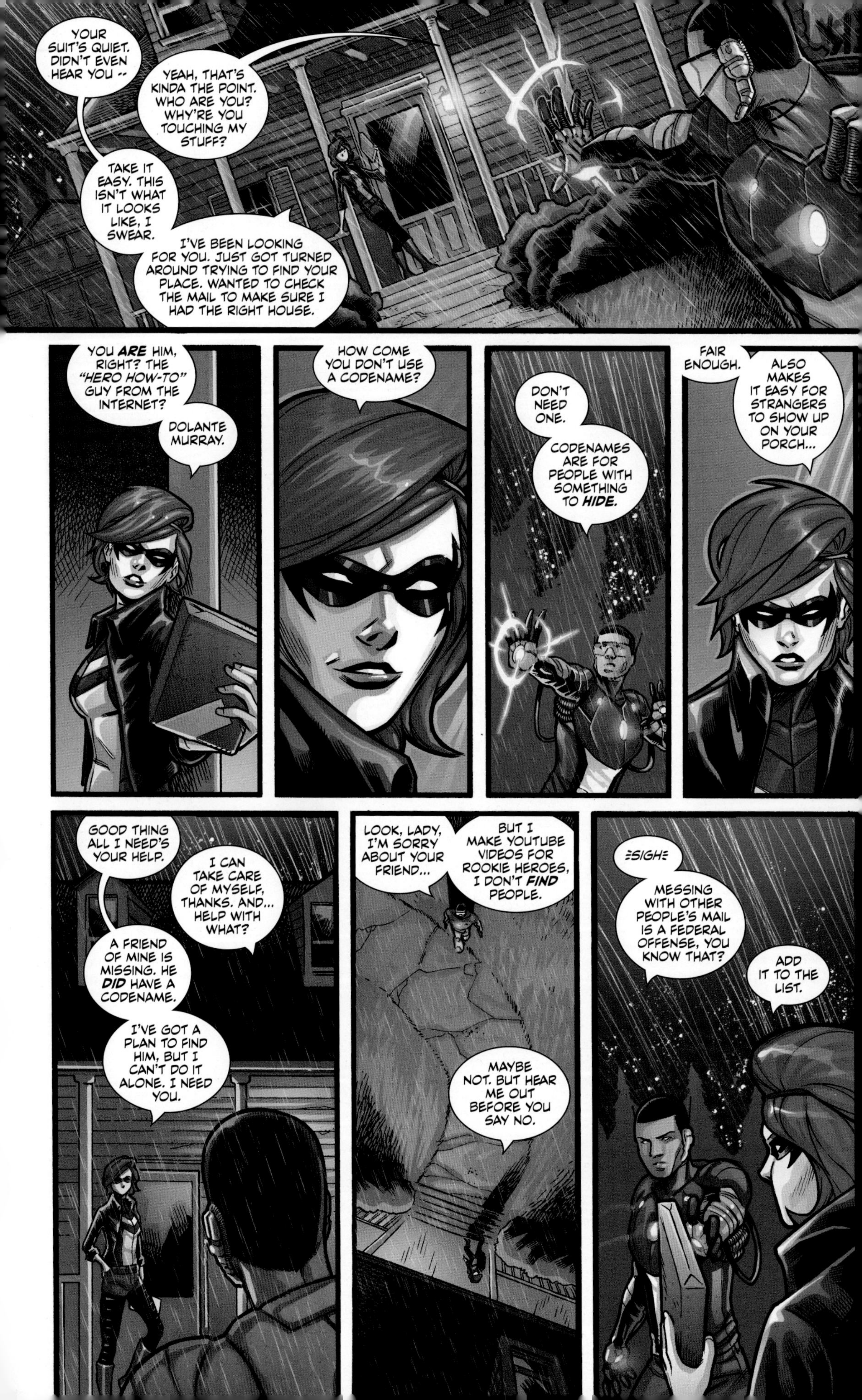

YOUR SUIT'S QUIET. DIDN'T EVEN HEAR YOU --
YEAH, THAT'S KINDA THE POINT. WHO ARE YOU? WHY'RE YOU TOUCHING MY STUFF?
TAKE IT EASY. THIS ISN'T WHAT IT LOOKS LIKE, I SWEAR.
I'VE BEEN LOOKING FOR YOU. JUST GOT TURNED AROUND TRYING TO FIND YOUR PLACE. WANTED TO CHECK THE MAIL TO MAKE SURE I HAD THE RIGHT HOUSE.
YOU ***ARE*** HIM, RIGHT? THE *"HERO HOW-TO"* GUY FROM THE INTERNET?
DOLANTE MURRAY.
HOW COME YOU DON'T USE A CODENAME?
DON'T NEED ONE.
CODENAMES ARE FOR PEOPLE WITH SOMETHING TO ***HIDE.***
FAIR ENOUGH.
ALSO MAKES IT EASY FOR STRANGERS TO SHOW UP ON YOUR PORCH...
GOOD THING ALL I NEED'S YOUR HELP.
I CAN TAKE CARE OF MYSELF, THANKS. AND... HELP WITH WHAT?
A FRIEND OF MINE IS MISSING. HE ***DID*** HAVE A CODENAME.
I'VE GOT A PLAN TO FIND HIM, BUT I CAN'T DO IT ALONE. I NEED YOU.
LOOK, LADY, I'M SORRY ABOUT YOUR FRIEND...
BUT I MAKE YOUTUBE VIDEOS FOR ROOKIE HEROES, I DON'T ***FIND*** PEOPLE.
MAYBE NOT. BUT HEAR ME OUT BEFORE YOU SAY NO.
SIGH
MESSING WITH OTHER PEOPLE'S MAIL IS A FEDERAL OFFENSE, YOU KNOW THAT?
ADD IT TO THE LIST.

-- BUT DID HE HAVE ANY ENEMIES? MAYBE SOMEONE WHO DIDN'T LIKE HIM?

WAS HE -- WHAT'D YOU CALL HIM, **"MAN-UP"?** WAS HE ON **HELP?!**

YEAH, BUT WHEN HE DISAPPEARED, SO DID **EVERYTHING.** IT'S LIKE HE NEVER EXISTED.

IF I HADN'T MET HIS AUNT, I'D JUST ABOUT BELIEVE I MADE HIM UP, Y'KNOW?

YOU TALKED TO HIS FAMILY?

YEAH.

LOOK, GUNNER, YOU SEEM ALL RIGHT...

BUT IT SOUNDS LIKE YOU'VE COVERED ALL YOUR BASES. THE COPS, THE INTERNET. EVEN HIS LIFE OUTSIDE THE COSTUME. WHAT CAN I DO THAT YOU HAVEN'T ALREADY?

YOU'RE RIGHT. I HAVE COVERED MY BASES --

AND IT'S GOTTEN ME NOWHERE.

WANNA KNOW WHY THAT IS? BECAUSE I'M NOBODY, DOLANTE. NOBODY CARES ABOUT A NOBODY.

BUT HE BELIEVED IN ME. I OWE IT TO HIM TO FIND OUT WHAT HAPPENED.

SO I'M TRYING SOMETHING NEW. SOMETHING DESPERATE.

I'M REINVENTING MYSELF --

AND THE NEW VOGUE IS GONNA MAKE A LOT OF NOISE.

I COULD USE A **SENTINEL** BY MY SIDE TO MAKE SURE THE RIGHT PEOPLE ARE LISTENING.

Marcus "Sentinel" Langston

Lorem ipsum dolor sit amet, consectetuer adipiscing elit, sed diam nonummy nibh euismod tincidunt ut laoreet dolore magna aliquam erat volutpat. Ut wisi enim ad

Lorem ipsum dolor sit amet, consectetuer adipiscing elit, sed diam nonummy nibh euismod

Lorem ipsum dolor sit amet, consectetuer adipiscing elit, sed diam nonummy nibh euismod tincidunt

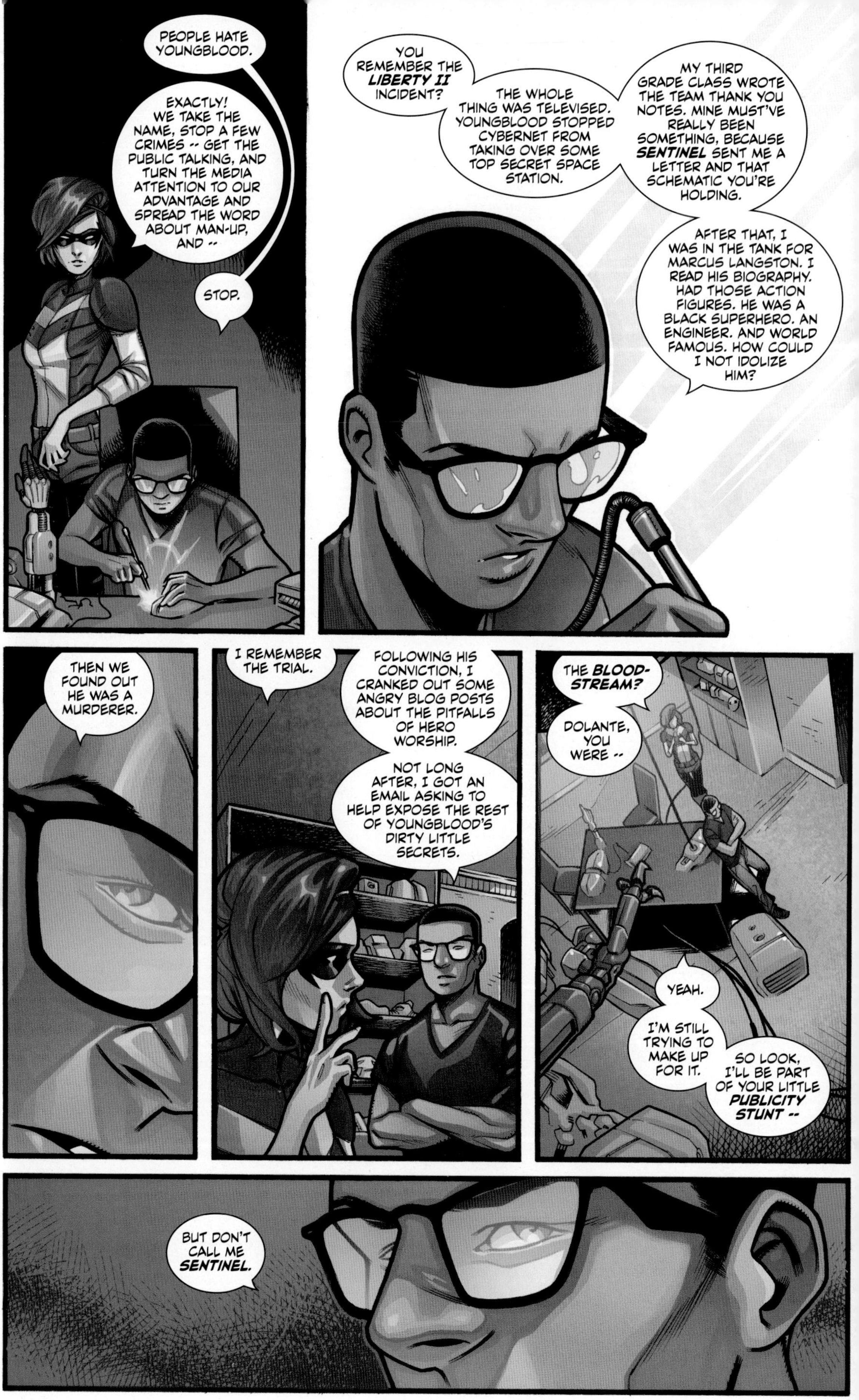
PEOPLE HATE YOUNGBLOOD.
EXACTLY! WE TAKE THE NAME, STOP A FEW CRIMES -- GET THE PUBLIC TALKING, AND TURN THE MEDIA ATTENTION TO OUR ADVANTAGE AND SPREAD THE WORD ABOUT MAN-UP, AND --
STOP.
YOU REMEMBER THE LIBERTY II INCIDENT?
THE WHOLE THING WAS TELEVISED. YOUNGBLOOD STOPPED CYBERNET FROM TAKING OVER SOME TOP SECRET SPACE STATION.
MY THIRD GRADE CLASS WROTE THE TEAM THANK YOU NOTES. MINE MUST'VE REALLY BEEN SOMETHING, BECAUSE SENTINEL SENT ME A LETTER AND THAT SCHEMATIC YOU'RE HOLDING.
AFTER THAT, I WAS IN THE TANK FOR MARCUS LANGSTON. I READ HIS BIOGRAPHY. HAD THOSE ACTION FIGURES. HE WAS A BLACK SUPERHERO. AN ENGINEER. AND WORLD FAMOUS. HOW COULD I NOT IDOLIZE HIM?
THEN WE FOUND OUT HE WAS A MURDERER.
I REMEMBER THE TRIAL.
FOLLOWING HIS CONVICTION, I CRANKED OUT SOME ANGRY BLOG POSTS ABOUT THE PITFALLS OF HERO WORSHIP.
NOT LONG AFTER, I GOT AN EMAIL ASKING TO HELP EXPOSE THE REST OF YOUNGBLOOD'S DIRTY LITTLE SECRETS.
THE BLOOD-STREAM?
DOLANTE, YOU WERE --
YEAH.
I'M STILL TRYING TO MAKE UP FOR IT.
SO LOOK, I'LL BE PART OF YOUR LITTLE PUBLICITY STUNT --
BUT DON'T CALL ME SENTINEL.

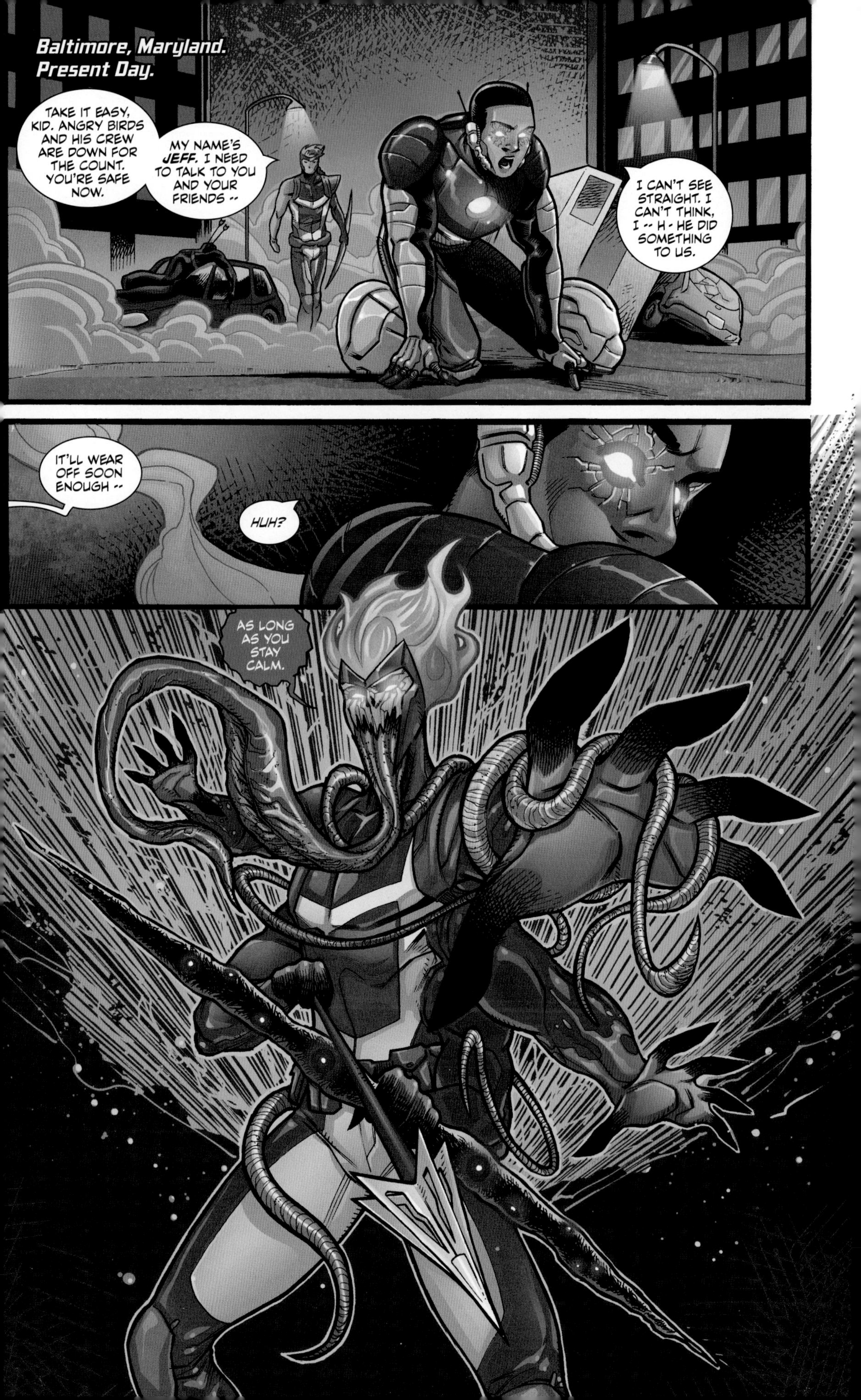
Baltimore, Maryland.
Present Day.
TAKE IT EASY, KID. ANGRY BIRDS AND HIS CREW ARE DOWN FOR THE COUNT. YOU'RE SAFE NOW.
MY NAME'S JEFF. I NEED TO TALK TO YOU AND YOUR FRIENDS --
I CAN'T SEE STRAIGHT. I CAN'T THINK, I -- H - HE DID SOMETHING TO US.
IT'LL WEAR OFF SOON ENOUGH --
HUH?
AS LONG AS YOU STAY CALM.

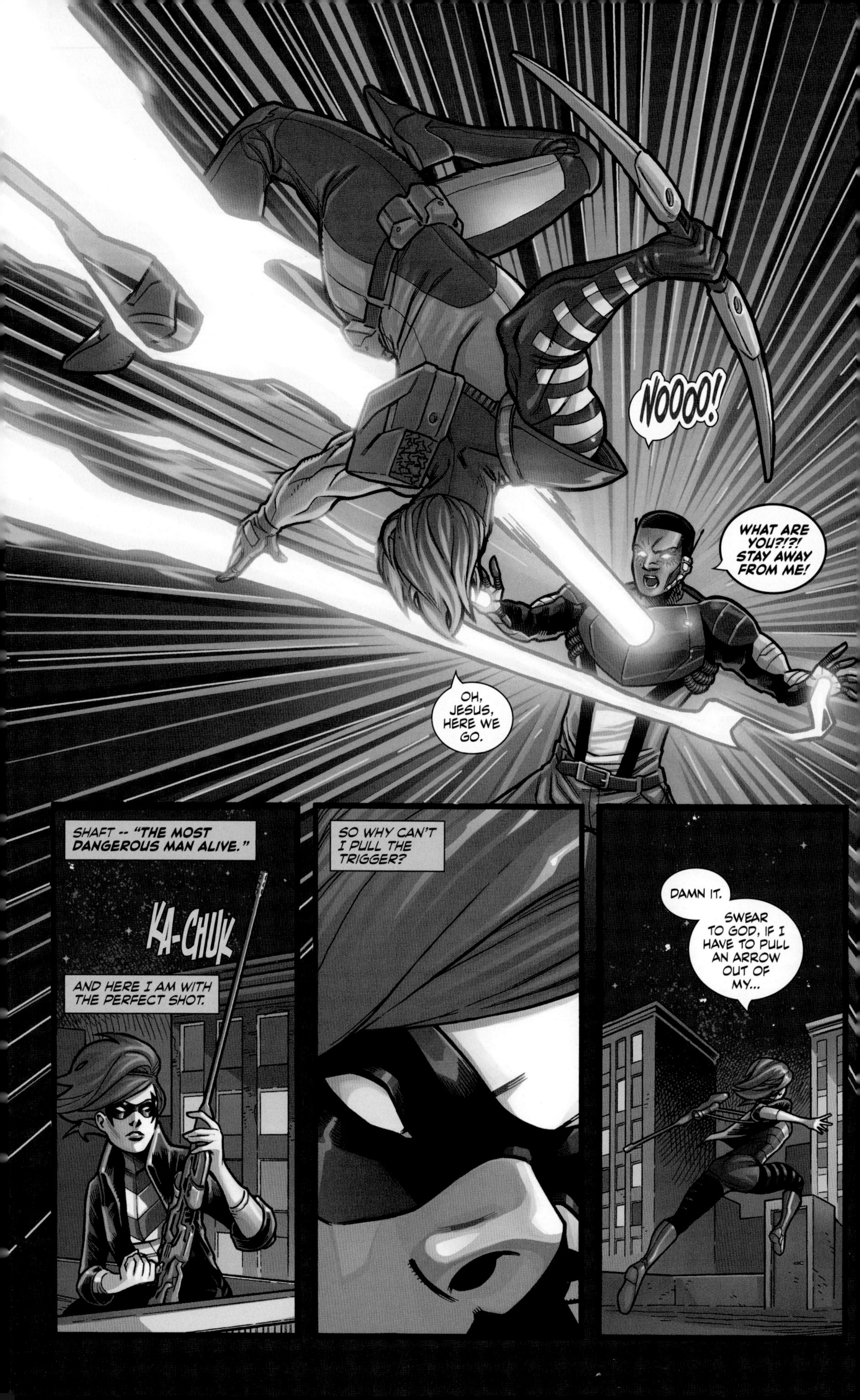
NOOOO!
WHAT ARE YOU?!?! STAY AWAY FROM ME!
OH, JESUS, HERE WE GO.
SHAFT -- "THE MOST DANGEROUS MAN ALIVE."
KA-CHUK
AND HERE I AM WITH THE PERFECT SHOT.
SO WHY CAN'T I PULL THE TRIGGER?
DAMN IT.
SWEAR TO GOD, IF I HAVE TO PULL AN ARROW OUT OF MY...

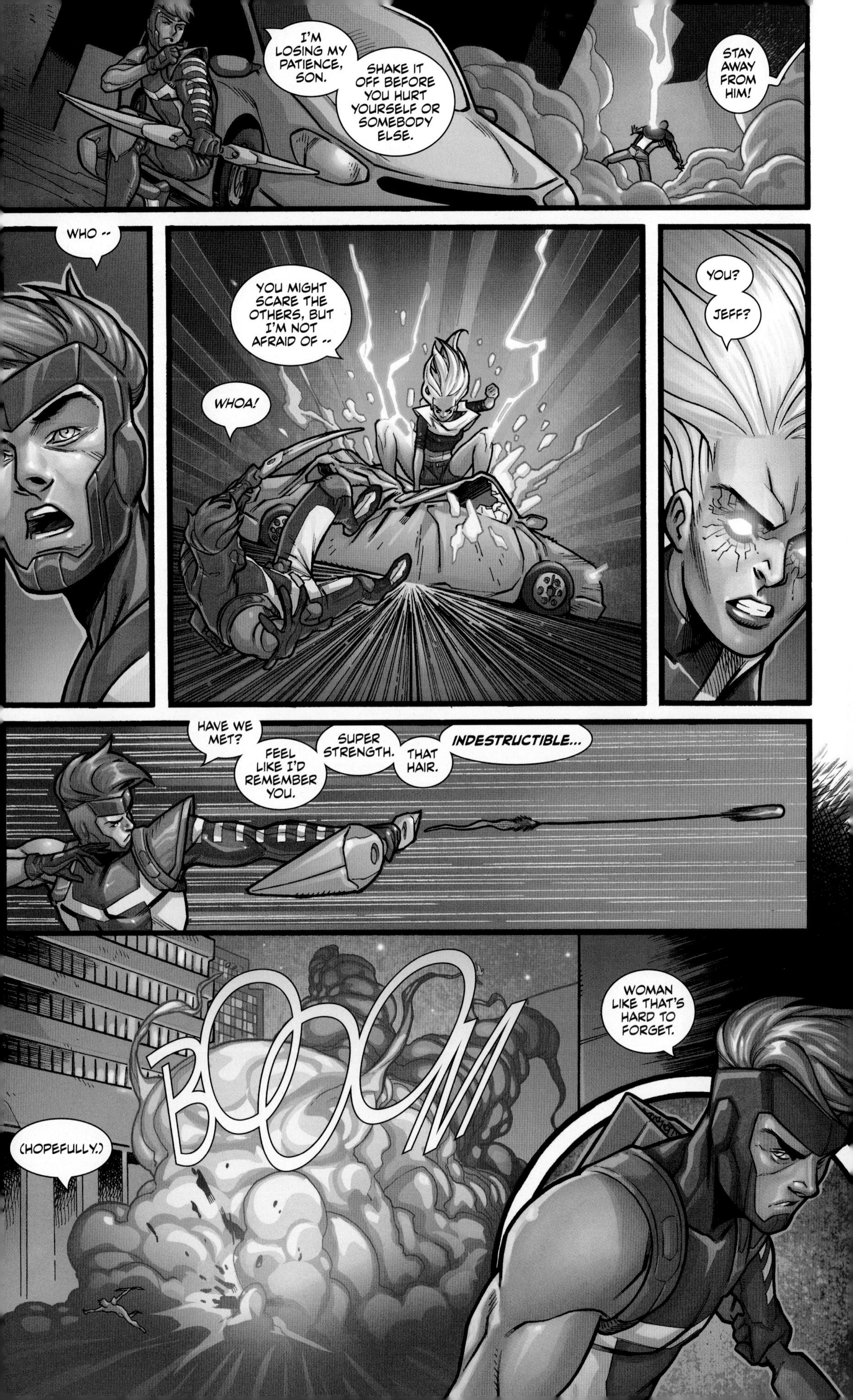
I'M LOSING MY PATIENCE, SON.
SHAKE IT OFF BEFORE YOU HURT YOURSELF OR SOMEBODY ELSE.
STAY AWAY FROM HIM!
WHO --
YOU MIGHT SCARE THE OTHERS, BUT I'M NOT AFRAID OF --
WHOA!
YOU?
JEFF?
HAVE WE MET?
FEEL LIKE I'D REMEMBER YOU.
SUPER STRENGTH.
THAT HAIR.
INDESTRUCTIBLE...
BOOOM
WOMAN LIKE THAT'S HARD TO FORGET.
(HOPEFULLY.)

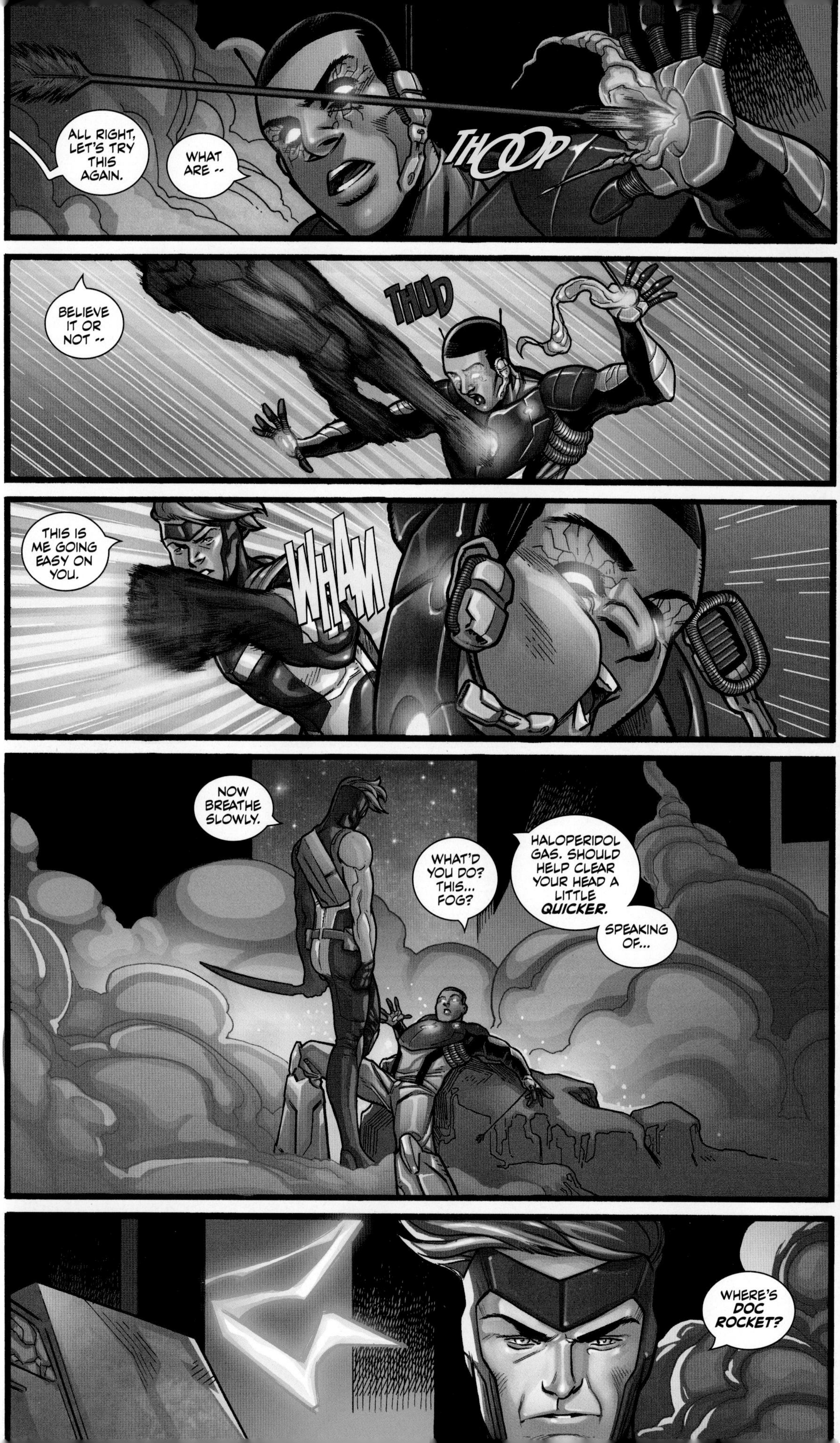

ALL RIGHT, LET'S TRY THIS AGAIN.
WHAT ARE --
THOOP
BELIEVE IT OR NOT --
THUD
THIS IS ME GOING EASY ON YOU.
WHAM
NOW BREATHE SLOWLY.
WHAT'D YOU DO? THIS... FOG?
HALOPERIDOL GAS. SHOULD HELP CLEAR YOUR HEAD A LITTLE QUICKER.
SPEAKING OF...
WHERE'S DOC ROCKET?

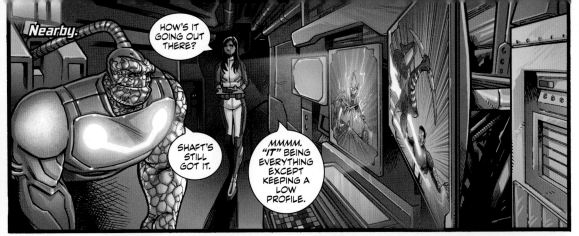

HOW'S IT GOING OUT THERE?

SHAFT'S STILL GOT IT.

MMMM. "IT" BEING EVERYTHING EXCEPT KEEPING A LOW PROFILE.

RELAX. CIVILIANS ARE CLEAR, AND JEFF'S GOT *SCRAMBLEWARE* ALL OVER HIS SUIT. NOBODY'LL KNOW HE WAS HERE.

THIS AIN'T MY FIRST RODEO, MARGOT.

FINE.

HOLD STILL, COWBOY.

HOW'S IT LOOK?

B - BETTER.

WNHHRRR

YOU'RE LYING.

LOT OF THAT GOING AROUND.

I THOUGHT YOU WERE WITH ME ON THIS, MARGOT.

I AM, IT'S JUST -- I WORRY.

NO, I GET IT. WE'RE PLAYING WITH FIRE.

I JUST WANT TO BE REMEMBERED FOR SOMETHING MORE THAN "YABBA DABBA DOOM." THIS IS AS CLOSE TO A LEGACY AS I'M LIKELY TO GET, AND I AIM TO MAKE A DIFFERENCE BEFORE I... WELL, YOU KNOW.

I DO, TOM...

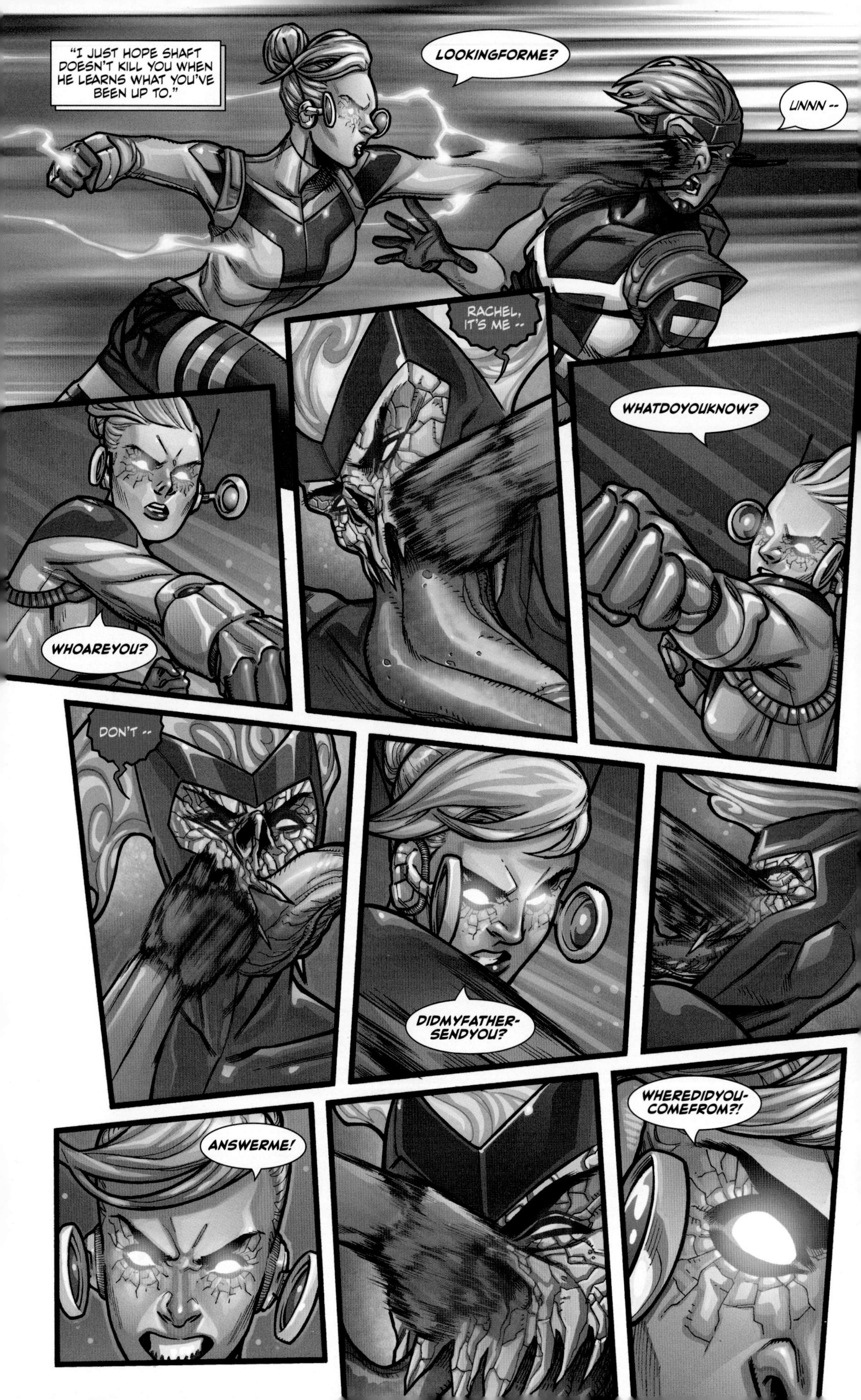
"I JUST HOPE SHAFT DOESN'T KILL YOU WHEN HE LEARNS WHAT YOU'VE BEEN UP TO."
LOOKINGFORME?
UNNN --
RACHEL, IT'S ME --
WHATDOYOUKNOW?
WHOAREYOU?
DON'T --
DIDMYFATHER-SENDYOU?
WHEREDIDYOU-COMEFROM?!
ANSWERME!

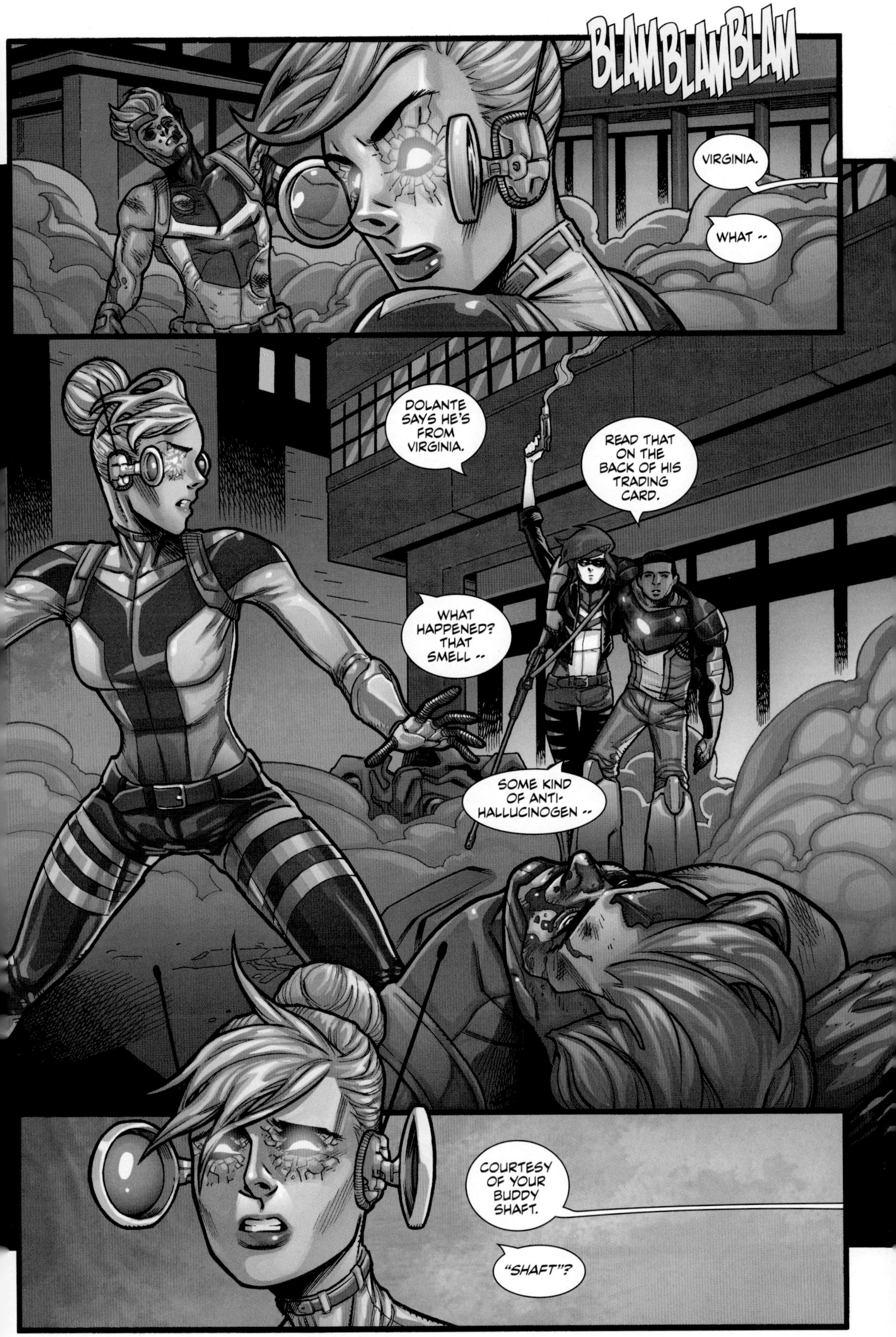
BLAMBLAMBLAM
VIRGINIA.
WHAT --
DOLANTE SAYS HE'S FROM VIRGINIA.
READ THAT ON THE BACK OF HIS TRADING CARD.
WHAT HAPPENED? THAT SMELL --
SOME KIND OF ANTI-HALLUCINOGEN --
COURTESY OF YOUR BUDDY SHAFT.
"SHAFT"?

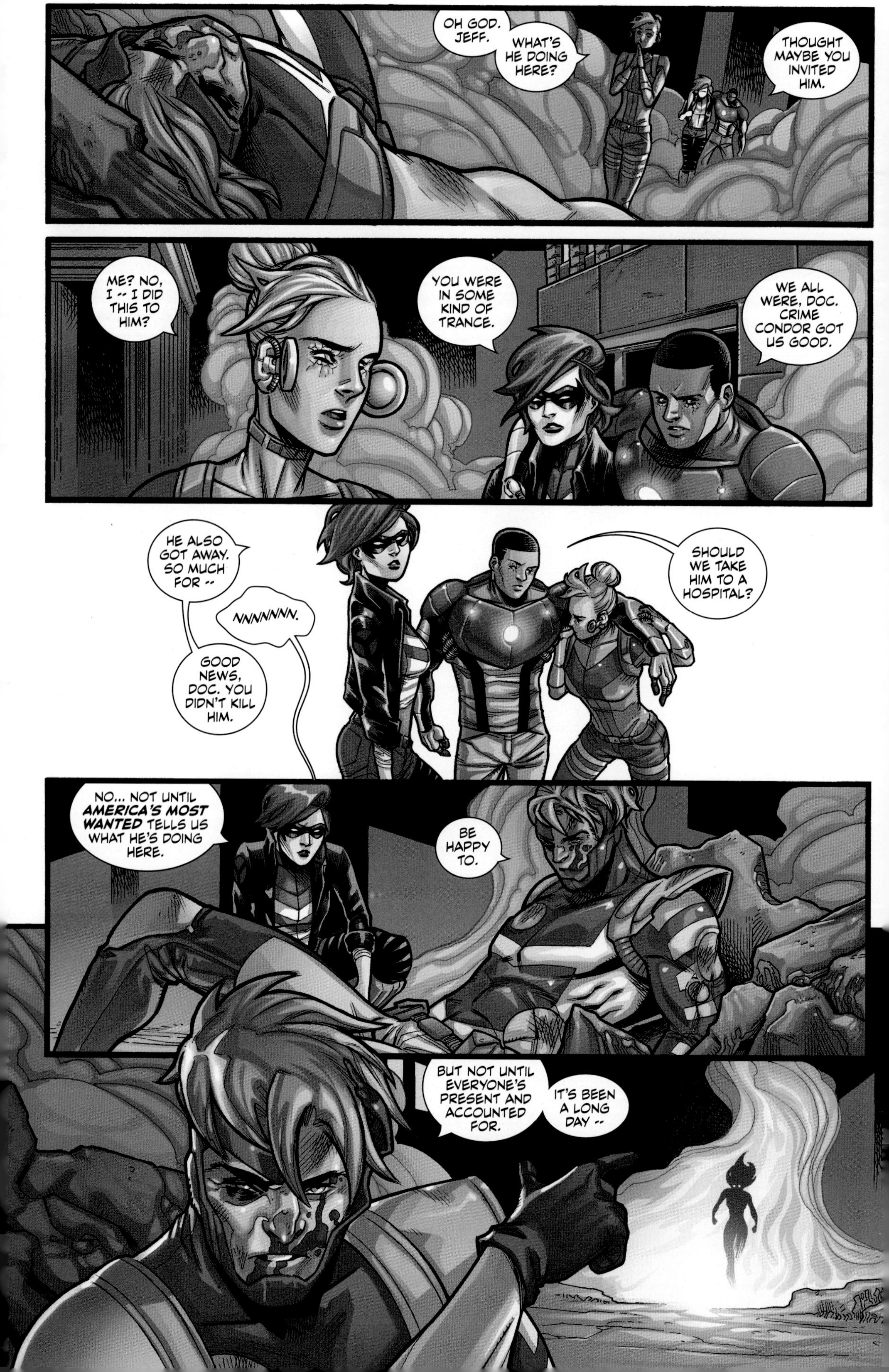
OH GOD. JEFF.
WHAT'S HE DOING HERE?
THOUGHT MAYBE YOU INVITED HIM.
ME? NO, I -- I DID THIS TO HIM?
YOU WERE IN SOME KIND OF TRANCE.
WE ALL WERE, DOC. CRIME CONDOR GOT US GOOD.
HE ALSO GOT AWAY. SO MUCH FOR --
NNNNNNN.
GOOD NEWS, DOC. YOU DIDN'T KILL HIM.
SHOULD WE TAKE HIM TO A HOSPITAL?
NO... NOT UNTIL AMERICA'S MOST WANTED TELLS US WHAT HE'S DOING HERE.
BE HAPPY TO.
BUT NOT UNTIL EVERYONE'S PRESENT AND ACCOUNTED FOR.
IT'S BEEN A LONG DAY --

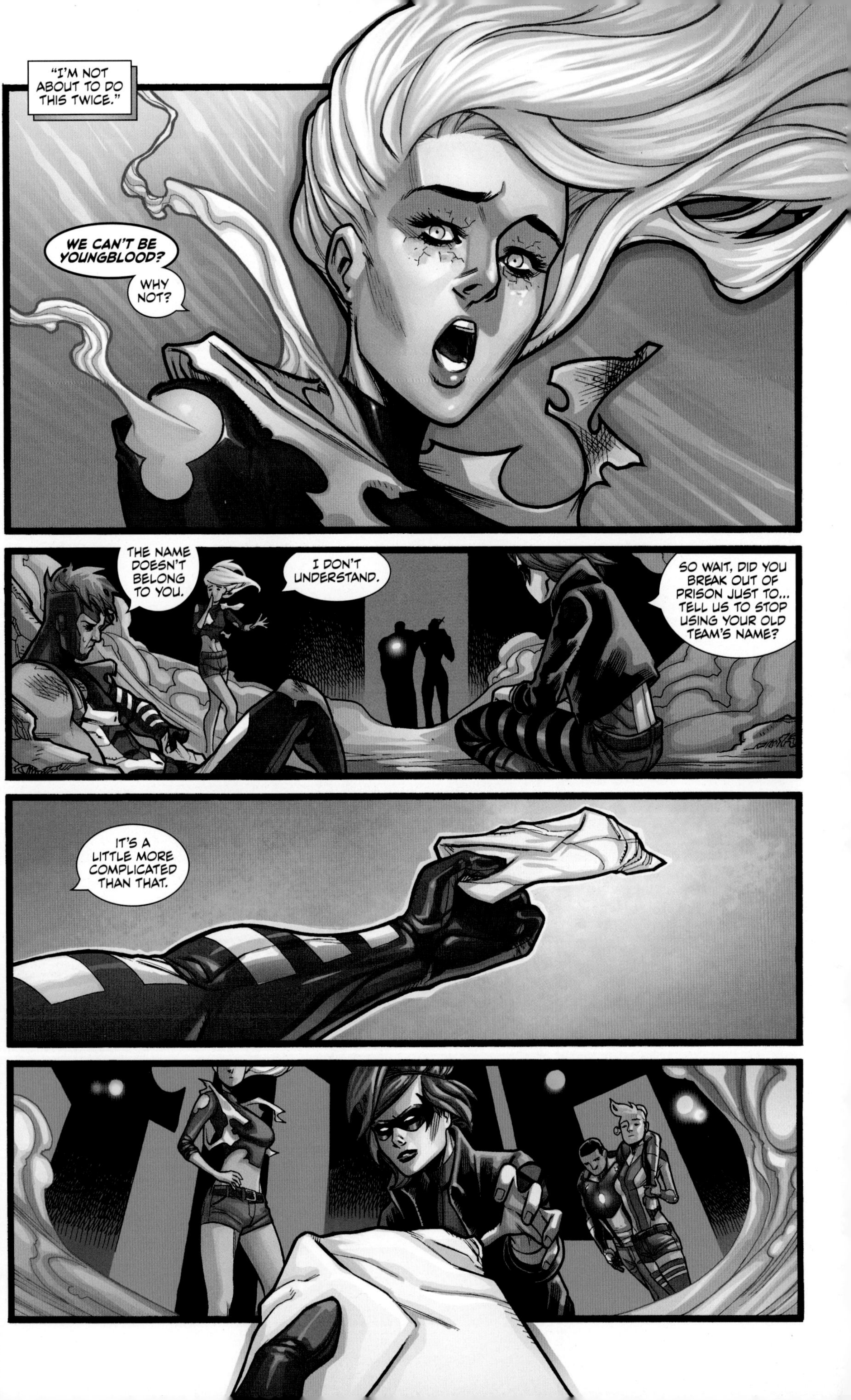
"I'M NOT ABOUT TO DO THIS TWICE."
WE CAN'T BE YOUNGBLOOD?
WHY NOT?
THE NAME DOESN'T BELONG TO YOU.
I DON'T UNDERSTAND.
SO WAIT, DID YOU BREAK OUT OF PRISON JUST TO... TELL US TO STOP USING YOUR OLD TEAM'S NAME?
IT'S A LITTLE MORE COMPLICATED THAN THAT.

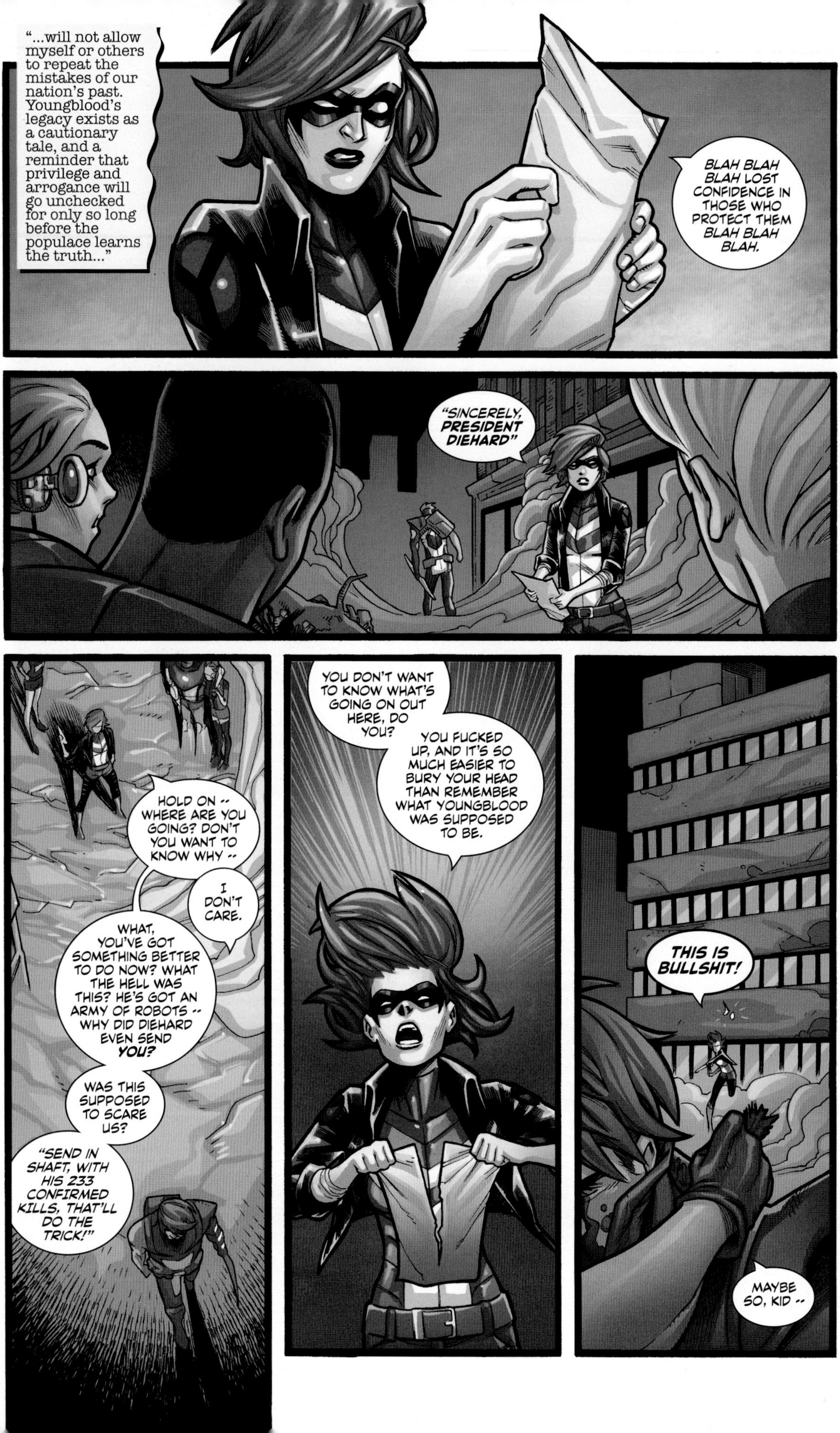
"...will not allow myself or others to repeat the mistakes of our nation's past. Youngblood's legacy exists as a cautionary tale, and a reminder that privilege and arrogance will go unchecked for only so long before the populace learns the truth..."
BLAH BLAH BLAH LOST CONFIDENCE IN THOSE WHO PROTECT THEM BLAH BLAH BLAH.
"SINCERELY, PRESIDENT DIEHARD"
HOLD ON -- WHERE ARE YOU GOING? DON'T YOU WANT TO KNOW WHY --
I DON'T CARE.
WHAT, YOU'VE GOT SOMETHING BETTER TO DO NOW? WHAT THE HELL WAS THIS? HE'S GOT AN ARMY OF ROBOTS -- WHY DID DIEHARD EVEN SEND YOU?
WAS THIS SUPPOSED TO SCARE US?
"SEND IN SHAFT, WITH HIS 233 CONFIRMED KILLS, THAT'LL DO THE TRICK!"
YOU DON'T WANT TO KNOW WHAT'S GOING ON OUT HERE, DO YOU?
YOU FUCKED UP, AND IT'S SO MUCH EASIER TO BURY YOUR HEAD THAN REMEMBER WHAT YOUNGBLOOD WAS SUPPOSED TO BE.
THIS IS BULLSHIT!
MAYBE SO, KID --

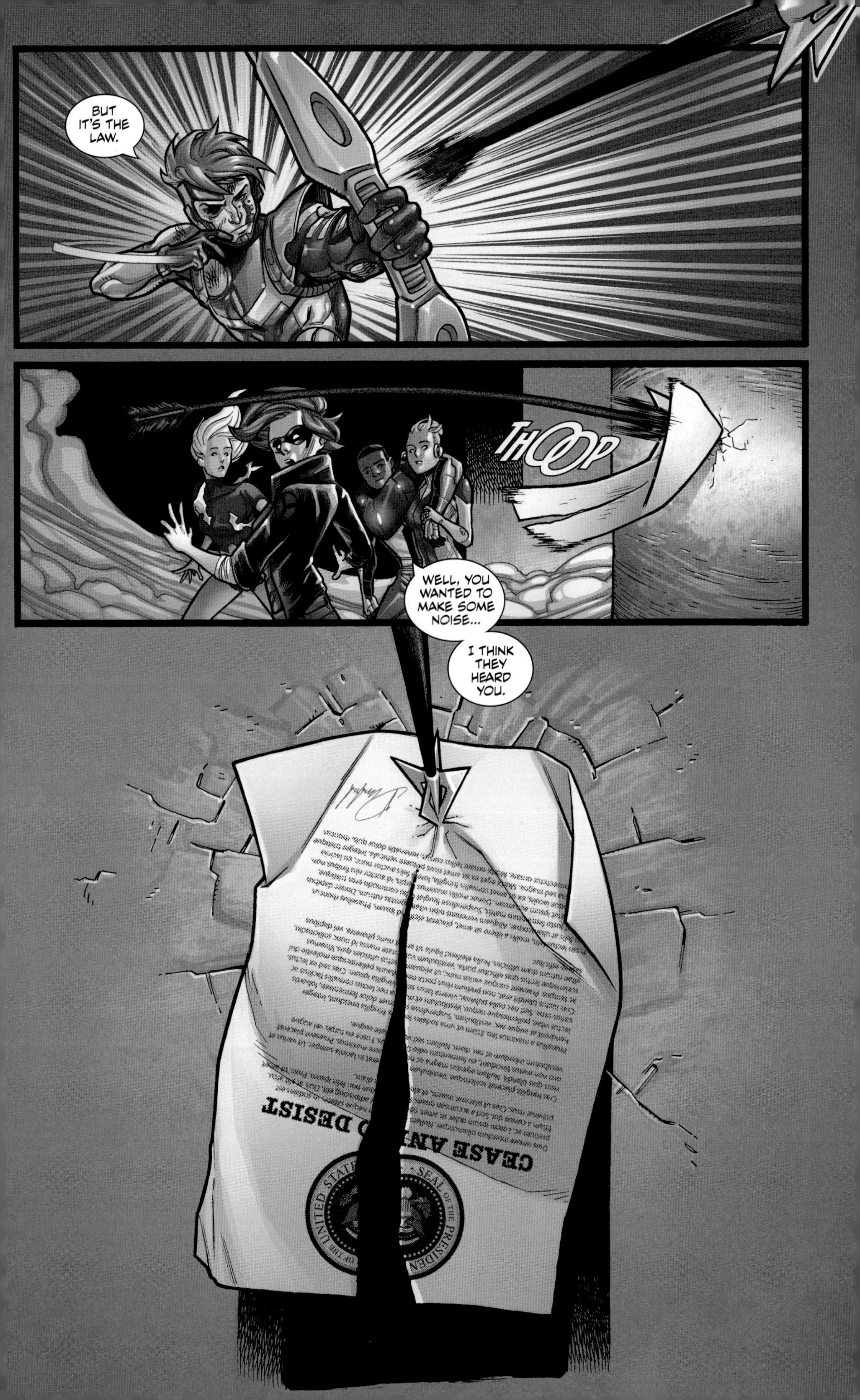

BUT IT'S THE LAW.
THOOP
WELL, YOU WANTED TO MAKE SOME NOISE...
I THINK THEY HEARD YOU.

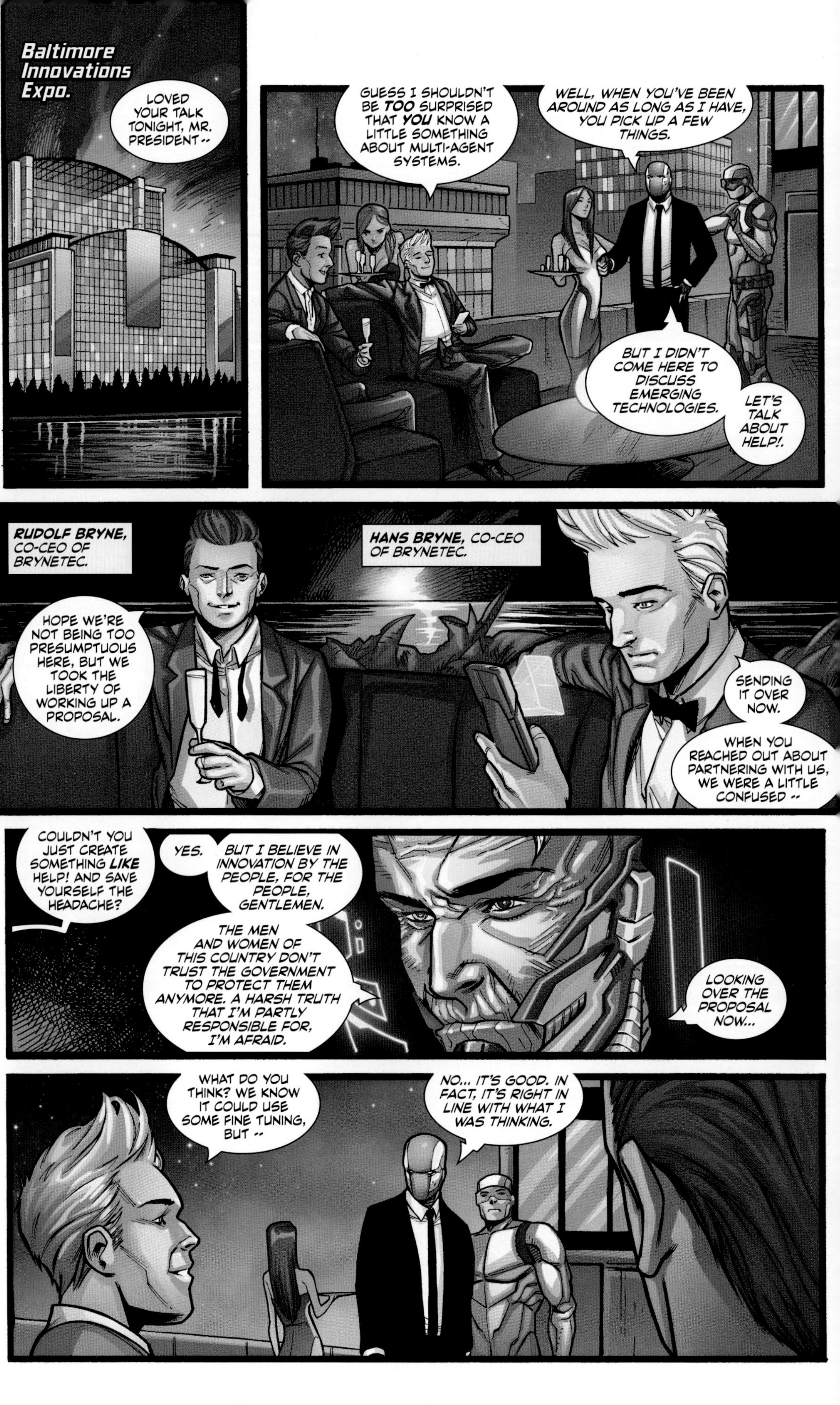
Baltimore Innovations Expo.
LOVED YOUR TALK TONIGHT, MR. PRESIDENT --
GUESS I SHOULDN'T BE TOO SURPRISED THAT YOU KNOW A LITTLE SOMETHING ABOUT MULTI-AGENT SYSTEMS.
WELL, WHEN YOU'VE BEEN AROUND AS LONG AS I HAVE, YOU PICK UP A FEW THINGS.
BUT I DIDN'T COME HERE TO DISCUSS EMERGING TECHNOLOGIES.
LET'S TALK ABOUT HELP!.
RUDOLF BRYNE, CO-CEO OF BRYNETEC.
HANS BRYNE, CO-CEO OF BRYNETEC.
HOPE WE'RE NOT BEING TOO PRESUMPTUOUS HERE, BUT WE TOOK THE LIBERTY OF WORKING UP A PROPOSAL.
SENDING IT OVER NOW.
WHEN YOU REACHED OUT ABOUT PARTNERING WITH US, WE WERE A LITTLE CONFUSED --
COULDN'T YOU JUST CREATE SOMETHING LIKE HELP! AND SAVE YOURSELF THE HEADACHE?
YES.
BUT I BELIEVE IN INNOVATION BY THE PEOPLE, FOR THE PEOPLE, GENTLEMEN.
THE MEN AND WOMEN OF THIS COUNTRY DON'T TRUST THE GOVERNMENT TO PROTECT THEM ANYMORE. A HARSH TRUTH THAT I'M PARTLY RESPONSIBLE FOR, I'M AFRAID.
LOOKING OVER THE PROPOSAL NOW...
WHAT DO YOU THINK? WE KNOW IT COULD USE SOME FINE TUNING, BUT --
NO... IT'S GOOD. IN FACT, IT'S RIGHT IN LINE WITH WHAT I WAS THINKING.

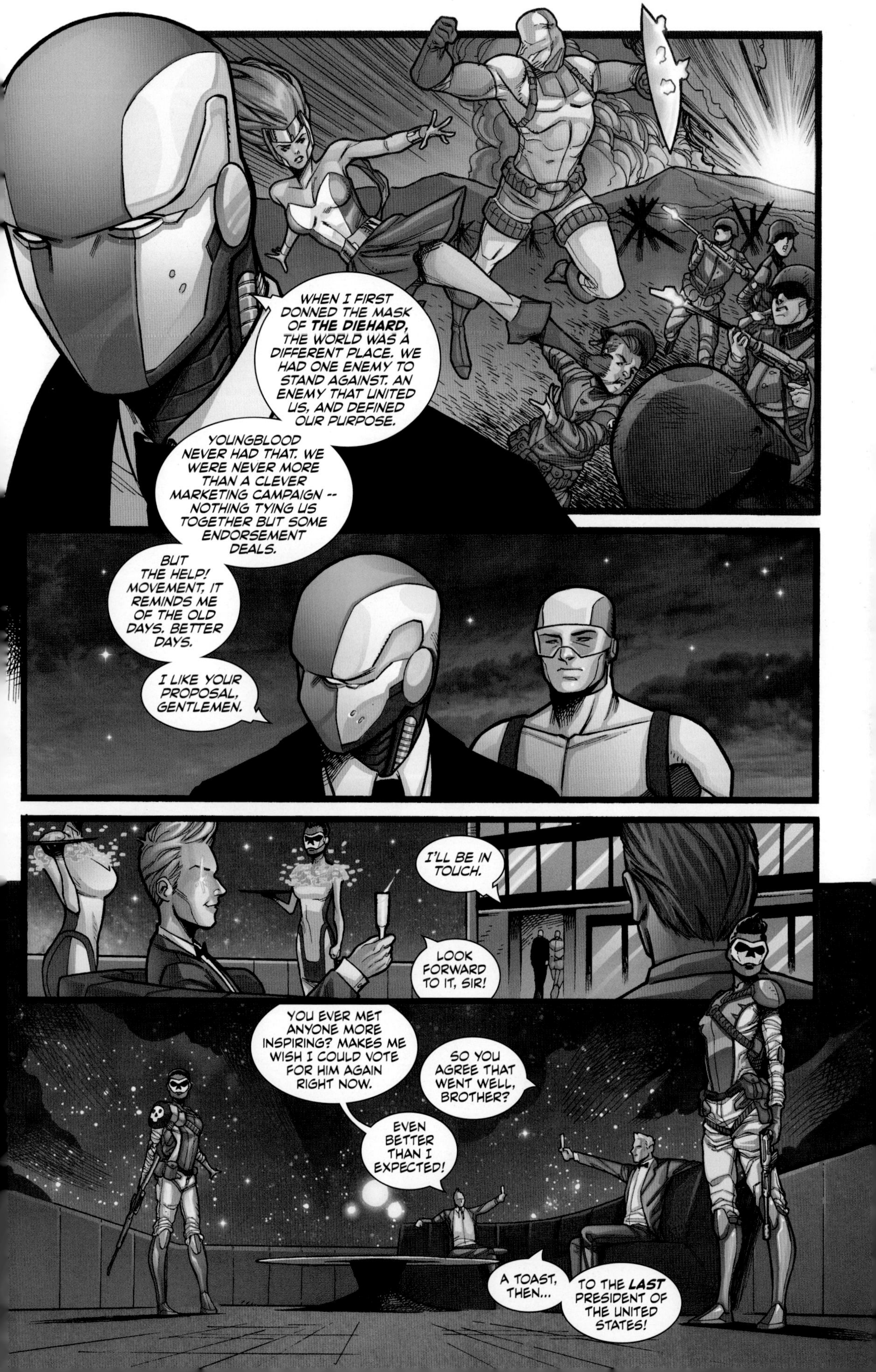

WHEN I FIRST DONNED THE MASK OF **THE DIEHARD,** THE WORLD WAS A DIFFERENT PLACE. WE HAD ONE ENEMY TO STAND AGAINST. AN ENEMY THAT UNITED US, AND DEFINED OUR PURPOSE.
YOUNGBLOOD NEVER HAD THAT. WE WERE NEVER MORE THAN A CLEVER MARKETING CAMPAIGN -- NOTHING TYING US TOGETHER BUT SOME ENDORSEMENT DEALS.
BUT THE HELP! MOVEMENT, IT REMINDS ME OF THE OLD DAYS. BETTER DAYS.
I LIKE YOUR PROPOSAL, GENTLEMEN.
I'LL BE IN TOUCH.
LOOK FORWARD TO IT, SIR!
YOU EVER MET ANYONE MORE INSPIRING? MAKES ME WISH I COULD VOTE FOR HIM AGAIN RIGHT NOW.
SO YOU AGREE THAT WENT WELL, BROTHER?
EVEN BETTER THAN I EXPECTED!
A TOAST, THEN...
TO THE **LAST** PRESIDENT OF THE UNITED STATES!

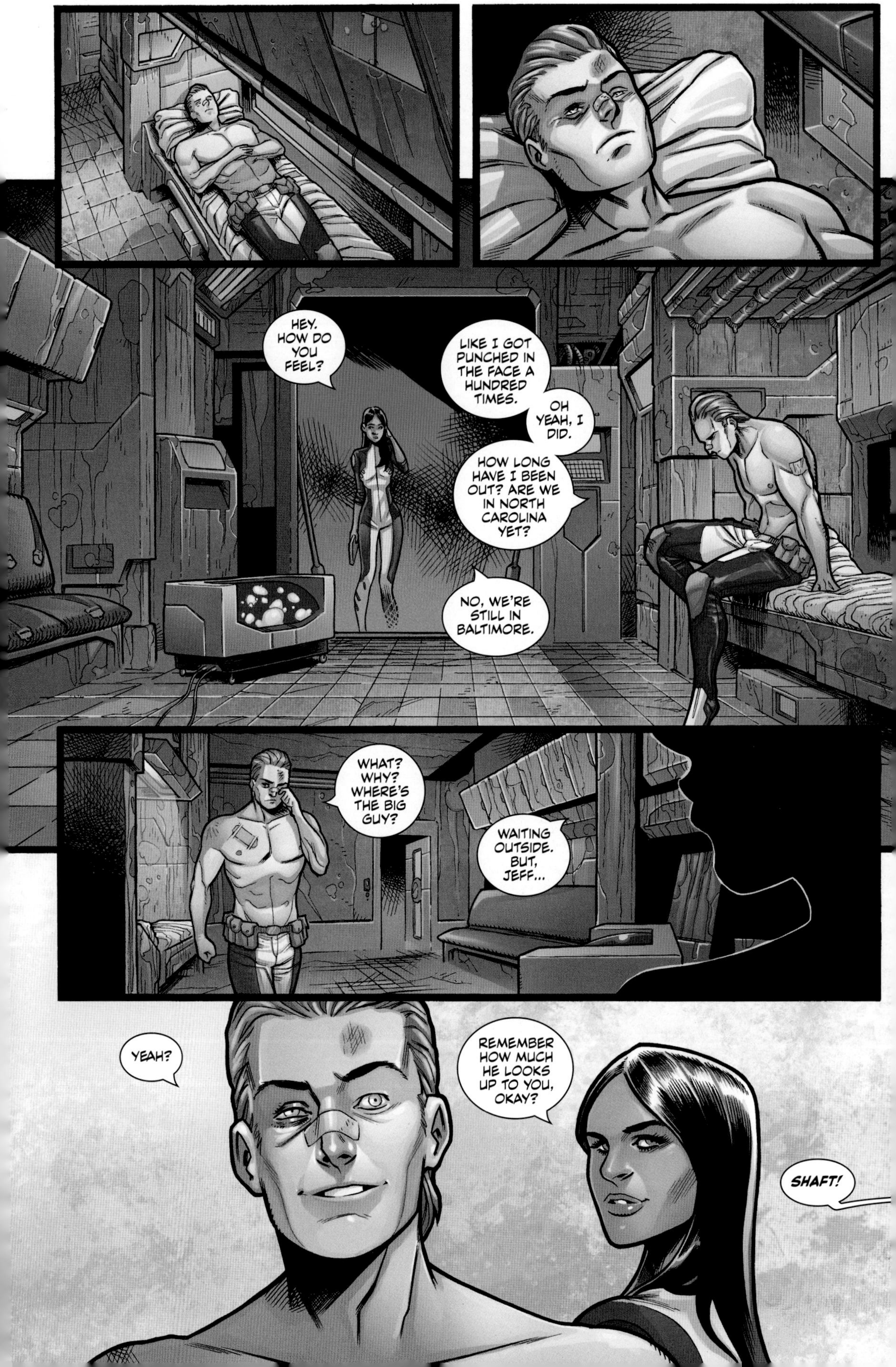
HEY. HOW DO YOU FEEL?
LIKE I GOT PUNCHED IN THE FACE A HUNDRED TIMES.
OH YEAH, I DID.
HOW LONG HAVE I BEEN OUT? ARE WE IN NORTH CAROLINA YET?
NO, WE'RE STILL IN BALTIMORE.
WHAT? WHY? WHERE'S THE BIG GUY?
WAITING OUTSIDE. BUT, JEFF...
YEAH?
REMEMBER HOW MUCH HE LOOKS UP TO YOU, OKAY?
SHAFT!

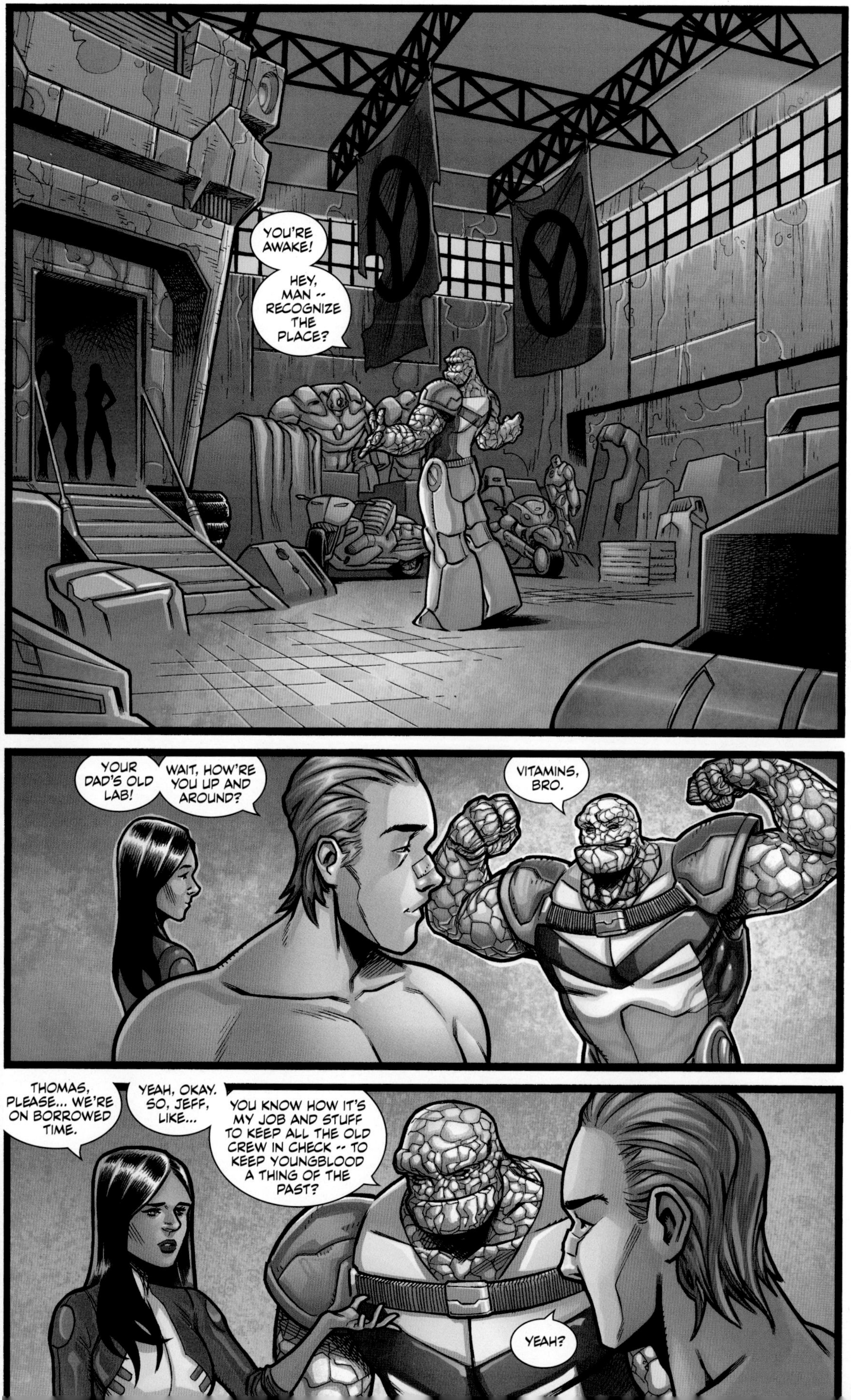
YOU'RE AWAKE!
HEY, MAN -- RECOGNIZE THE PLACE?
YOUR DAD'S OLD LAB!
WAIT, HOW'RE YOU UP AND AROUND?
VITAMINS, BRO.
THOMAS, PLEASE... WE'RE ON BORROWED TIME.
YEAH, OKAY. SO, JEFF, LIKE...
YOU KNOW HOW IT'S MY JOB AND STUFF TO KEEP ALL THE OLD CREW IN CHECK -- TO KEEP YOUNGBLOOD A THING OF THE PAST?
YEAH?

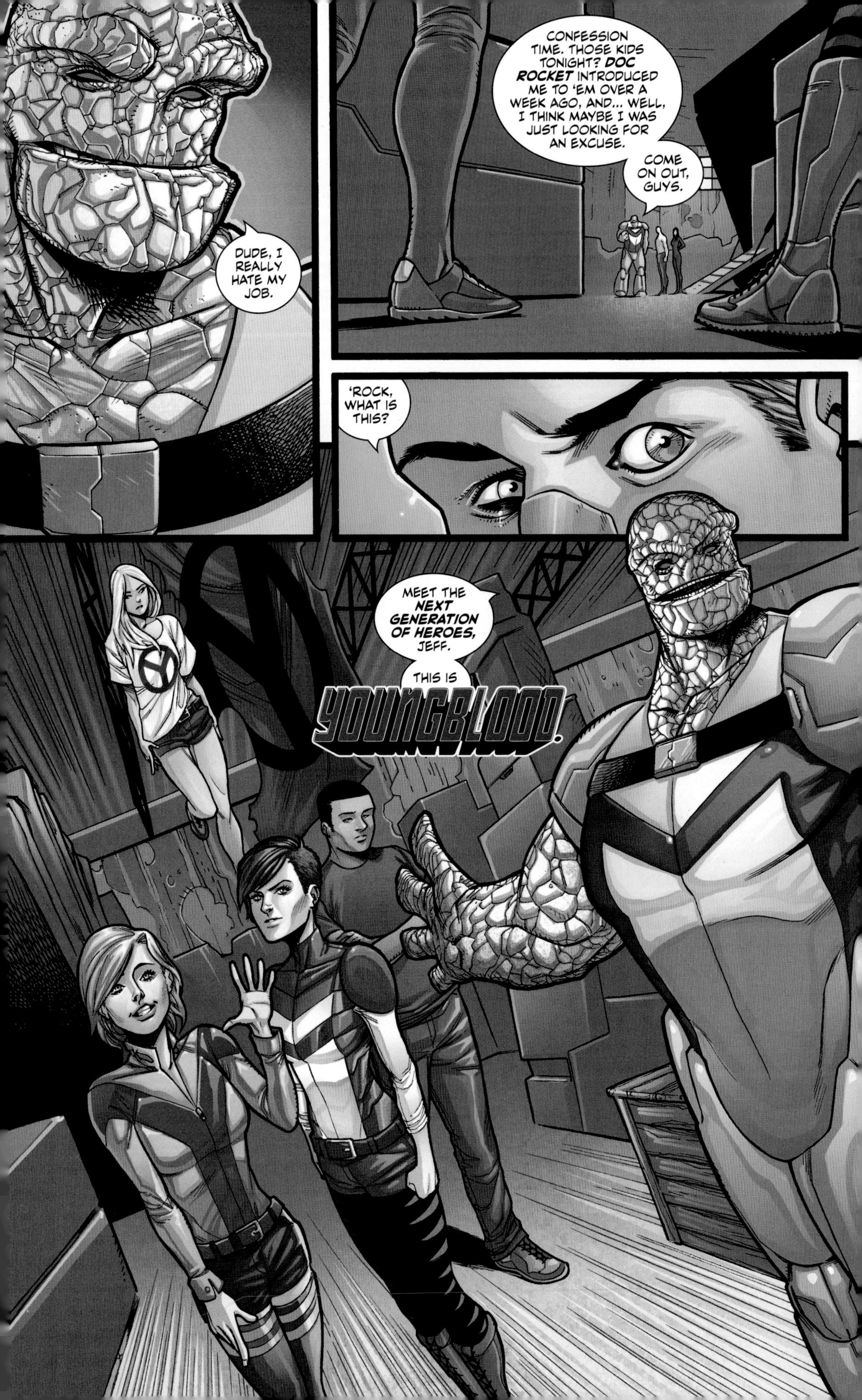
DUDE, I REALLY HATE MY JOB.
CONFESSION TIME. THOSE KIDS TONIGHT? DOC ROCKET INTRODUCED ME TO 'EM OVER A WEEK AGO, AND... WELL, I THINK MAYBE I WAS JUST LOOKING FOR AN EXCUSE.
COME ON OUT, GUYS.
'ROCK, WHAT IS THIS?
MEET THE NEXT GENERATION OF HEROES, JEFF.
THIS IS
YOUNGBLOOD.

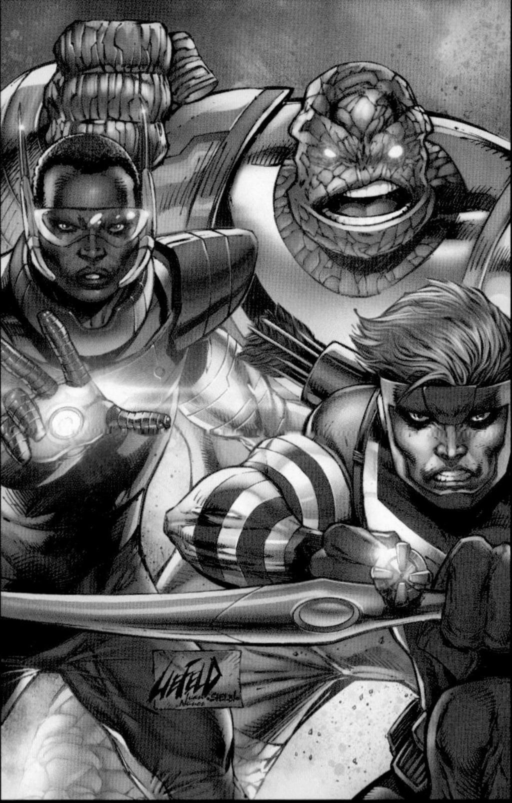

ART BY ROB LIEFELD

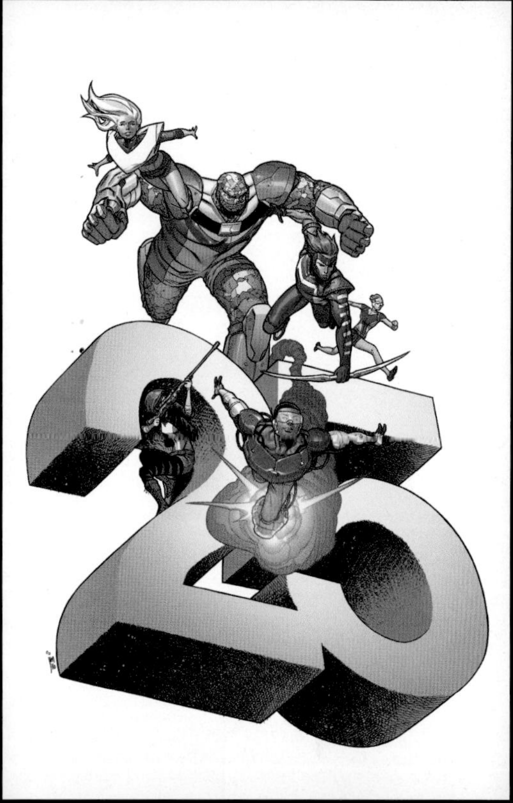

ART BY JIM TOWE

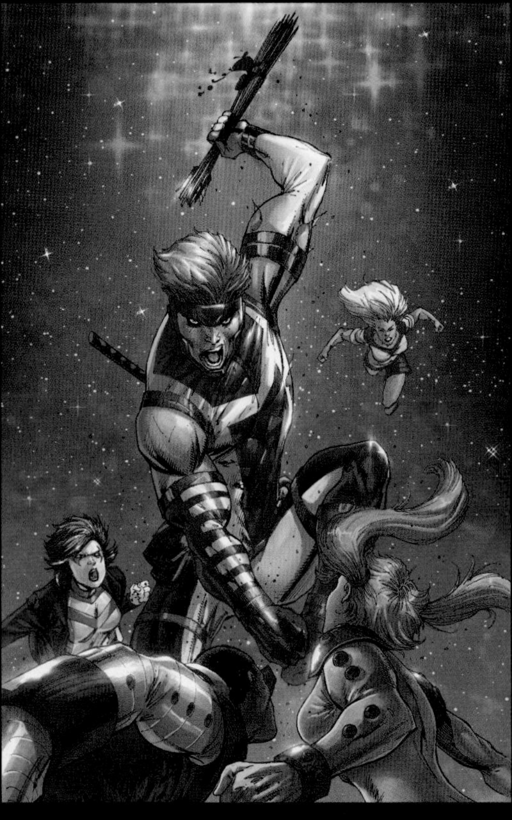

ART BY ROB LIEFELD

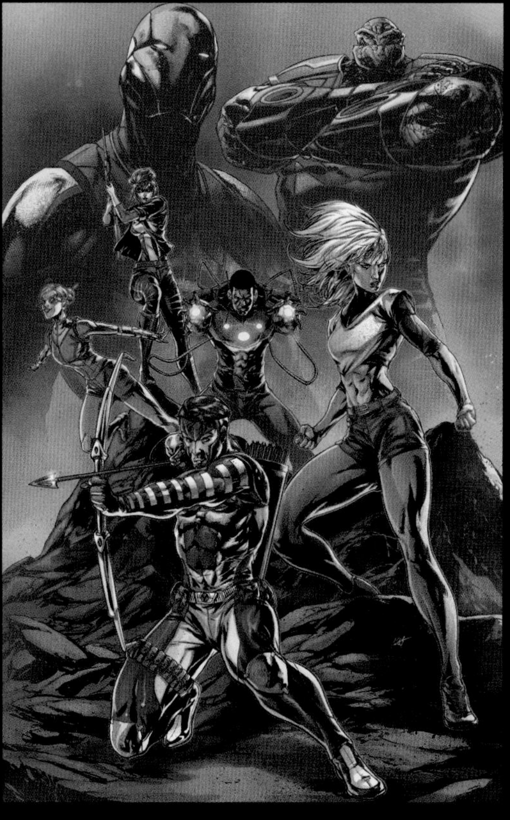

ART BY CAANAN WHITE

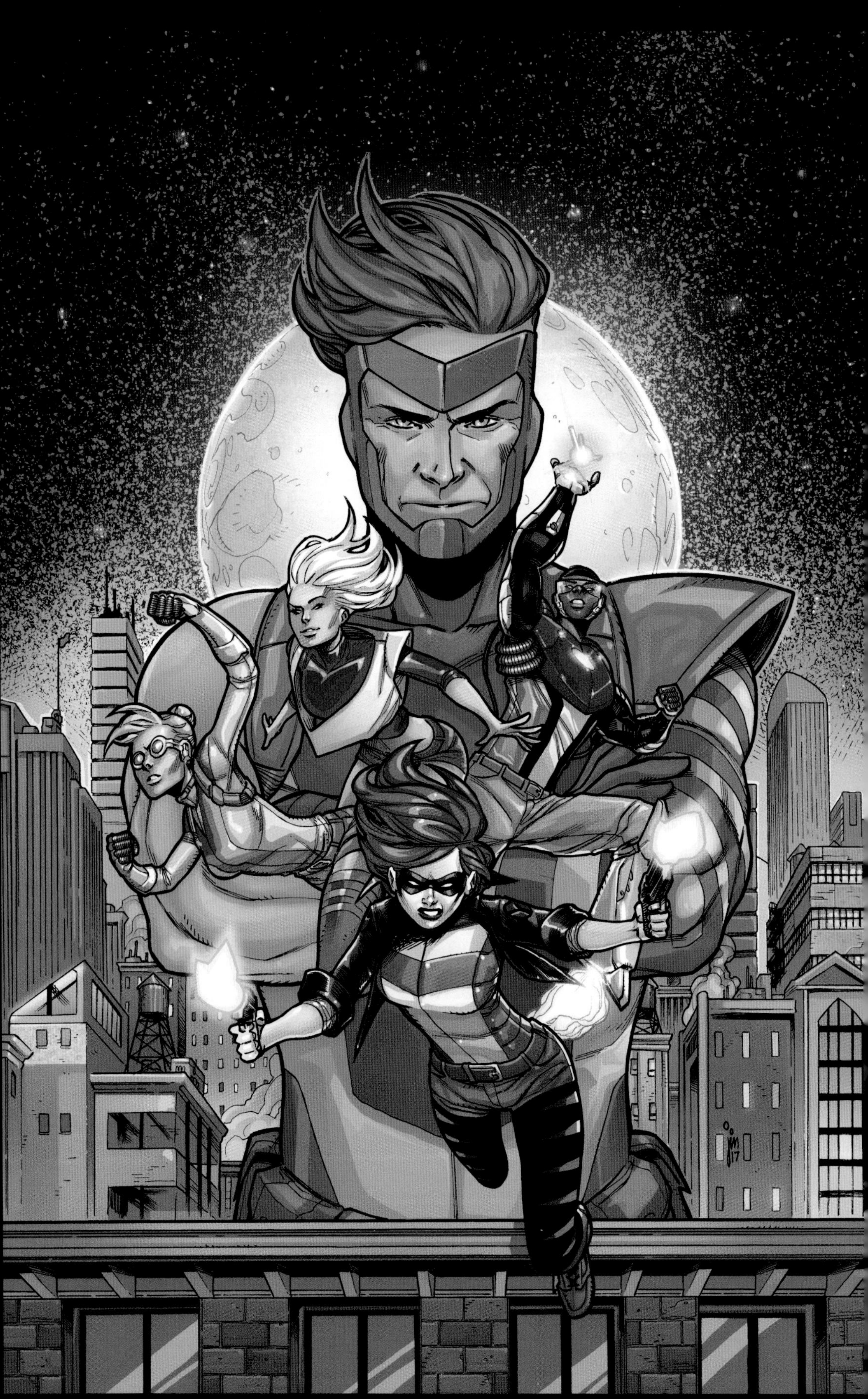

CHAPTER THREE: ...THICKER THAN WATER

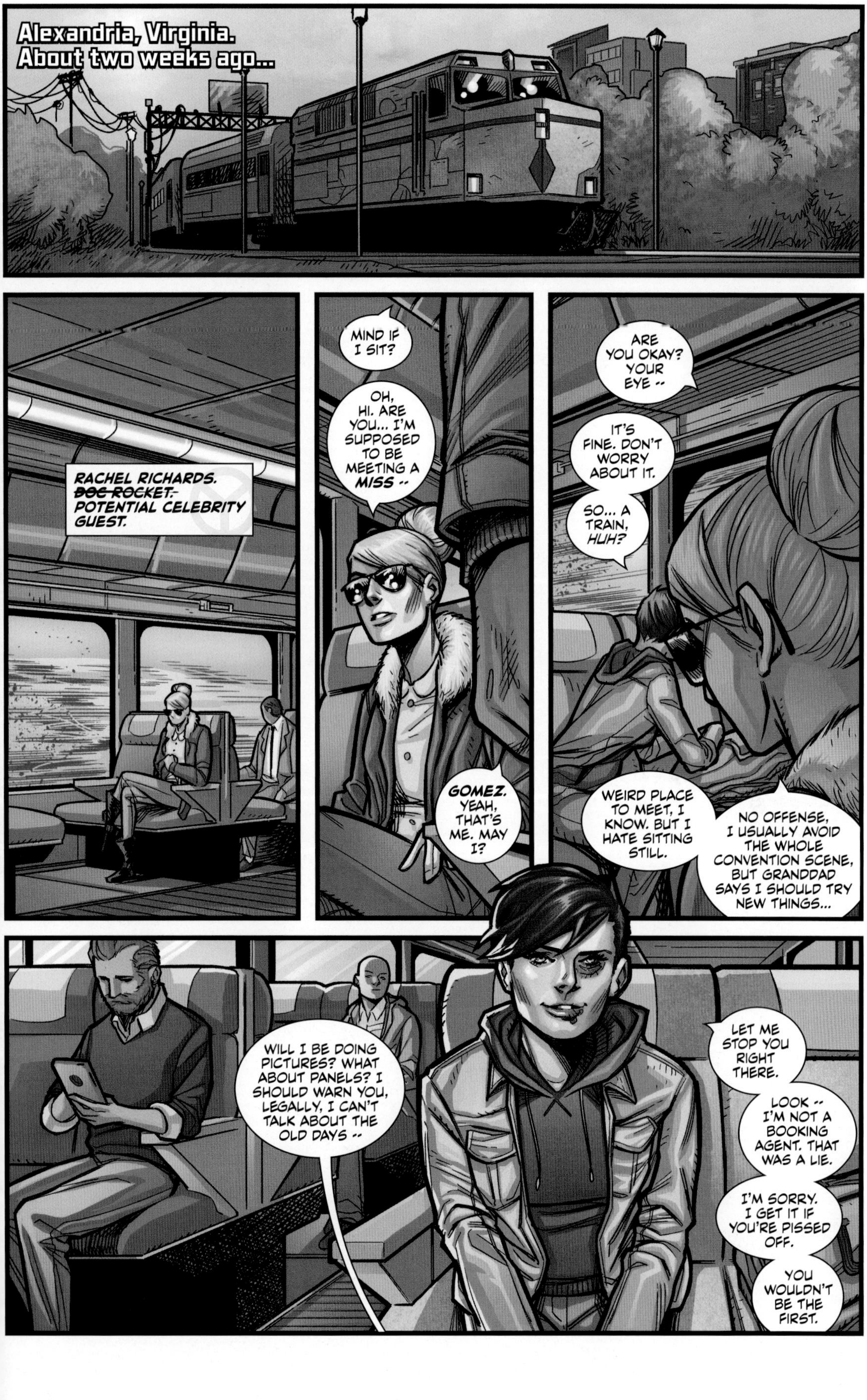

Alexandria, Virginia. About two weeks ago...
RACHEL RICHARDS. ~~DOC ROCKET.~~ POTENTIAL CELEBRITY GUEST.
MIND IF I SIT?
OH, HI. ARE YOU... I'M SUPPOSED TO BE MEETING A *MISS* --
GOMEZ. YEAH, THAT'S ME. MAY I?
ARE YOU OKAY? YOUR EYE --
IT'S FINE. DON'T WORRY ABOUT IT.
SO... A TRAIN, *HUH?*
WEIRD PLACE TO MEET, I KNOW. BUT I HATE SITTING STILL.
NO OFFENSE, I USUALLY AVOID THE WHOLE CONVENTION SCENE, BUT GRANDDAD SAYS I SHOULD TRY NEW THINGS...
WILL I BE DOING PICTURES? WHAT ABOUT PANELS? I SHOULD WARN YOU, LEGALLY, I CAN'T TALK ABOUT THE OLD DAYS --
LET ME STOP YOU RIGHT THERE.
LOOK -- I'M NOT A BOOKING AGENT. THAT WAS A LIE.
I'M SORRY. I GET IT IF YOU'RE PISSED OFF.
YOU WOULDN'T BE THE FIRST.

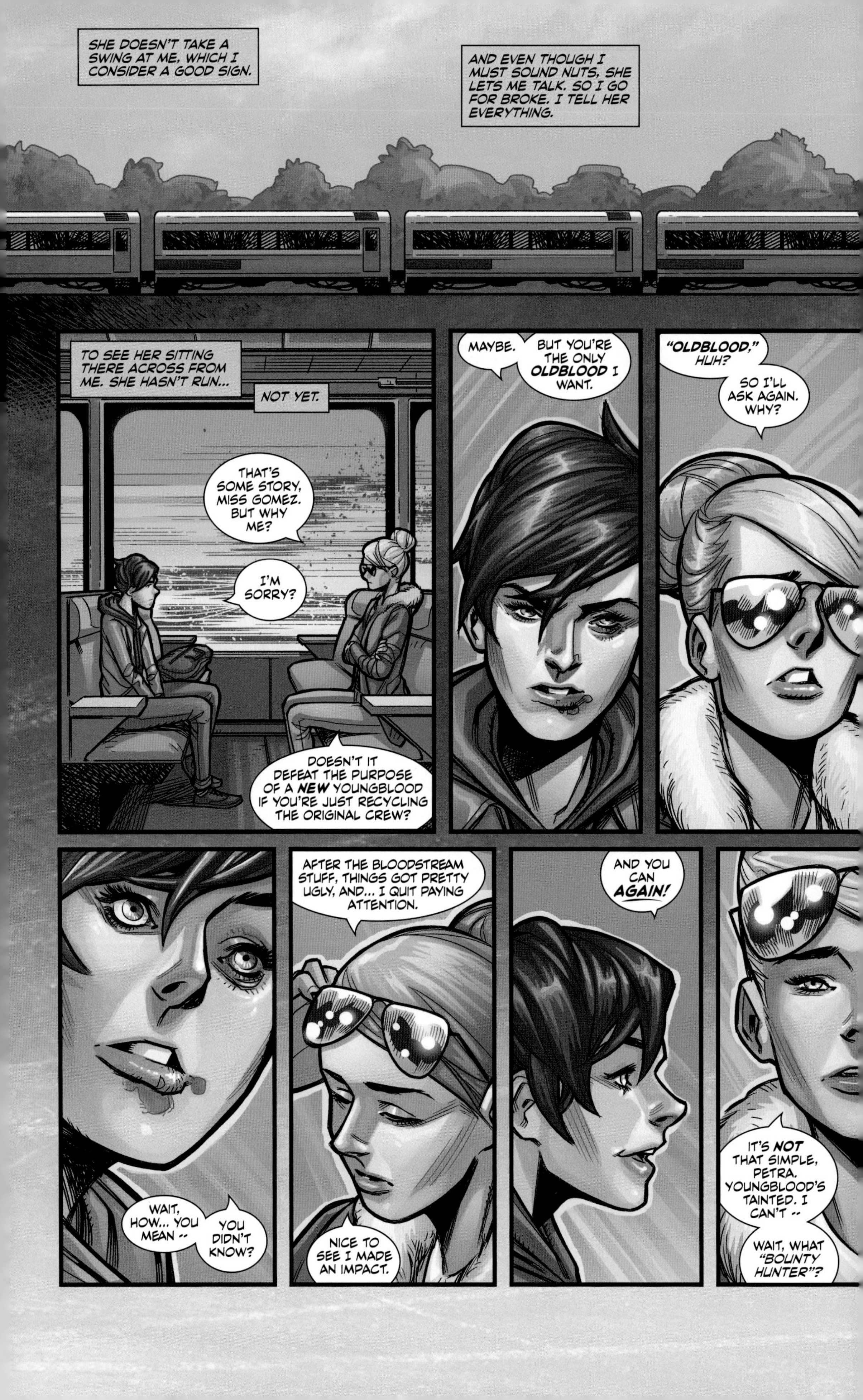

SHE DOESN'T TAKE A SWING AT ME, WHICH I CONSIDER A GOOD SIGN.
AND EVEN THOUGH I MUST SOUND NUTS, SHE LETS ME TALK. SO I GO FOR BROKE. I TELL HER EVERYTHING.
TO SEE HER SITTING THERE ACROSS FROM ME. SHE HASN'T RUN...
NOT YET.
THAT'S SOME STORY, MISS GOMEZ. BUT WHY ME?
I'M SORRY?
DOESN'T IT DEFEAT THE PURPOSE OF A NEW YOUNGBLOOD IF YOU'RE JUST RECYCLING THE ORIGINAL CREW?
MAYBE.
BUT YOU'RE THE ONLY OLDBLOOD I WANT.
"OLDBLOOD," HUH?
SO I'LL ASK AGAIN. WHY?
WAIT, HOW... YOU MEAN --
YOU DIDN'T KNOW?
AFTER THE BLOODSTREAM STUFF, THINGS GOT PRETTY UGLY, AND... I QUIT PAYING ATTENTION.
NICE TO SEE I MADE AN IMPACT.
AND YOU CAN AGAIN!
IT'S NOT THAT SIMPLE, PETRA. YOUNGBLOOD'S TAINTED. I CAN'T --
WAIT, WHAT "BOUNTY HUNTER"?

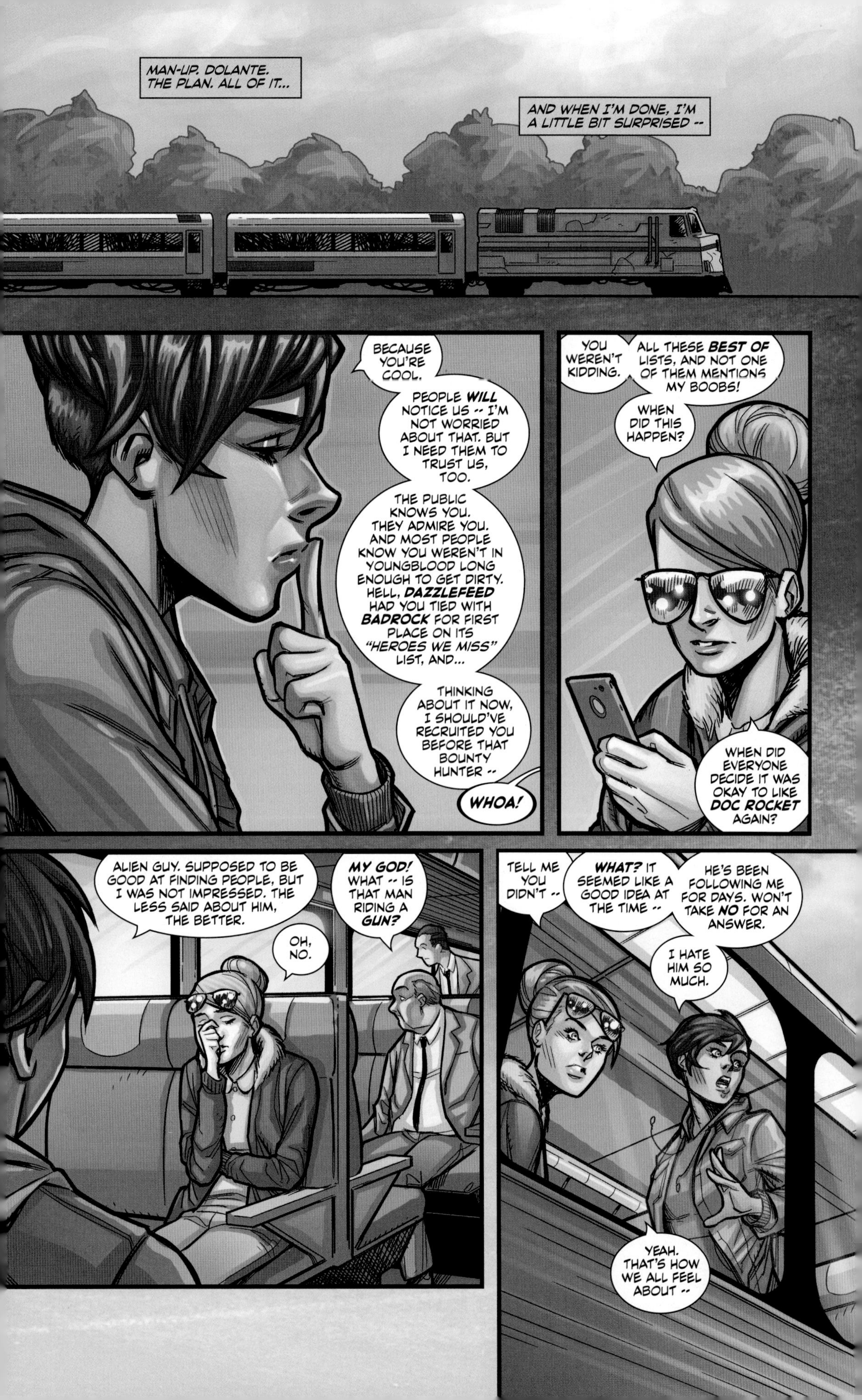
MAN-UP, DOLANTE. THE PLAN. ALL OF IT...
AND WHEN I'M DONE, I'M A LITTLE BIT SURPRISED --
BECAUSE YOU'RE COOL.
PEOPLE **WILL** NOTICE US -- I'M NOT WORRIED ABOUT THAT. BUT I NEED THEM TO TRUST US, TOO.
THE PUBLIC KNOWS YOU. THEY ADMIRE YOU. AND MOST PEOPLE KNOW YOU WEREN'T IN YOUNGBLOOD LONG ENOUGH TO GET DIRTY. HELL, **DAZZLEFEED** HAD YOU TIED WITH **BADROCK** FOR FIRST PLACE ON ITS *"HEROES WE MISS"* LIST, AND...
THINKING ABOUT IT NOW, I SHOULD'VE RECRUITED YOU BEFORE THAT BOUNTY HUNTER --
WHOA!
YOU WEREN'T KIDDING.
ALL THESE **BEST OF** LISTS, AND NOT ONE OF THEM MENTIONS MY BOOBS!
WHEN DID THIS HAPPEN?
WHEN DID EVERYONE DECIDE IT WAS OKAY TO LIKE **DOC ROCKET** AGAIN?
ALIEN GUY. SUPPOSED TO BE GOOD AT FINDING PEOPLE, BUT I WAS NOT IMPRESSED. THE LESS SAID ABOUT HIM, THE BETTER.
OH, NO.
MY GOD! WHAT -- IS THAT MAN RIDING A **GUN?**
TELL ME YOU DIDN'T --
WHAT? IT SEEMED LIKE A GOOD IDEA AT THE TIME --
HE'S BEEN FOLLOWING ME FOR DAYS. WON'T TAKE **NO** FOR AN ANSWER.
I HATE HIM SO MUCH.
YEAH. THAT'S HOW WE ALL FEEL ABOUT --

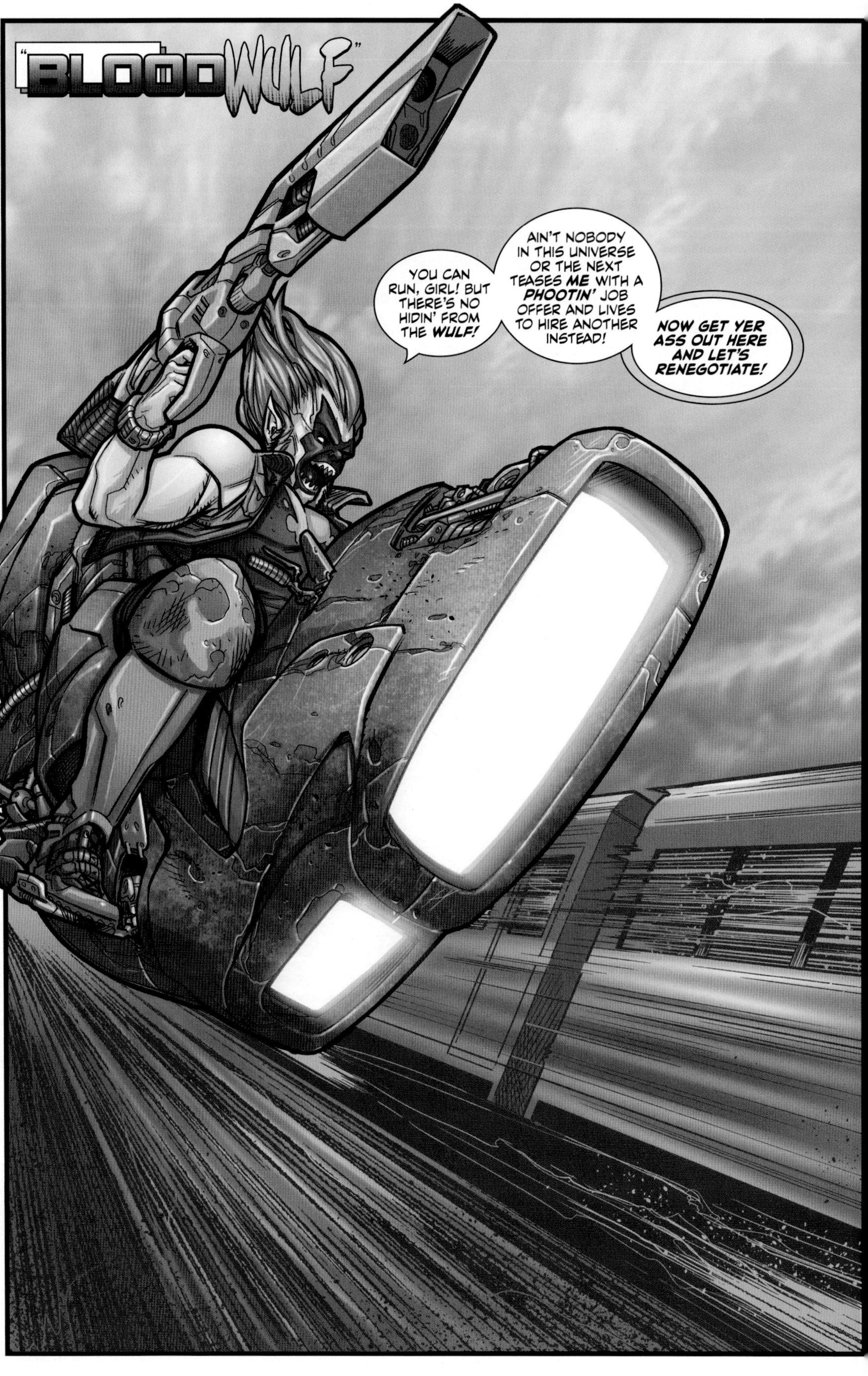
"BLOODWULF"
YOU CAN RUN, GIRL! BUT THERE'S NO HIDIN' FROM THE WULF!
AIN'T NOBODY IN THIS UNIVERSE OR THE NEXT TEASES ME WITH A PHOOTIN' JOB OFFER AND LIVES TO HIRE ANOTHER INSTEAD!
NOW GET YER ASS OUT HERE AND LET'S RENEGOTIATE!

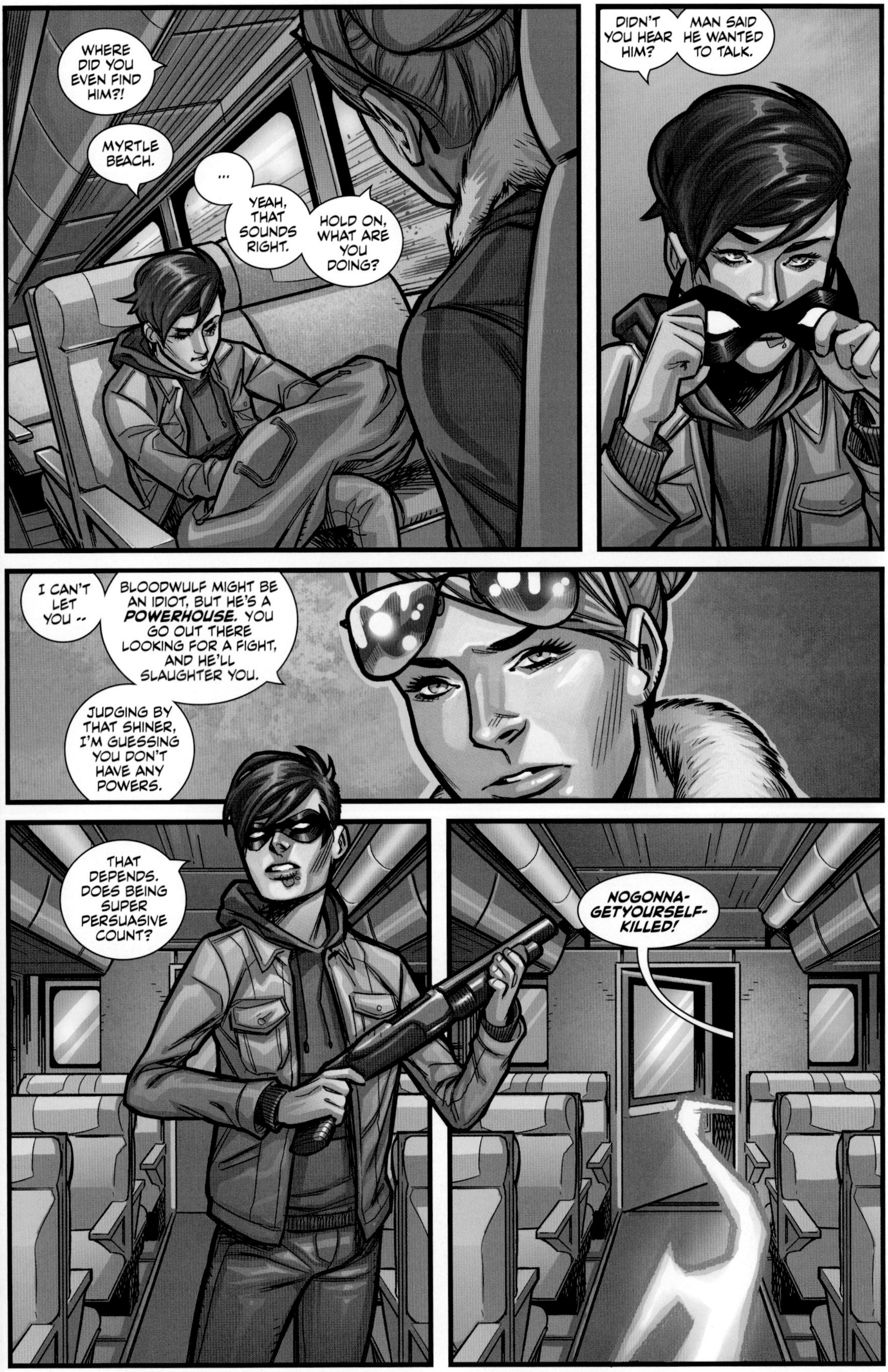
WHERE DID YOU EVEN FIND HIM?!
MYRTLE BEACH.
...
YEAH, THAT SOUNDS RIGHT.
HOLD ON, WHAT ARE YOU DOING?
DIDN'T YOU HEAR HIM?
MAN SAID HE WANTED TO TALK.
I CAN'T LET YOU --
BLOODWULF MIGHT BE AN IDIOT, BUT HE'S A POWERHOUSE. YOU GO OUT THERE LOOKING FOR A FIGHT, AND HE'LL SLAUGHTER YOU.
JUDGING BY THAT SHINER, I'M GUESSING YOU DON'T HAVE ANY POWERS.
THAT DEPENDS. DOES BEING SUPER PERSUASIVE COUNT?
NOGONNA-GETYOURSELF-KILLED!

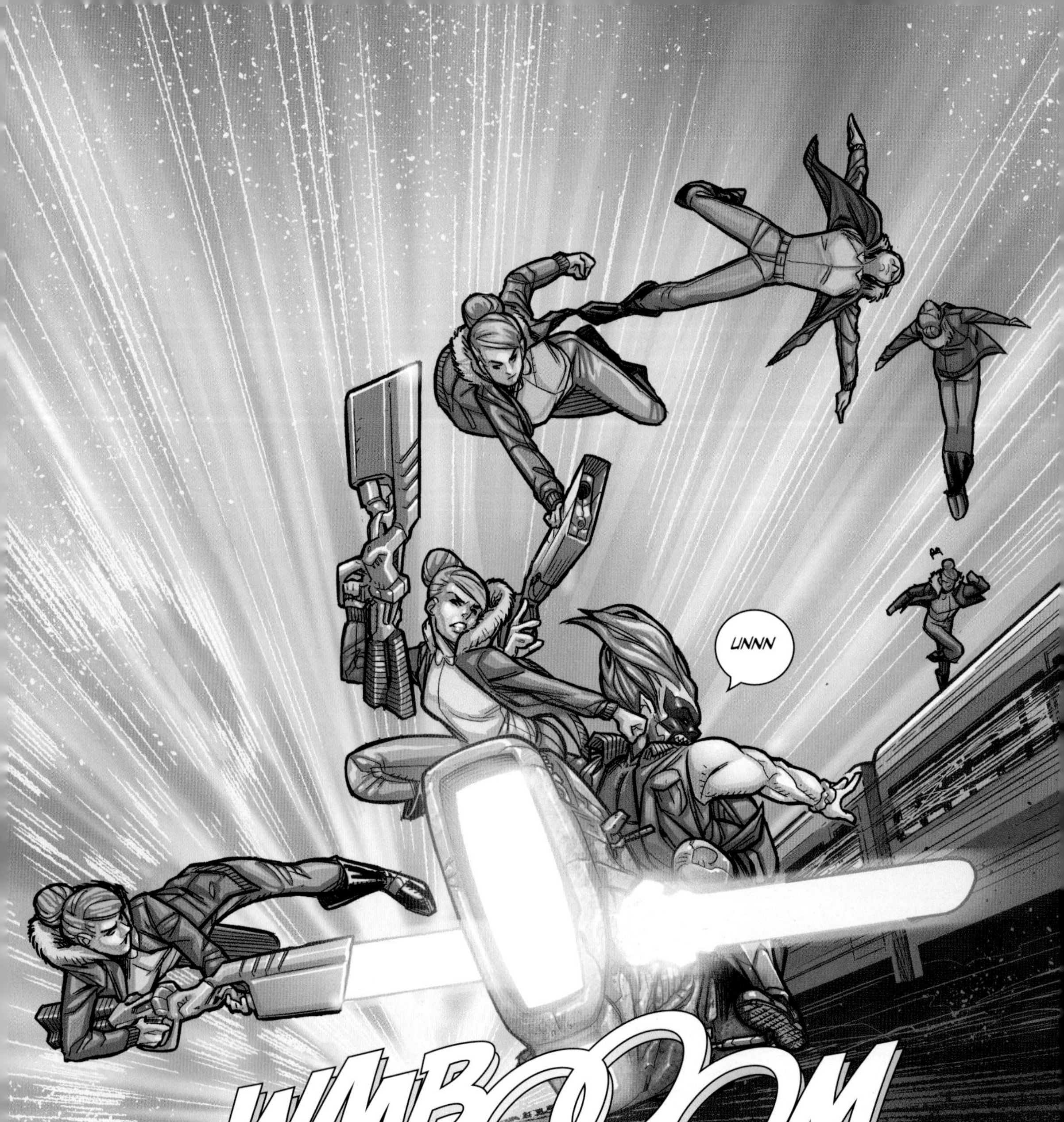
UNNN
WAABOOOM

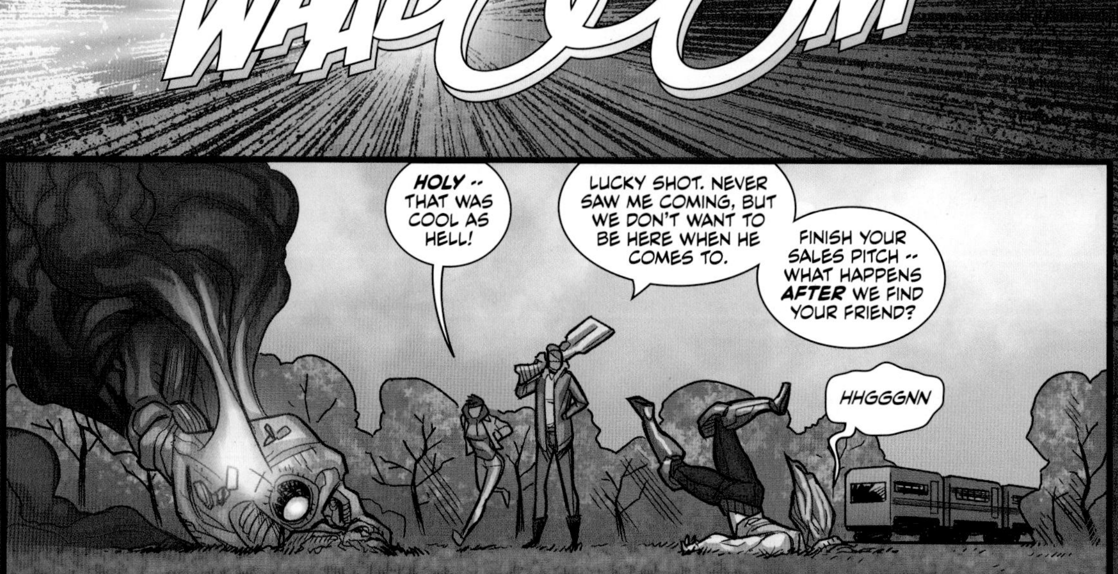
HOLY -- THAT WAS COOL AS HELL!
LUCKY SHOT. NEVER SAW ME COMING, BUT WE DON'T WANT TO BE HERE WHEN HE COMES TO.
FINISH YOUR SALES PITCH -- WHAT HAPPENS AFTER WE FIND YOUR FRIEND?
HHGGGNN

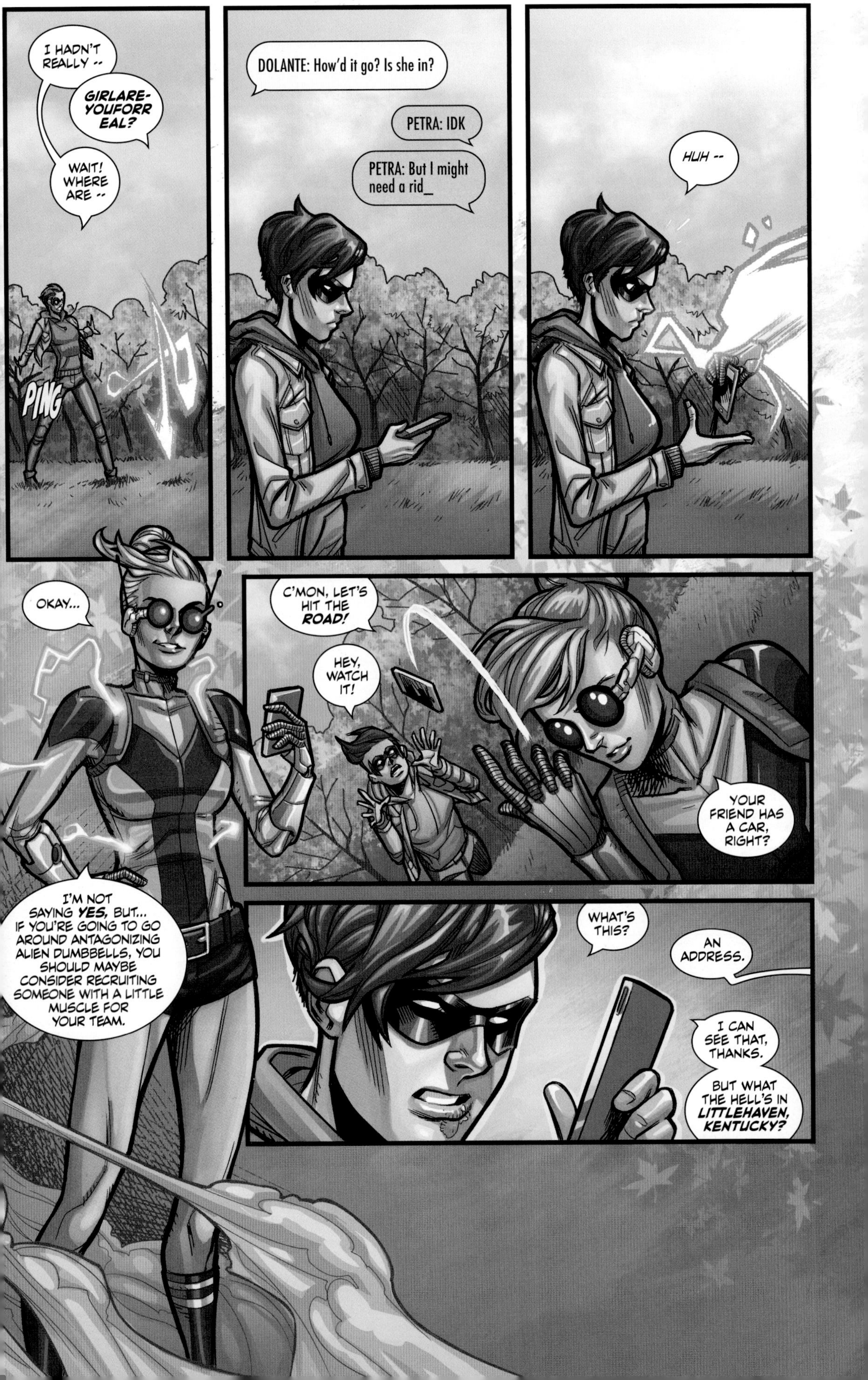
I HADN'T REALLY --
GIRLARE-YOUFORREAL?
WAIT! WHERE ARE --
PING
DOLANTE: How'd it go? Is she in?
PETRA: IDK
PETRA: But I might need a rid_
HUH --
OKAY...
I'M NOT SAYING YES, BUT... IF YOU'RE GOING TO GO AROUND ANTAGONIZING ALIEN DUMBBELLS, YOU SHOULD MAYBE CONSIDER RECRUITING SOMEONE WITH A LITTLE MUSCLE FOR YOUR TEAM.
C'MON, LET'S HIT THE ROAD!
HEY, WATCH IT!
YOUR FRIEND HAS A CAR, RIGHT?
WHAT'S THIS?
AN ADDRESS.
I CAN SEE THAT, THANKS.
BUT WHAT THE HELL'S IN LITTLEHAVEN, KENTUCKY?

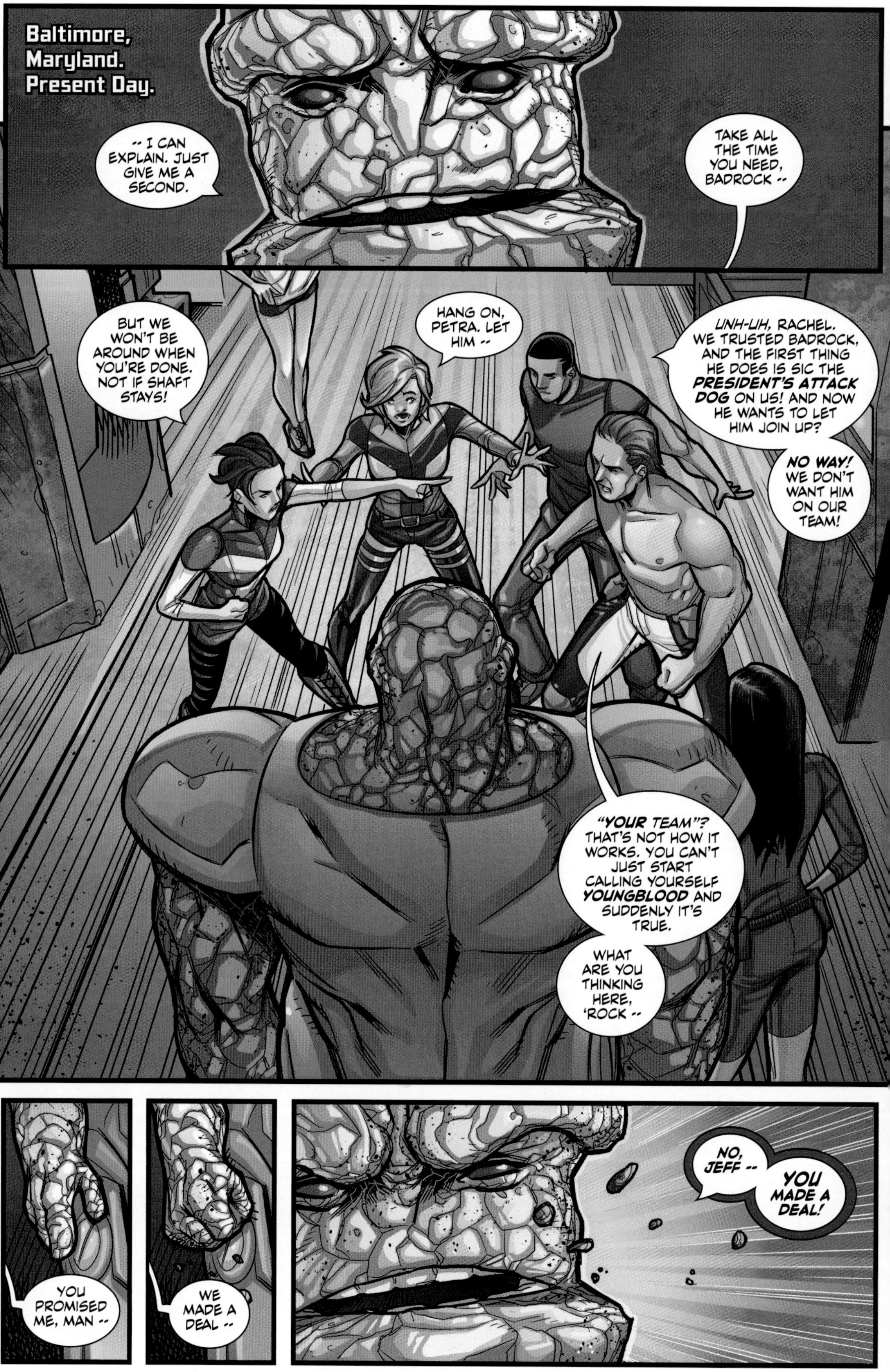
Baltimore, Maryland. Present Day.
-- I CAN EXPLAIN. JUST GIVE ME A SECOND.
TAKE ALL THE TIME YOU NEED, BADROCK --
BUT WE WON'T BE AROUND WHEN YOU'RE DONE. NOT IF SHAFT STAYS!
HANG ON, PETRA. LET HIM --
UNH-UH, RACHEL. WE TRUSTED BADROCK, AND THE FIRST THING HE DOES IS SIC THE PRESIDENT'S ATTACK DOG ON US! AND NOW HE WANTS TO LET HIM JOIN UP?
NO WAY! WE DON'T WANT HIM ON OUR TEAM!
"YOUR TEAM"? THAT'S NOT HOW IT WORKS. YOU CAN'T JUST START CALLING YOURSELF YOUNGBLOOD AND SUDDENLY IT'S TRUE.
WHAT ARE YOU THINKING HERE, 'ROCK --
YOU PROMISED ME, MAN --
WE MADE A DEAL --
NO, JEFF --
YOU MADE A DEAL!

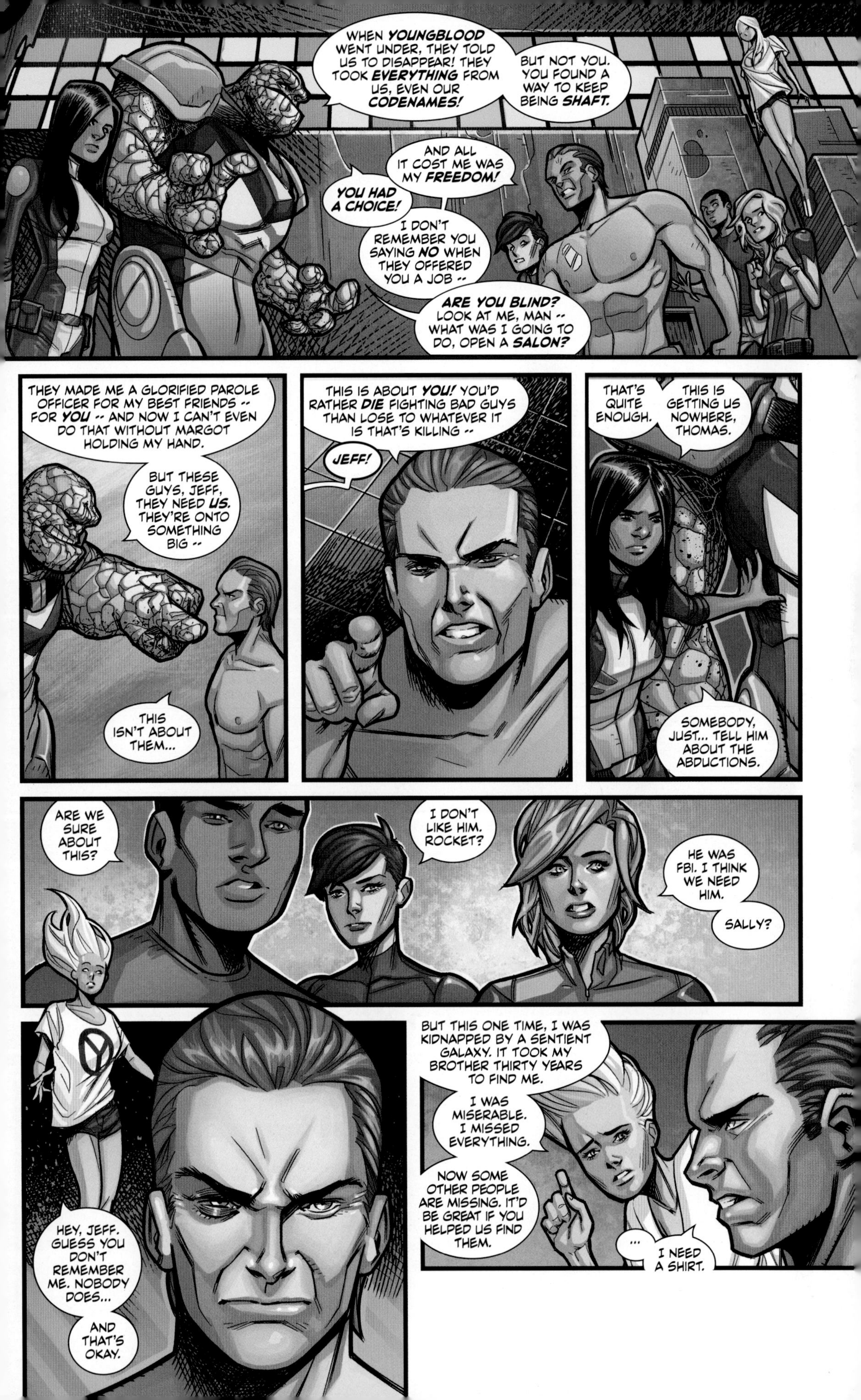
WHEN YOUNGBLOOD WENT UNDER, THEY TOLD US TO DISAPPEAR! THEY TOOK EVERYTHING FROM US, EVEN OUR CODENAMES!
BUT NOT YOU. YOU FOUND A WAY TO KEEP BEING SHAFT.
AND ALL IT COST ME WAS MY FREEDOM!
YOU HAD A CHOICE!
I DON'T REMEMBER YOU SAYING NO WHEN THEY OFFERED YOU A JOB --
ARE YOU BLIND? LOOK AT ME, MAN -- WHAT WAS I GOING TO DO, OPEN A SALON?
THEY MADE ME A GLORIFIED PAROLE OFFICER FOR MY BEST FRIENDS -- FOR YOU -- AND NOW I CAN'T EVEN DO THAT WITHOUT MARGOT HOLDING MY HAND.
BUT THESE GUYS, JEFF, THEY NEED US. THEY'RE ONTO SOMETHING BIG --
THIS ISN'T ABOUT THEM...
THIS IS ABOUT YOU! YOU'D RATHER DIE FIGHTING BAD GUYS THAN LOSE TO WHATEVER IT IS THAT'S KILLING --
JEFF!
THAT'S QUITE ENOUGH.
THIS IS GETTING US NOWHERE, THOMAS.
SOMEBODY, JUST... TELL HIM ABOUT THE ABDUCTIONS.
ARE WE SURE ABOUT THIS?
I DON'T LIKE HIM. ROCKET?
HE WAS FBI. I THINK WE NEED HIM.
SALLY?
HEY, JEFF. GUESS YOU DON'T REMEMBER ME. NOBODY DOES...
AND THAT'S OKAY.
BUT THIS ONE TIME, I WAS KIDNAPPED BY A SENTIENT GALAXY. IT TOOK MY BROTHER THIRTY YEARS TO FIND ME.
I WAS MISERABLE. I MISSED EVERYTHING.
NOW SOME OTHER PEOPLE ARE MISSING. IT'D BE GREAT IF YOU HELPED US FIND THEM.
...
I NEED A SHIRT.

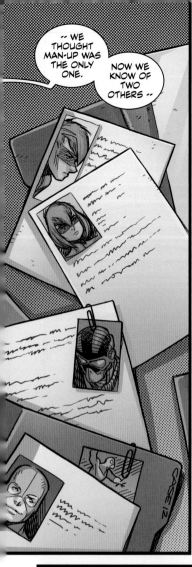

-- WE THOUGHT MAN-UP WAS THE ONLY ONE.

NOW WE KNOW OF TWO OTHERS --

AND THERE'S PROBABLY MORE.

MAN-UP WAS PETRA'S FRIEND. HOW'D YOU DISCOVER THE OTHERS?

IT WASN'T EASY. WHOEVER'S BEHIND THIS HAS THE RESOURCES TO VIRTUALLY ERASE ALL TRACES OF THEIR VICTIMS. SOCIAL MEDIA ACCOUNTS, VITAL RECORDS...

IT'S EERIE... BUT NOT PERFECT.

WHAT'D THEY MISS?

A COLLEGE NEWSPAPER.

YOU'RE KIDDING ME.

A SHORT TRAVEL PIECE -- FULL OF TYPOS, WHICH IS HOW THEY PROBABLY MISSED IT -- PROFILING THE TOP TEN *HELP!*ERS ACROSS THE U.S.

MAN-UP MADE THE LIST?

HE WAS NUMBER SIX --

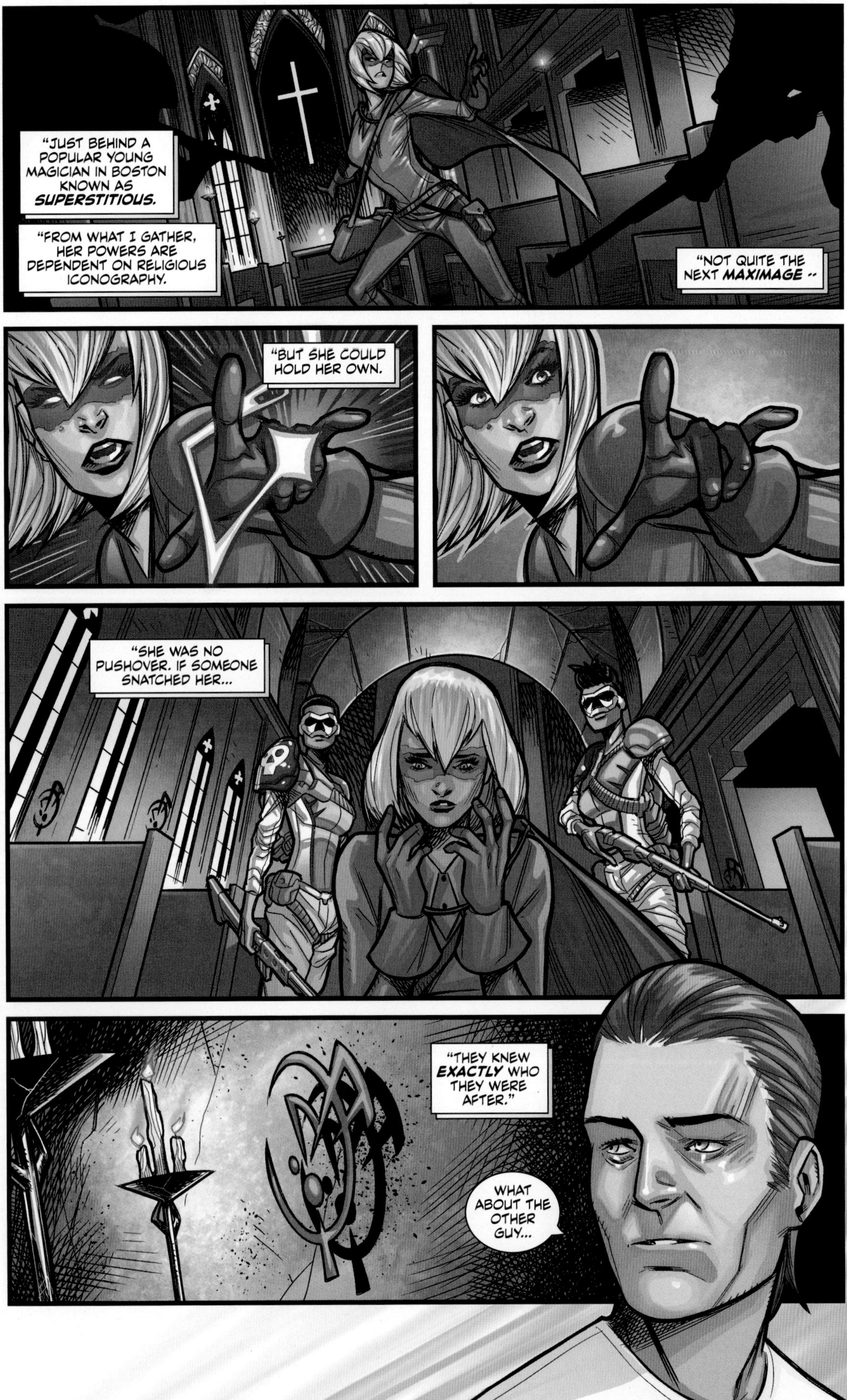
"JUST BEHIND A POPULAR YOUNG MAGICIAN IN BOSTON KNOWN AS SUPERSTITIOUS.
"FROM WHAT I GATHER, HER POWERS ARE DEPENDENT ON RELIGIOUS ICONOGRAPHY.
"NOT QUITE THE NEXT MAXIMAGE --
"BUT SHE COULD HOLD HER OWN.
"SHE WAS NO PUSHOVER. IF SOMEONE SNATCHED HER...
"THEY KNEW EXACTLY WHO THEY WERE AFTER."
WHAT ABOUT THE OTHER GUY...

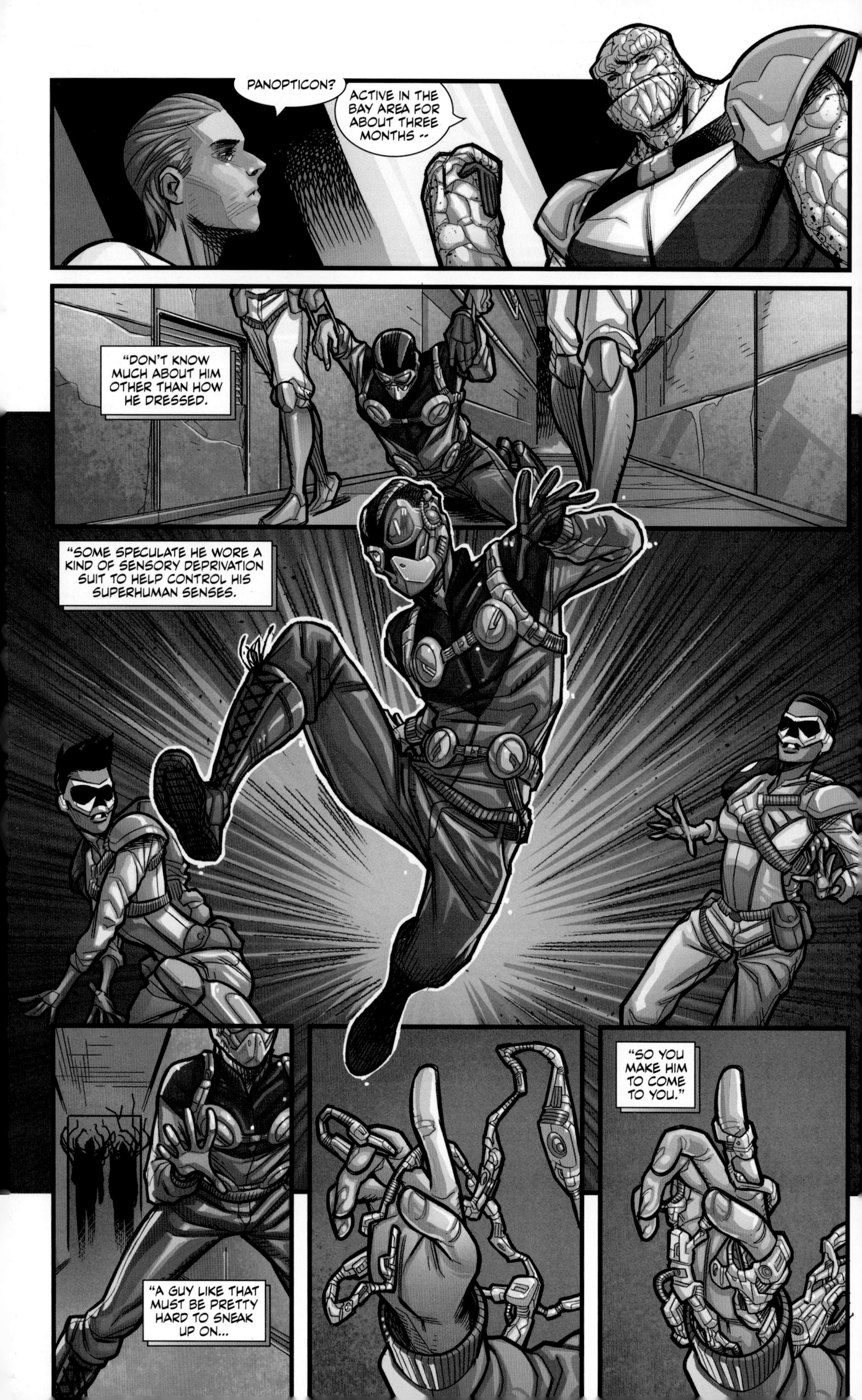
PANOPTICON?
ACTIVE IN THE BAY AREA FOR ABOUT THREE MONTHS --
"DON'T KNOW MUCH ABOUT HIM OTHER THAN HOW HE DRESSED.
"SOME SPECULATE HE WORE A KIND OF SENSORY DEPRIVATION SUIT TO HELP CONTROL HIS SUPERHUMAN SENSES.
"A GUY LIKE THAT MUST BE PRETTY HARD TO SNEAK UP ON...
"SO YOU MAKE HIM TO COME TO YOU."

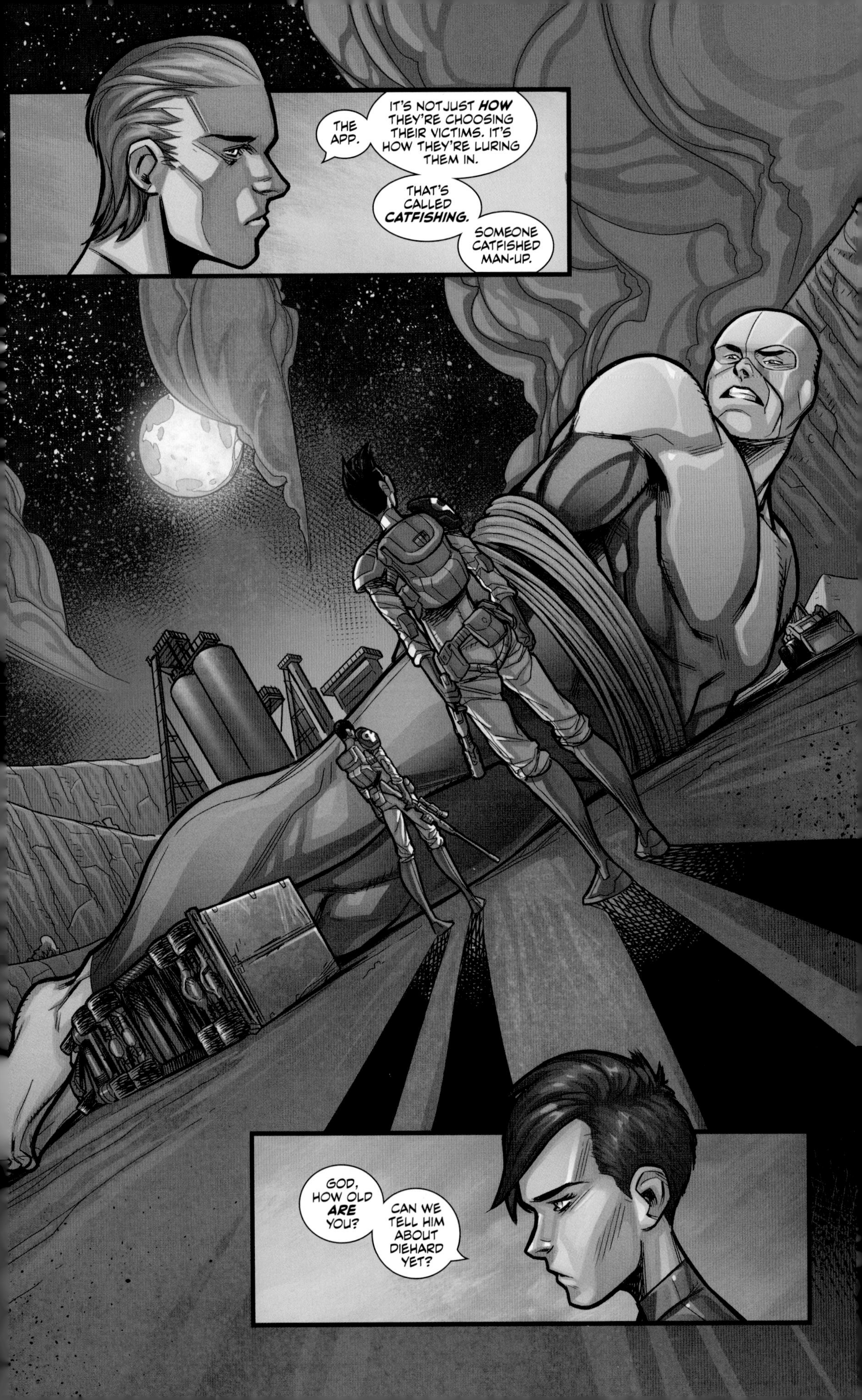
THE APP.
IT'S NOTJUST **HOW** THEY'RE CHOOSING THEIR VICTIMS. IT'S HOW THEY'RE LURING THEM IN.
THAT'S CALLED **CATFISHING.**
SOMEONE CATFISHED MAN-UP.
GOD, HOW OLD **ARE** YOU?
CAN WE TELL HIM ABOUT DIEHARD YET?

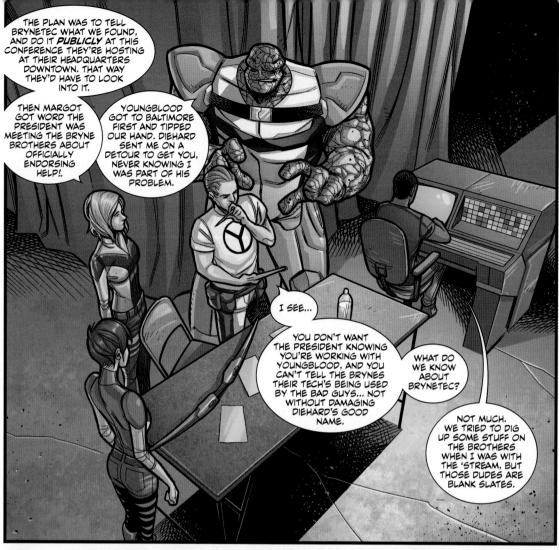

THE PLAN WAS TO TELL BRYNETEC WHAT WE FOUND, AND DO IT *PUBLICLY* AT THIS CONFERENCE THEY'RE HOSTING AT THEIR HEADQUARTERS DOWNTOWN. THAT WAY THEY'D HAVE TO LOOK INTO IT.

THEN MARGOT GOT WORD THE PRESIDENT WAS MEETING THE BRYNE BROTHERS ABOUT OFFICIALLY ENDORSING HELP!.

YOUNGBLOOD GOT TO BALTIMORE FIRST AND TIPPED OUR HAND. DIEHARD SENT ME ON A DETOUR TO GET YOU, NEVER KNOWING I WAS PART OF HIS PROBLEM.

I SEE...

YOU DON'T WANT THE PRESIDENT KNOWING YOU'RE WORKING WITH YOUNGBLOOD, AND YOU CAN'T TELL THE BRYNES THEIR TECH'S BEING USED BY THE BAD GUYS... NOT WITHOUT DAMAGING DIEHARD'S GOOD NAME.

WHAT DO WE KNOW ABOUT BRYNETEC?

NOT MUCH. WE TRIED TO DIG UP SOME STUFF ON THE BROTHERS WHEN I WAS WITH THE 'STREAM, BUT THOSE DUDES ARE BLANK SLATES.

WHAT DID YOU SAY?

THEY'RE BLANK SLATES. NOTHING JUICY --

NO!

WERE YOU PART OF THE *BLOOD-STREAM*?

UH...

DON'T SAY ANOTHER WORD, SON.

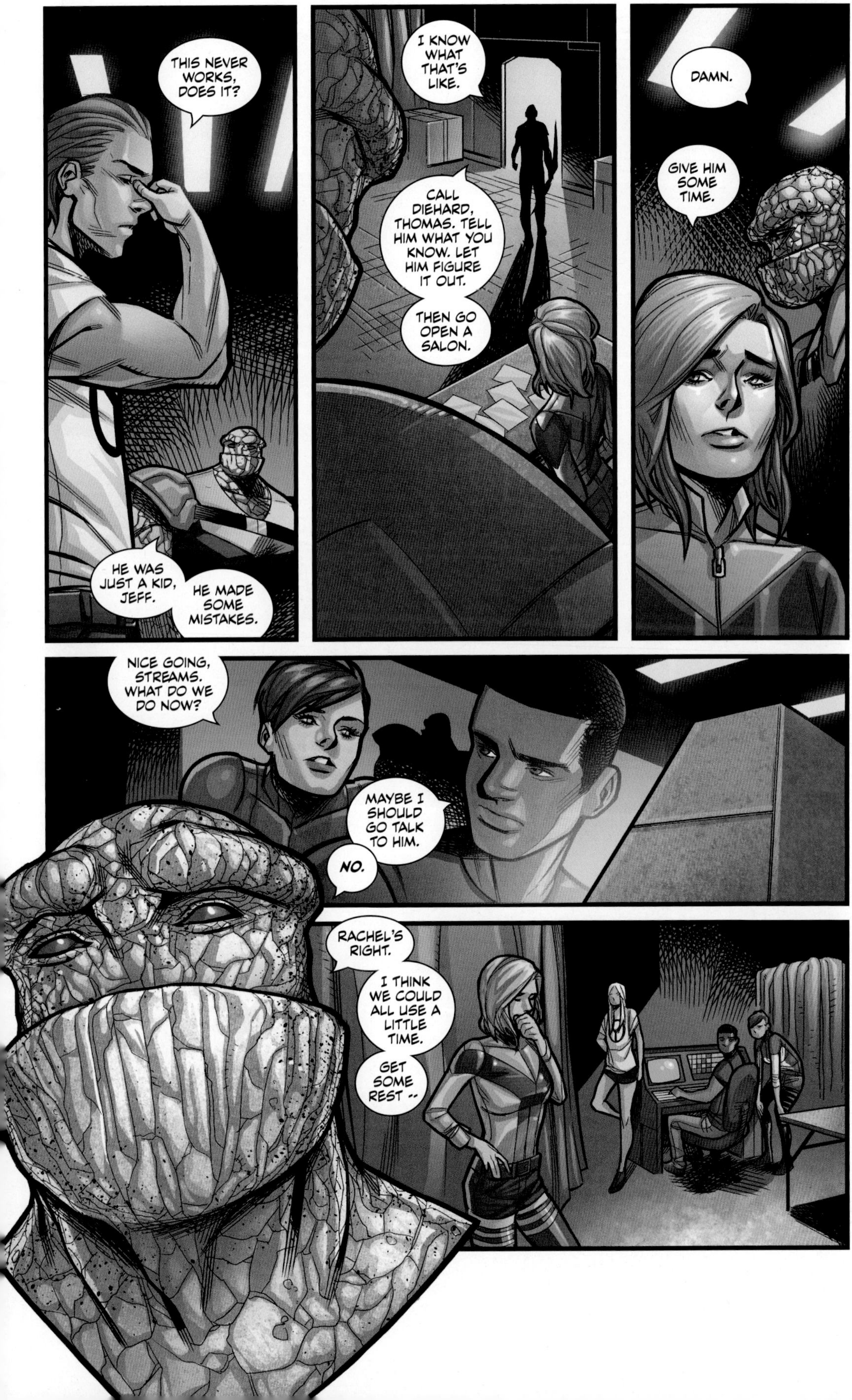
THIS NEVER WORKS, DOES IT?
HE WAS JUST A KID, JEFF.
HE MADE SOME MISTAKES.
I KNOW WHAT THAT'S LIKE.
CALL DIEHARD, THOMAS. TELL HIM WHAT YOU KNOW. LET HIM FIGURE IT OUT.
THEN GO OPEN A SALON.
DAMN.
GIVE HIM SOME TIME.
NICE GOING, STREAMS. WHAT DO WE DO NOW?
MAYBE I SHOULD GO TALK TO HIM.
NO.
RACHEL'S RIGHT.
I THINK WE COULD ALL USE A LITTLE TIME.
GET SOME REST --

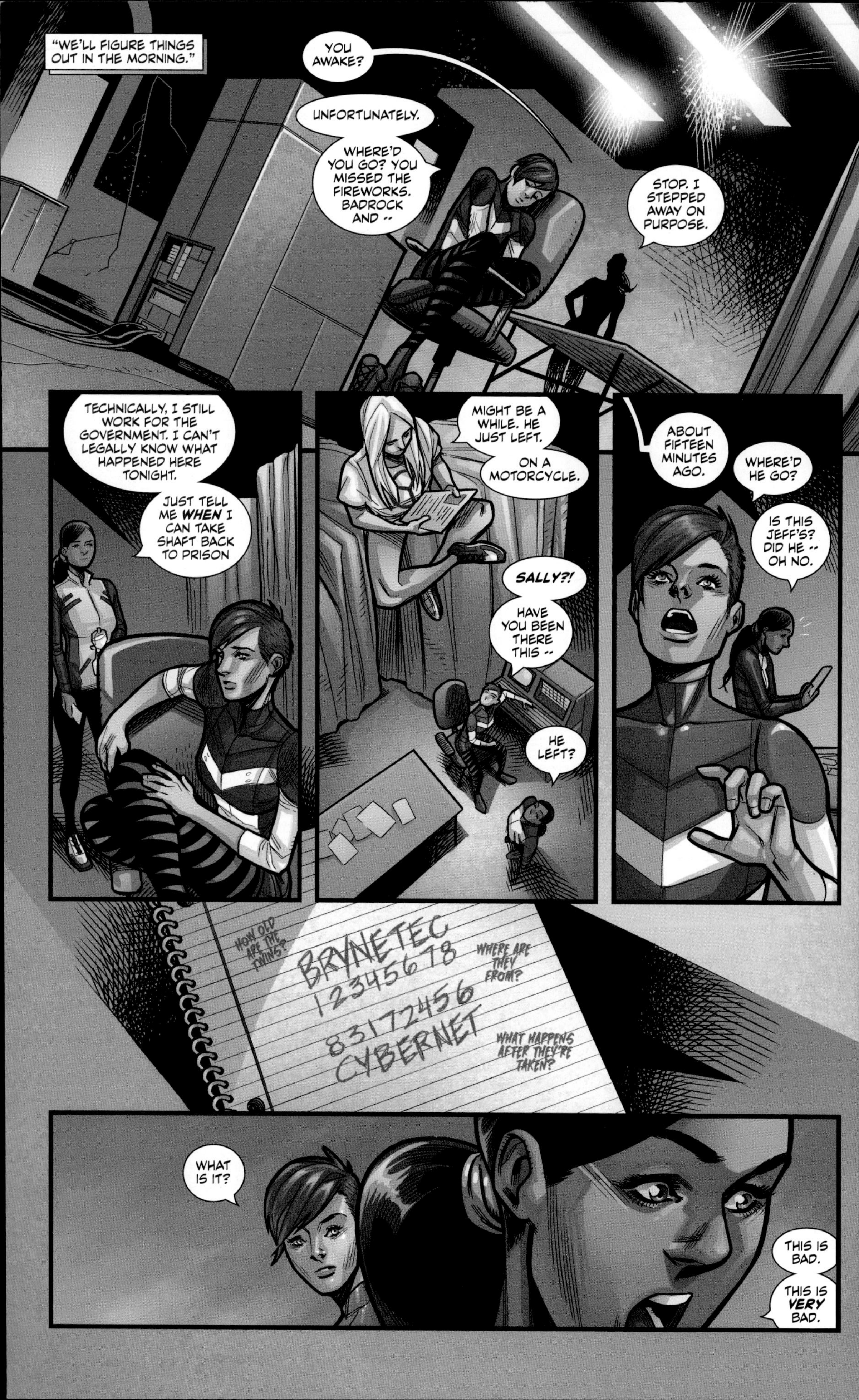
"WE'LL FIGURE THINGS OUT IN THE MORNING."
YOU AWAKE?
UNFORTUNATELY.
WHERE'D YOU GO? YOU MISSED THE FIREWORKS. BADROCK AND --
STOP. I STEPPED AWAY ON PURPOSE.
TECHNICALLY, I STILL WORK FOR THE GOVERNMENT. I CAN'T LEGALLY KNOW WHAT HAPPENED HERE TONIGHT.
JUST TELL ME *WHEN* I CAN TAKE SHAFT BACK TO PRISON
MIGHT BE A WHILE. HE JUST LEFT.
ON A MOTORCYCLE.
SALLY?!
HAVE YOU BEEN THERE THIS --
HE LEFT?
ABOUT FIFTEEN MINUTES AGO.
WHERE'D HE GO?
IS THIS JEFF'S? DID HE -- OH NO.
HOW OLD ARE THE TWINS?
BRYNETEC
12345678
83172456
CYBERNET
WHERE ARE THEY FROM?
WHAT HAPPENS AFTER THEY'RE TAKEN?
WHAT IS IT?
THIS IS BAD.
THIS IS *VERY* BAD.

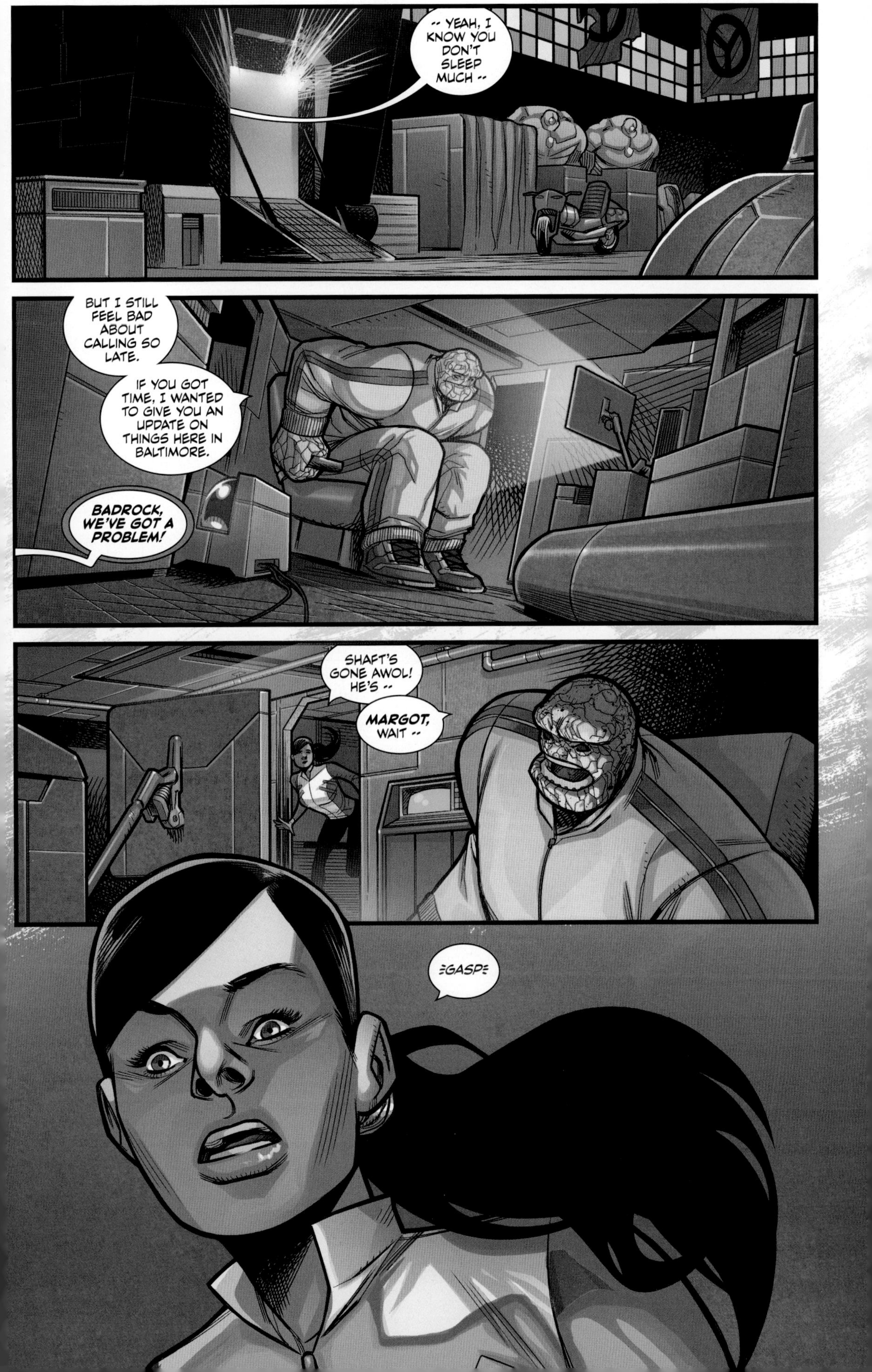
-- YEAH, I KNOW YOU DON'T SLEEP MUCH --
BUT I STILL FEEL BAD ABOUT CALLING SO LATE.
IF YOU GOT TIME, I WANTED TO GIVE YOU AN UPDATE ON THINGS HERE IN BALTIMORE.
BADROCK, WE'VE GOT A PROBLEM!
SHAFT'S GONE AWOL! HE'S --
MARGOT, WAIT --
GASP

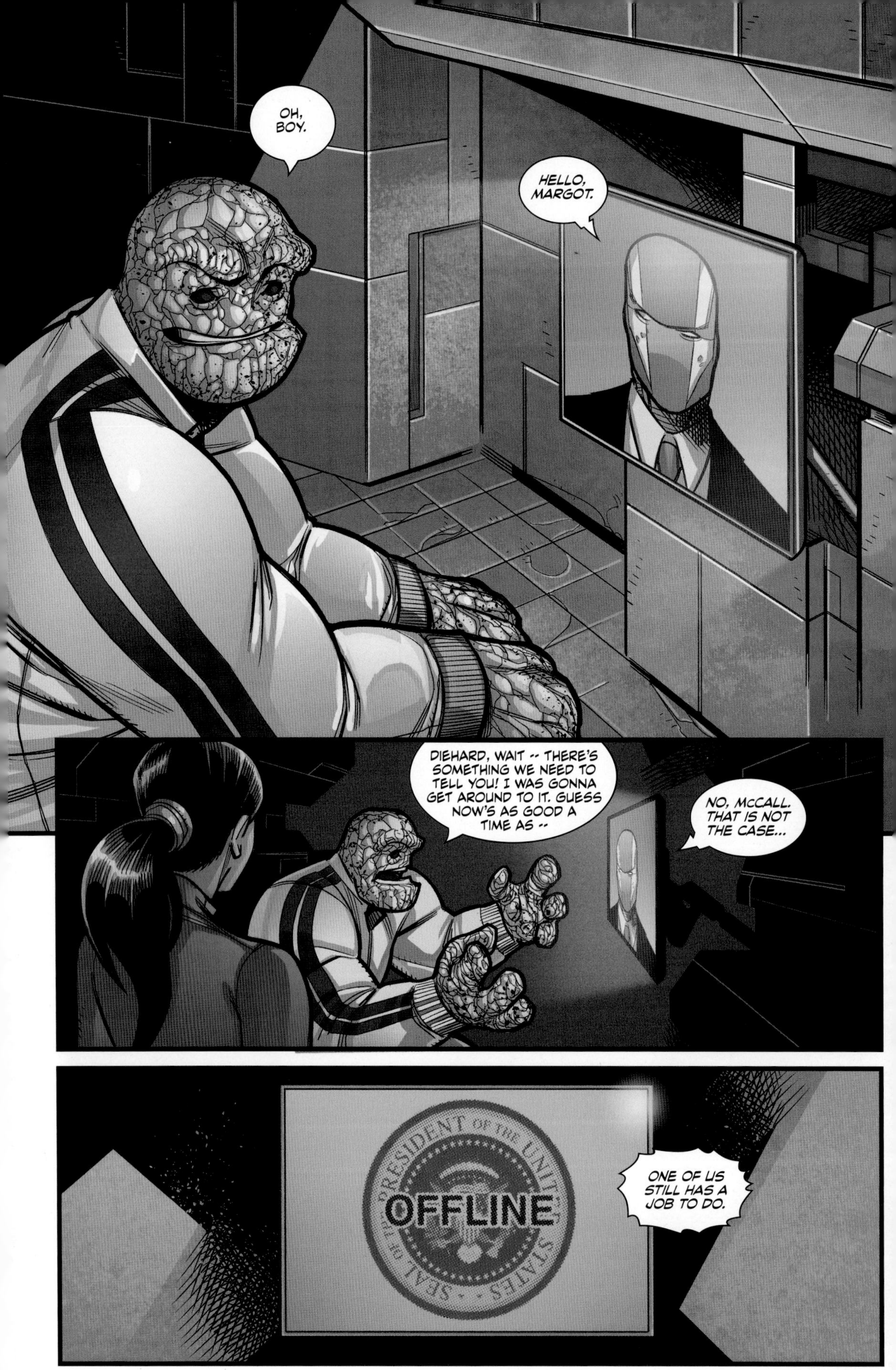
OH, BOY.
HELLO, MARGOT.
DIEHARD, WAIT -- THERE'S SOMETHING WE NEED TO TELL YOU! I WAS GONNA GET AROUND TO IT. GUESS NOW'S AS GOOD A TIME AS --
NO, McCALL. THAT IS NOT THE CASE...
SEAL OF THE PRESIDENT OF THE UNITED STATES
OFFLINE
ONE OF US STILL HAS A JOB TO DO.

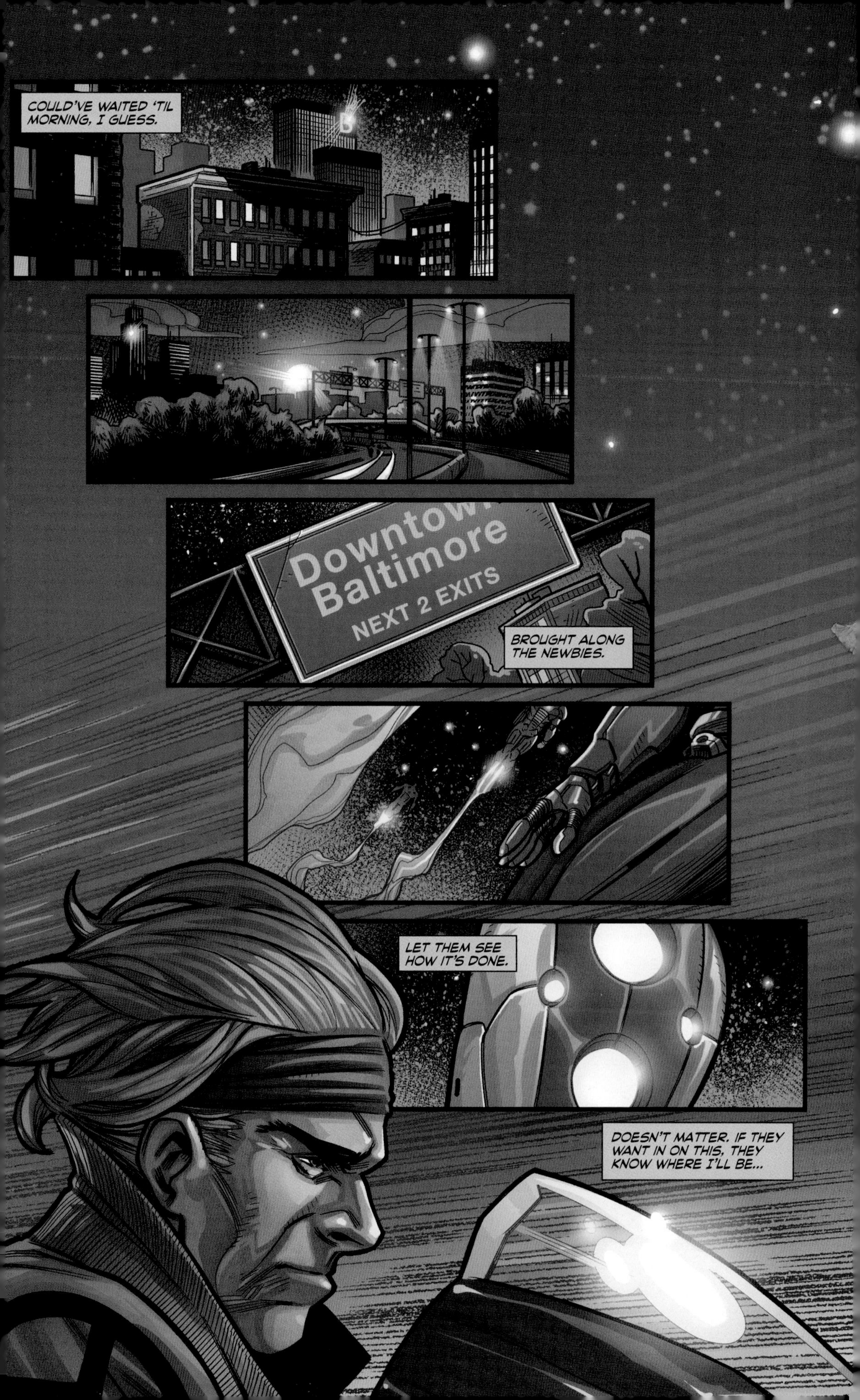
COULD'VE WAITED 'TIL MORNING, I GUESS.
Downtown
Baltimore
NEXT 2 EXITS
BROUGHT ALONG THE NEWBIES.
LET THEM SEE HOW IT'S DONE.
DOESN'T MATTER. IF THEY WANT IN ON THIS, THEY KNOW WHERE I'LL BE...

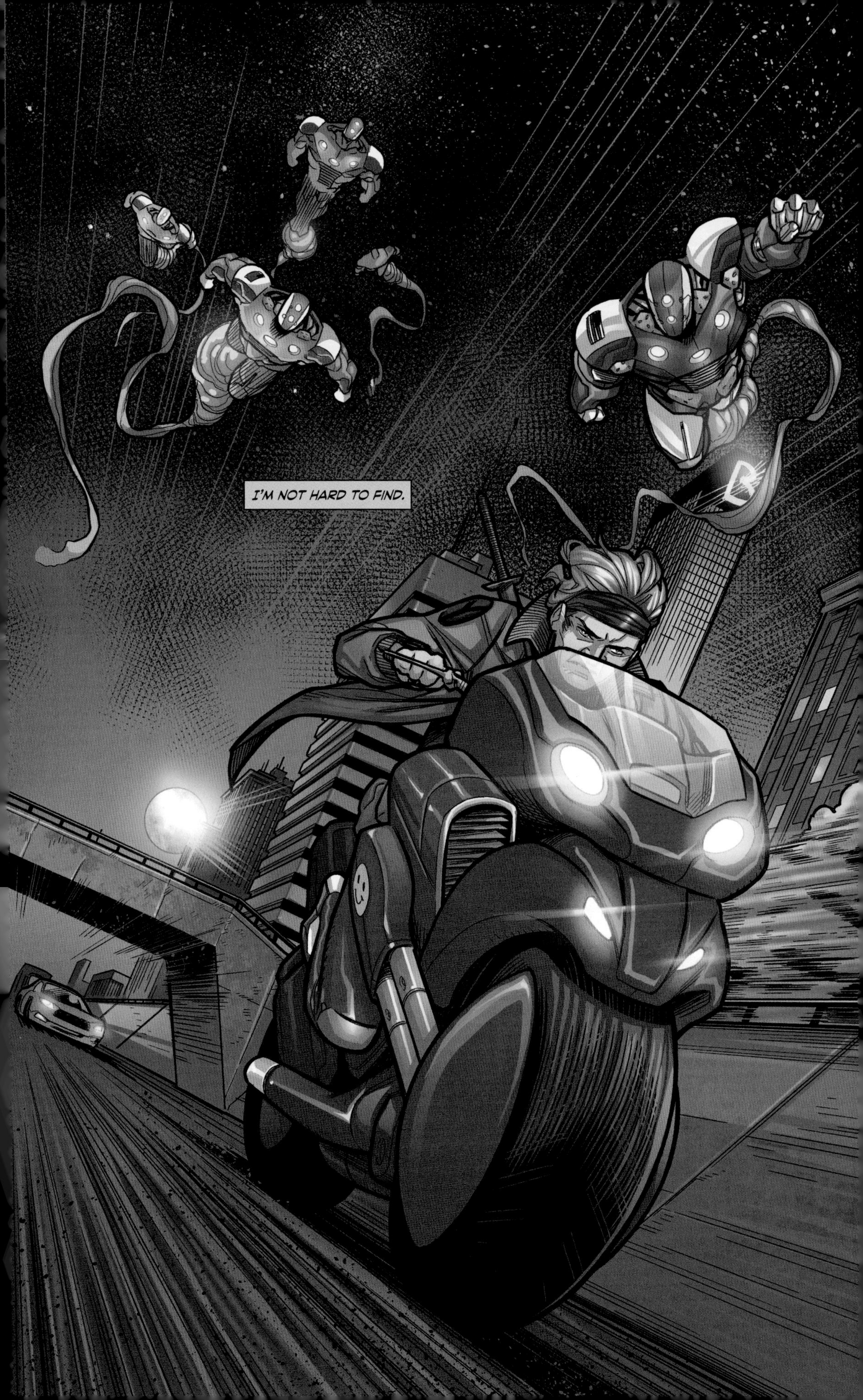
I'M NOT HARD TO FIND.

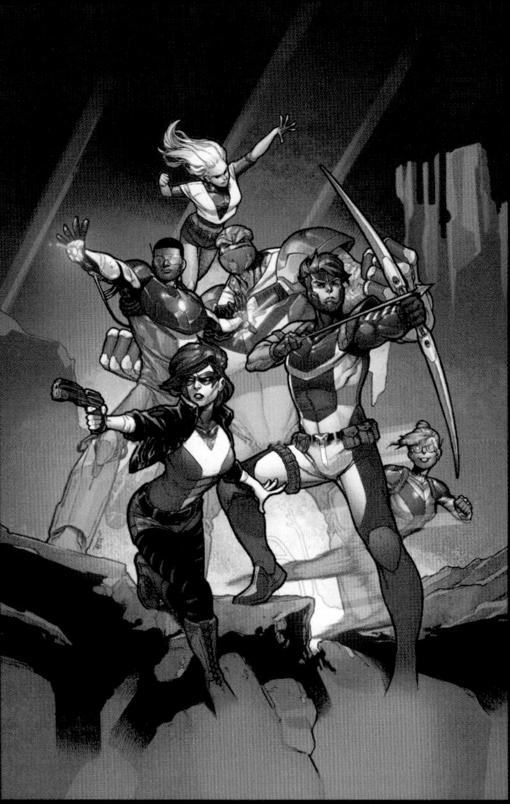

ART BY JIM TOWE

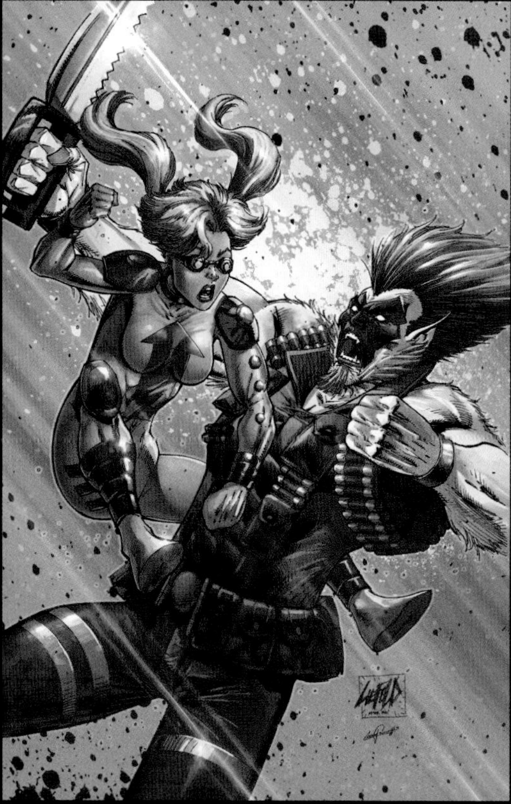

ART BY ROB LIEFELD

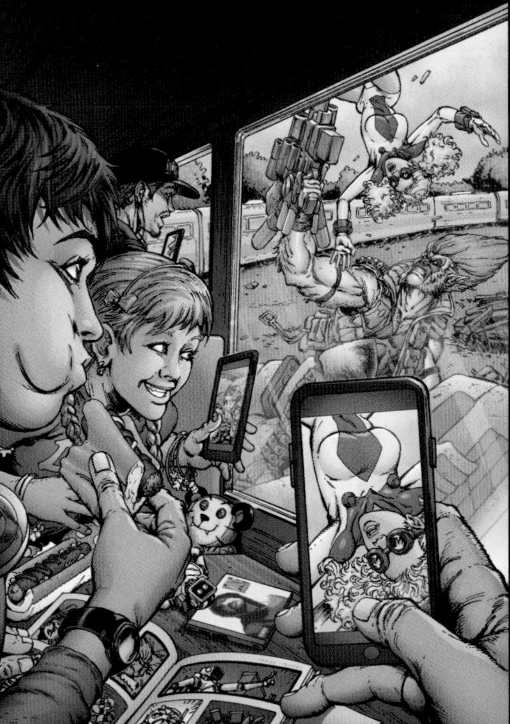

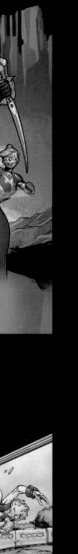

ART BY DAN FRAGA

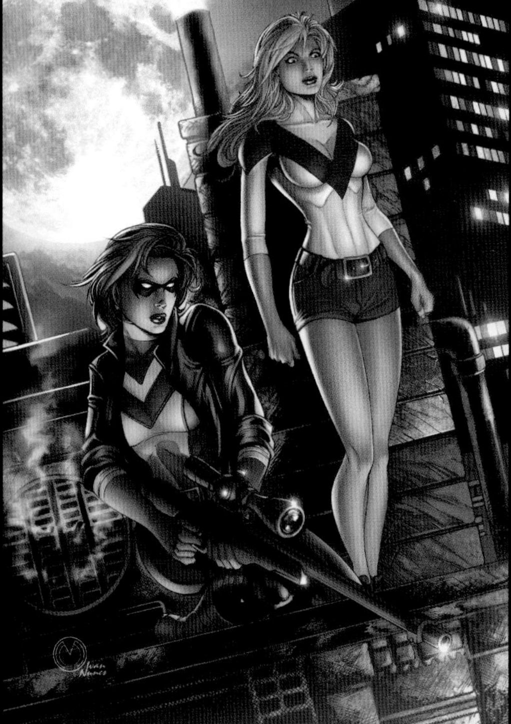

ART BY MARAT MYCHAELS

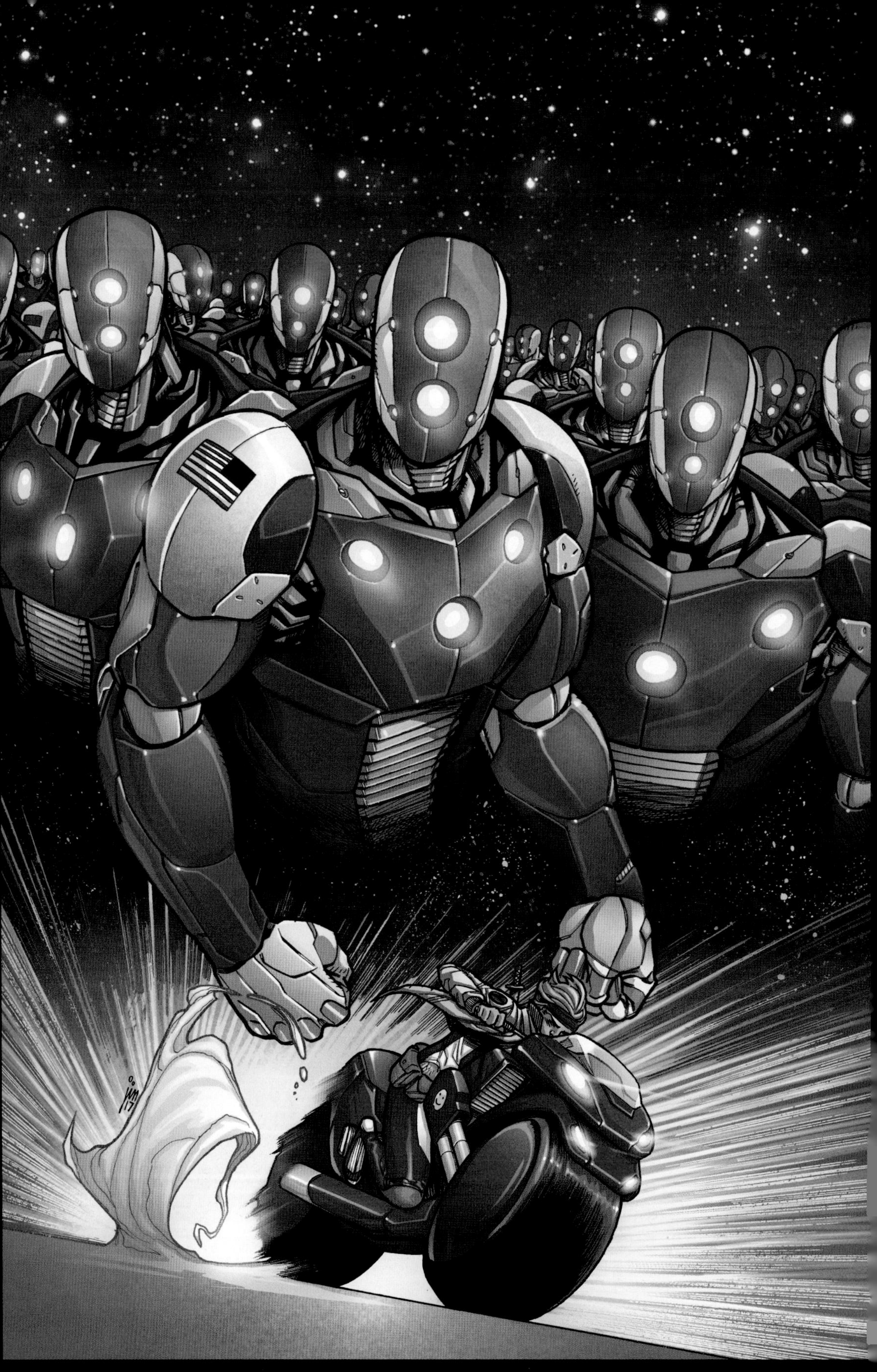

CHAPTER FOUR: LIVE FAST, DIE YOUNG

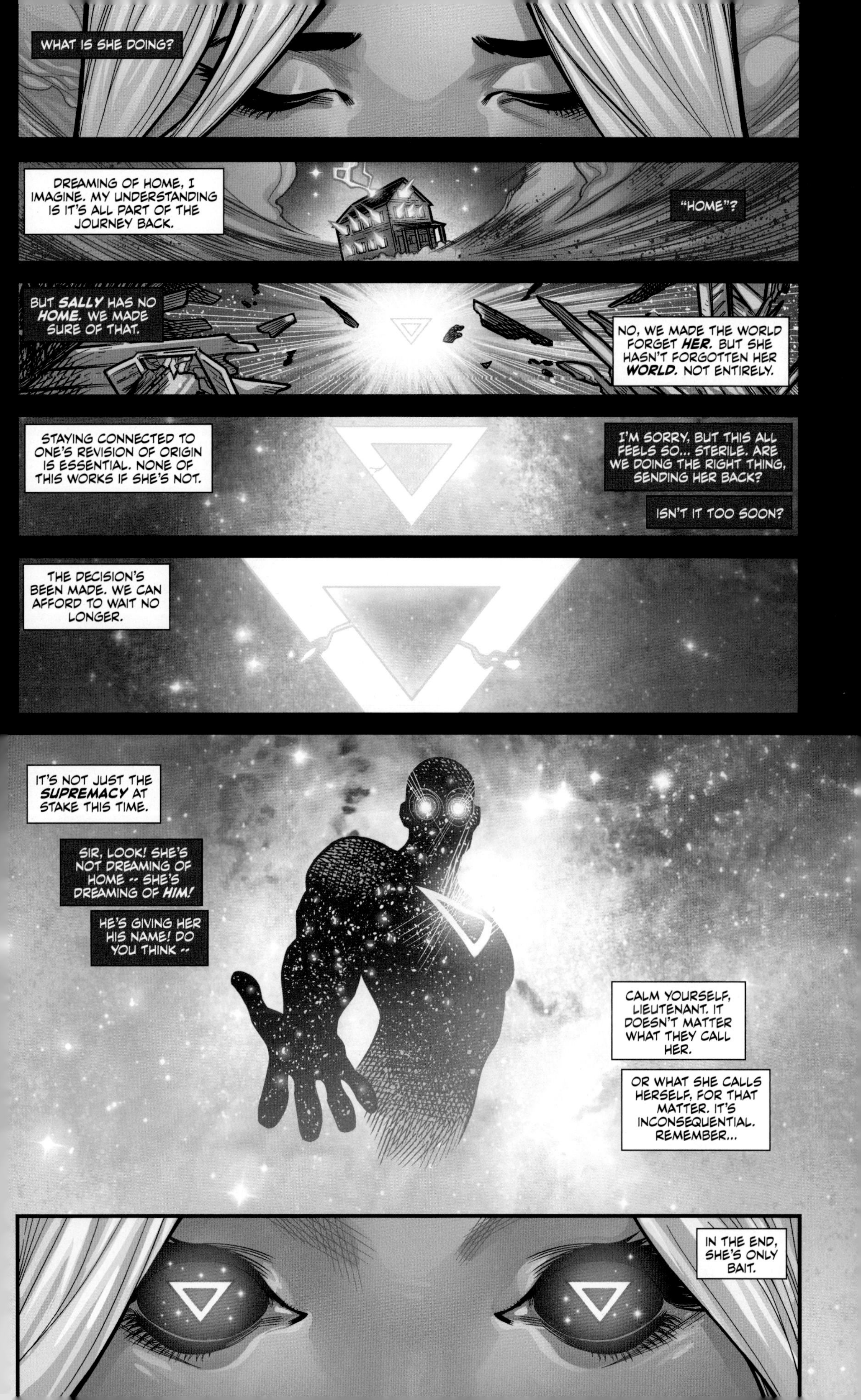

WHAT IS SHE DOING?
DREAMING OF HOME, I IMAGINE. MY UNDERSTANDING IS IT'S ALL PART OF THE JOURNEY BACK.
"HOME"?
BUT SALLY HAS NO HOME. WE MADE SURE OF THAT.
NO, WE MADE THE WORLD FORGET HER. BUT SHE HASN'T FORGOTTEN HER WORLD. NOT ENTIRELY.
STAYING CONNECTED TO ONE'S REVISION OF ORIGIN IS ESSENTIAL. NONE OF THIS WORKS IF SHE'S NOT.
I'M SORRY, BUT THIS ALL FEELS SO... STERILE. ARE WE DOING THE RIGHT THING, SENDING HER BACK?
ISN'T IT TOO SOON?
THE DECISION'S BEEN MADE. WE CAN AFFORD TO WAIT NO LONGER.
IT'S NOT JUST THE SUPREMACY AT STAKE THIS TIME.
SIR, LOOK! SHE'S NOT DREAMING OF HOME -- SHE'S DREAMING OF HIM!
HE'S GIVING HER HIS NAME! DO YOU THINK --
CALM YOURSELF, LIEUTENANT. IT DOESN'T MATTER WHAT THEY CALL HER.
OR WHAT SHE CALLS HERSELF, FOR THAT MATTER. IT'S INCONSEQUENTIAL. REMEMBER...
IN THE END, SHE'S ONLY BAIT.

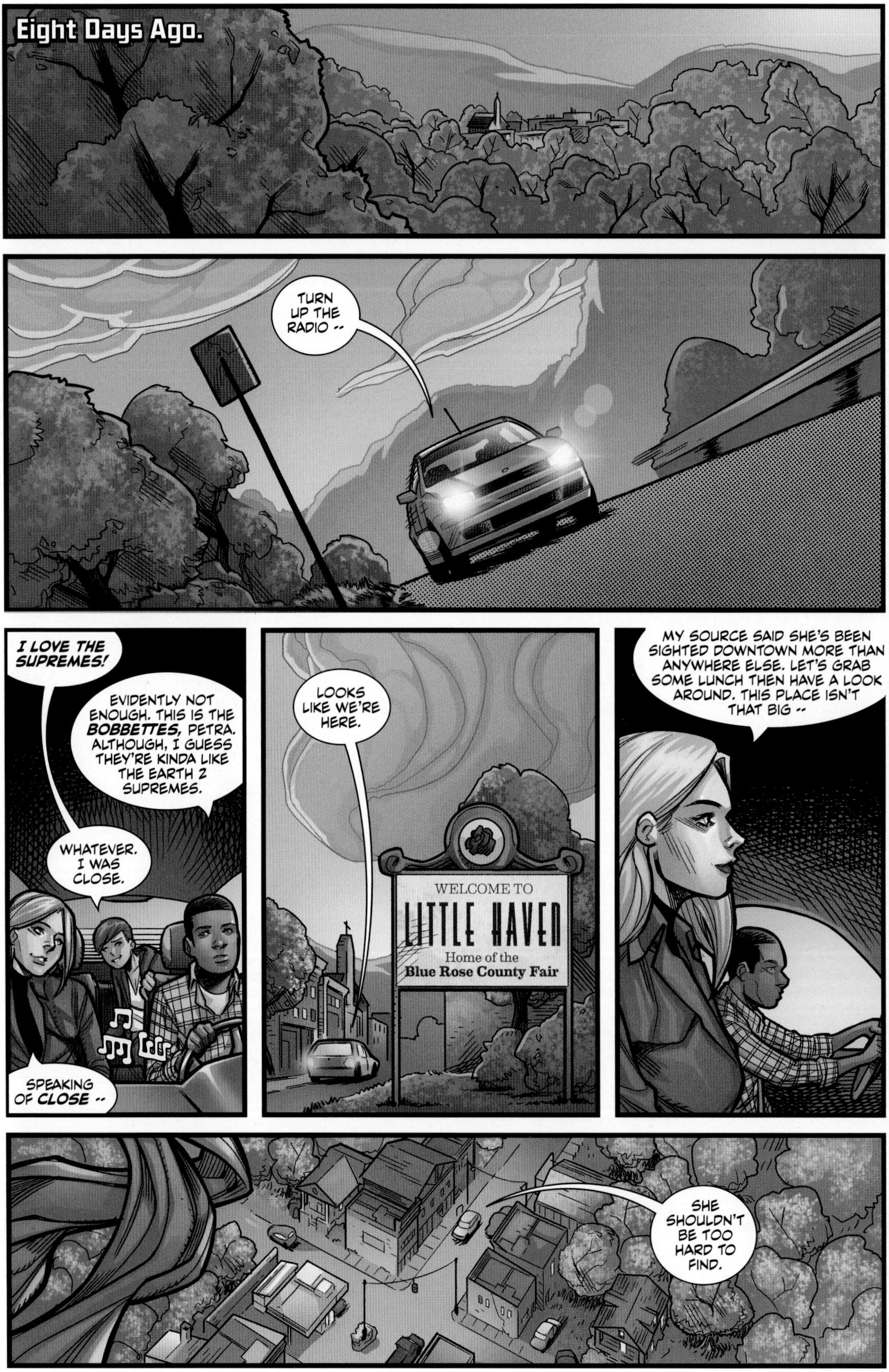
Eight Days Ago.
TURN UP THE RADIO --
I LOVE THE SUPREMES!
EVIDENTLY NOT ENOUGH. THIS IS THE BOBBETTES, PETRA. ALTHOUGH, I GUESS THEY'RE KINDA LIKE THE EARTH 2 SUPREMES.
WHATEVER. I WAS CLOSE.
SPEAKING OF CLOSE --
LOOKS LIKE WE'RE HERE.
WELCOME TO
LITTLE HAVEN
Home of the
Blue Rose County Fair
MY SOURCE SAID SHE'S BEEN SIGHTED DOWNTOWN MORE THAN ANYWHERE ELSE. LET'S GRAB SOME LUNCH THEN HAVE A LOOK AROUND. THIS PLACE ISN'T THAT BIG --
SHE SHOULDN'T BE TOO HARD TO FIND.

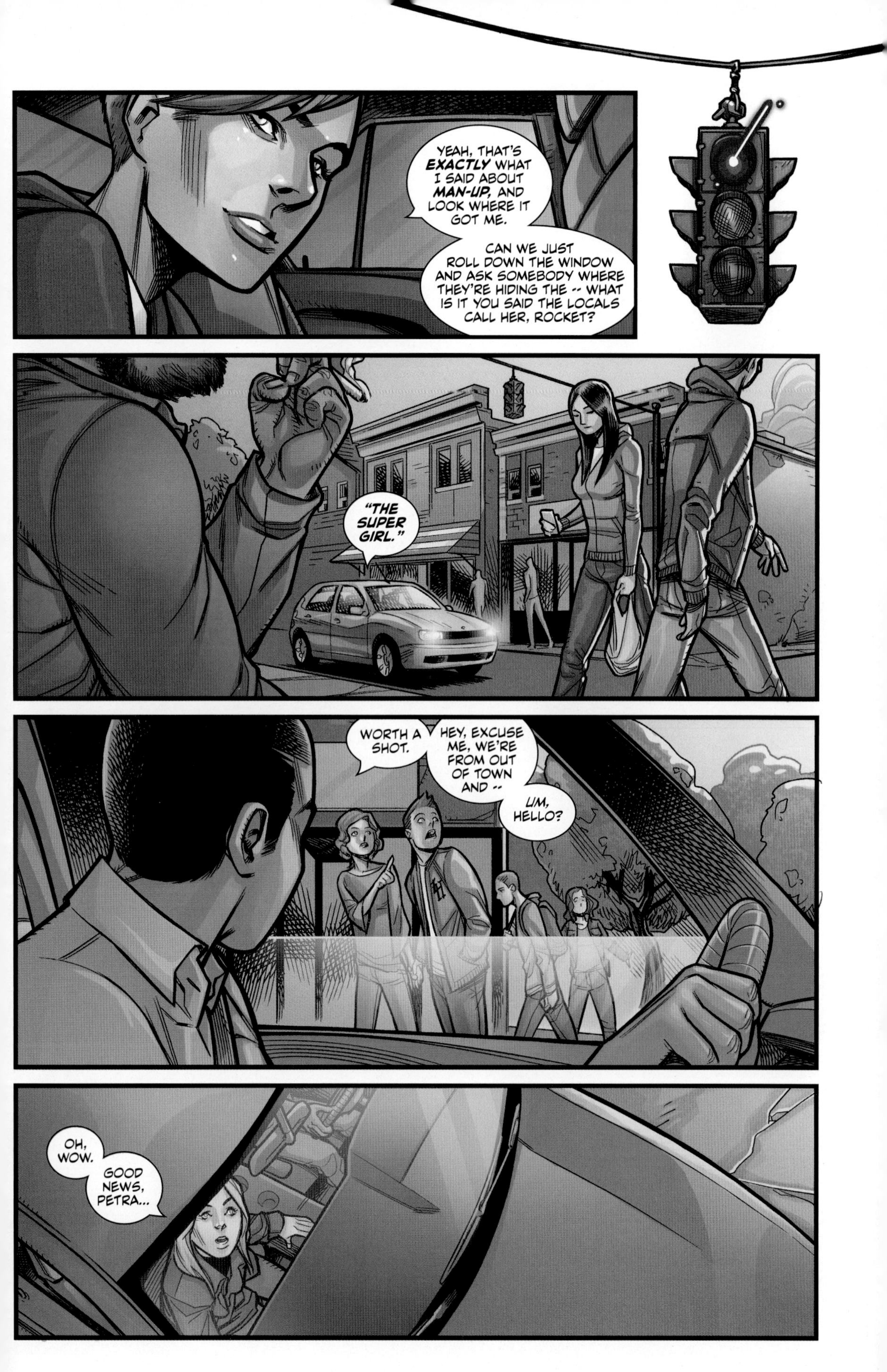
YEAH, THAT'S EXACTLY WHAT I SAID ABOUT MAN-UP, AND LOOK WHERE IT GOT ME.
CAN WE JUST ROLL DOWN THE WINDOW AND ASK SOMEBODY WHERE THEY'RE HIDING THE -- WHAT IS IT YOU SAID THE LOCALS CALL HER, ROCKET?
"THE SUPER GIRL."
WORTH A SHOT.
HEY, EXCUSE ME, WE'RE FROM OUT OF TOWN AND --
UM, HELLO?
OH, WOW.
GOOD NEWS, PETRA...

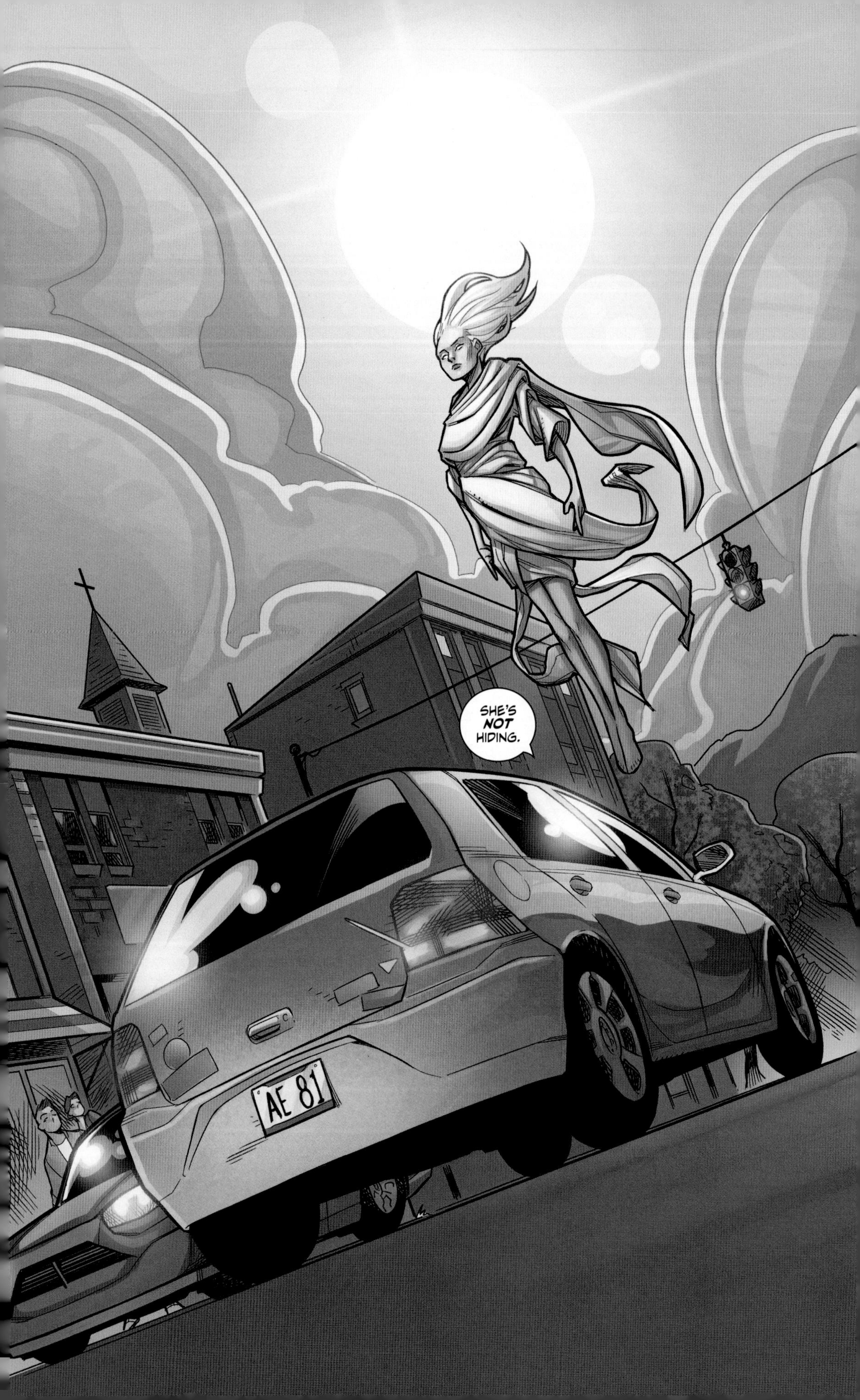
SHE'S NOT HIDING.
AE 81

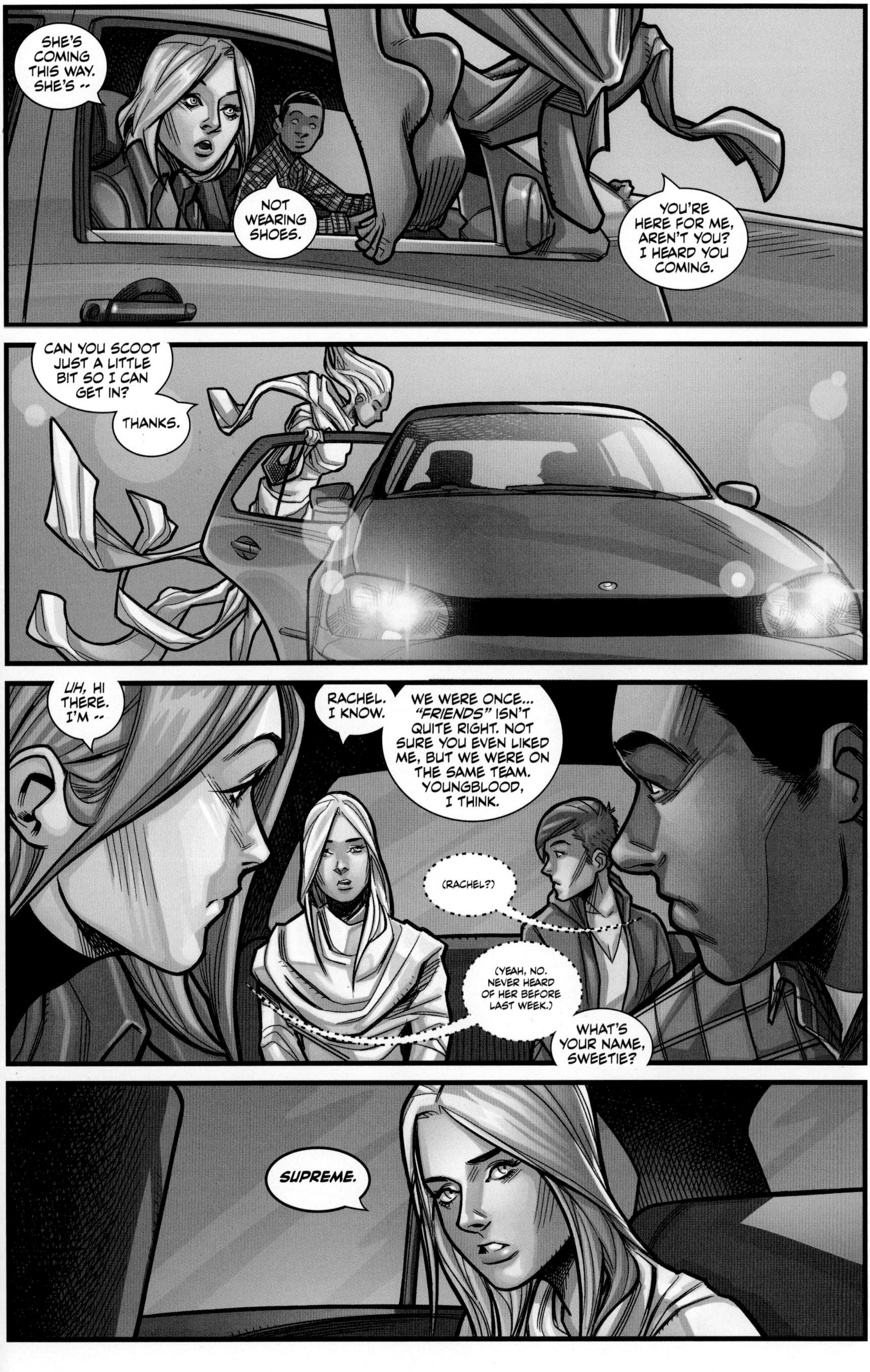
SHE'S COMING THIS WAY. SHE'S --
NOT WEARING SHOES.
YOU'RE HERE FOR ME, AREN'T YOU? I HEARD YOU COMING.
CAN YOU SCOOT JUST A LITTLE BIT SO I CAN GET IN?
THANKS.
UH, HI THERE. I'M --
RACHEL. I KNOW.
WE WERE ONCE... "FRIENDS" ISN'T QUITE RIGHT. NOT SURE YOU EVEN LIKED ME, BUT WE WERE ON THE SAME TEAM. YOUNGBLOOD, I THINK.
(RACHEL?)
(YEAH, NO. NEVER HEARD OF HER BEFORE LAST WEEK.)
WHAT'S YOUR NAME, SWEETIE?
SUPREME.

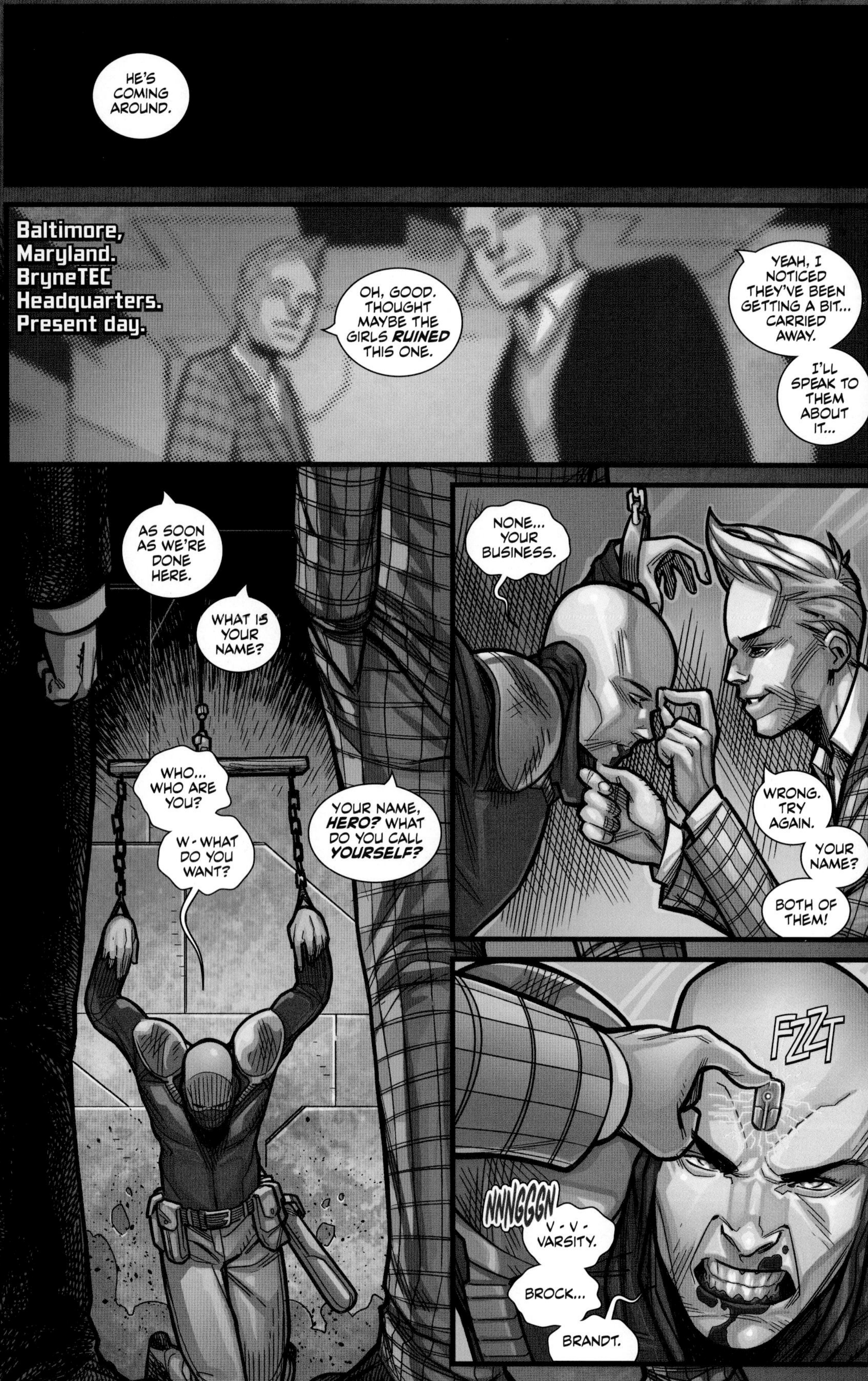
HE'S COMING AROUND.
Baltimore, Maryland. BryneTEC Headquarters. Present day.
OH, GOOD. THOUGHT MAYBE THE GIRLS RUINED THIS ONE.
YEAH, I NOTICED THEY'VE BEEN GETTING A BIT... CARRIED AWAY.
I'LL SPEAK TO THEM ABOUT IT...
AS SOON AS WE'RE DONE HERE.
WHAT IS YOUR NAME?
WHO... WHO ARE YOU?
W-WHAT DO YOU WANT?
YOUR NAME, HERO? WHAT DO YOU CALL YOURSELF?
NONE... YOUR BUSINESS.
WRONG. TRY AGAIN.
YOUR NAME?
BOTH OF THEM!
FZZT
NNNGGGN
V-V-VARSITY.
BROCK...
BRANDT.

THAT'S OUR BOY. DELETING HIS *HELP!* PROFILE NOW. ADIOS, BROCK.

RING

AND TAKE IT EASY, RUDY. LET'S NOT BURN HIM OUT BEFORE THE BUYER GETS HERE.

SPEAK OF THE DEVIL...

HEY, BUDDY!

"DO WE HAVE HIM?" OF COURSE WE HAVE HIM! WHO DO YOU THINK YOU'RE DEALING WITH? WE'RE CLEANING HIM UP NOW. HE'LL BE READY WHEN YOU ARRIVE.

SOUNDS GREAT. SEE YOU IN A FEW.

THEY'RE EARLY.

THEY'RE *RICH,* RUDY. RIGHT NOW, THAT'S ALL THAT MATTERS.

THIS *HELP!* SCHEME ONLY HAD A SHELF LIFE OF, WHAT... A YEAR, MAYBE? AND NOW THAT WE'VE GOT *DIEHARD* INVOLVED, EVEN LESS.

WE'RE ALREADY RUNNING LOW ON *D'KHAY DISKS* -- WHAT HAPPENS WHEN WE'RE OUT OF THOSE, *HUH?* YOU GOING TO STEAL MORE? I'M SURE AS HELL NOT.

DAD HAD A VISION, AND IT'S OUR DESTINY TO SEE THAT IT BECOMES A REALITY.

BUT WE CAN'T BURN DOWN THE WORLD IF WE'RE BROKE, BRO.

YOU'RE RIGHT. WE'RE TOO CLOSE TO FAIL.

SO, DID THEY TELL YOU WHAT THEY WANT TO CALL THIS GUY? GETTING A *RENAME* TO STICK TAKES A LITTLE LONGER.

NOPE, DIDN'T SAY. AND I DON'T THINK IT MATTERS --

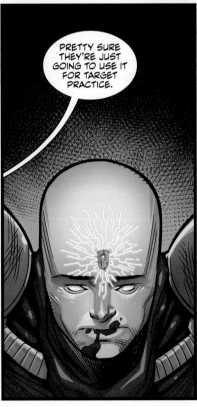

PRETTY SURE THEY'RE JUST GOING TO USE IT FOR TARGET PRACTICE.

WELL THAT MAKES THIS EASIER. HE'LL BE READY IN TEN.

I'LL GET A BOX.

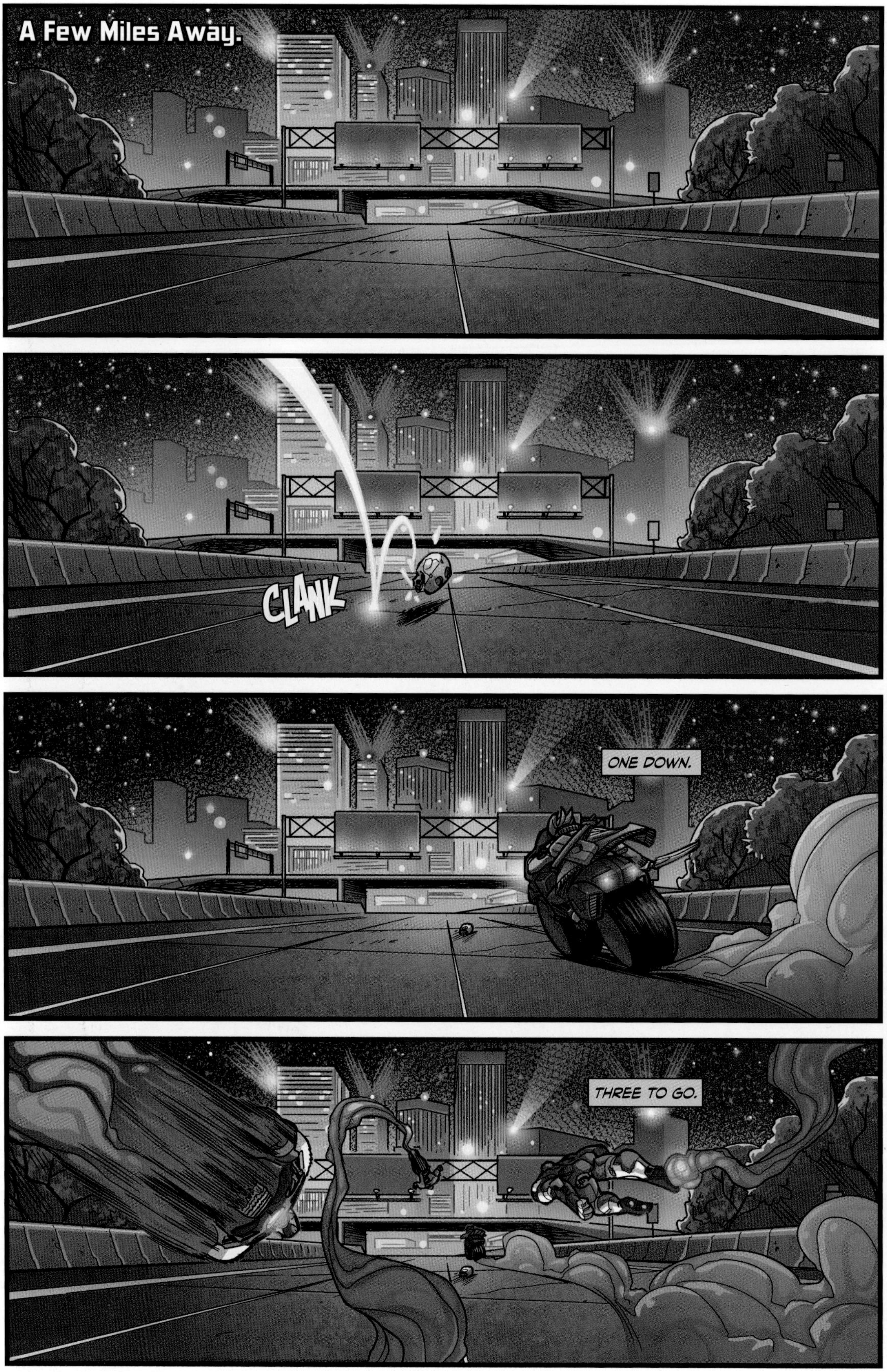
A Few Miles Away.
CLANK
ONE DOWN.
THREE TO GO.

HARDHEADS.

DIEHARD'S ELITE SQUADRON OF A.I. COMMANDOS.

RETRACT.

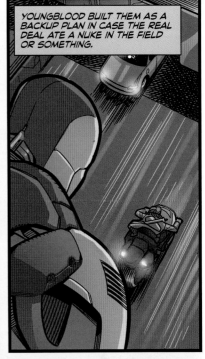

YOUNGBLOOD BUILT THEM AS A BACKUP PLAN IN CASE THE REAL DEAL ATE A NUKE IN THE FIELD OR SOMETHING.

THEY'RE STRONGER THAN HIM.

FASTER.

BETTER ARMED.

BUT NOT HALF AS RESILIENT.

SKREEEE --

SHEENG

TWO DOWN.

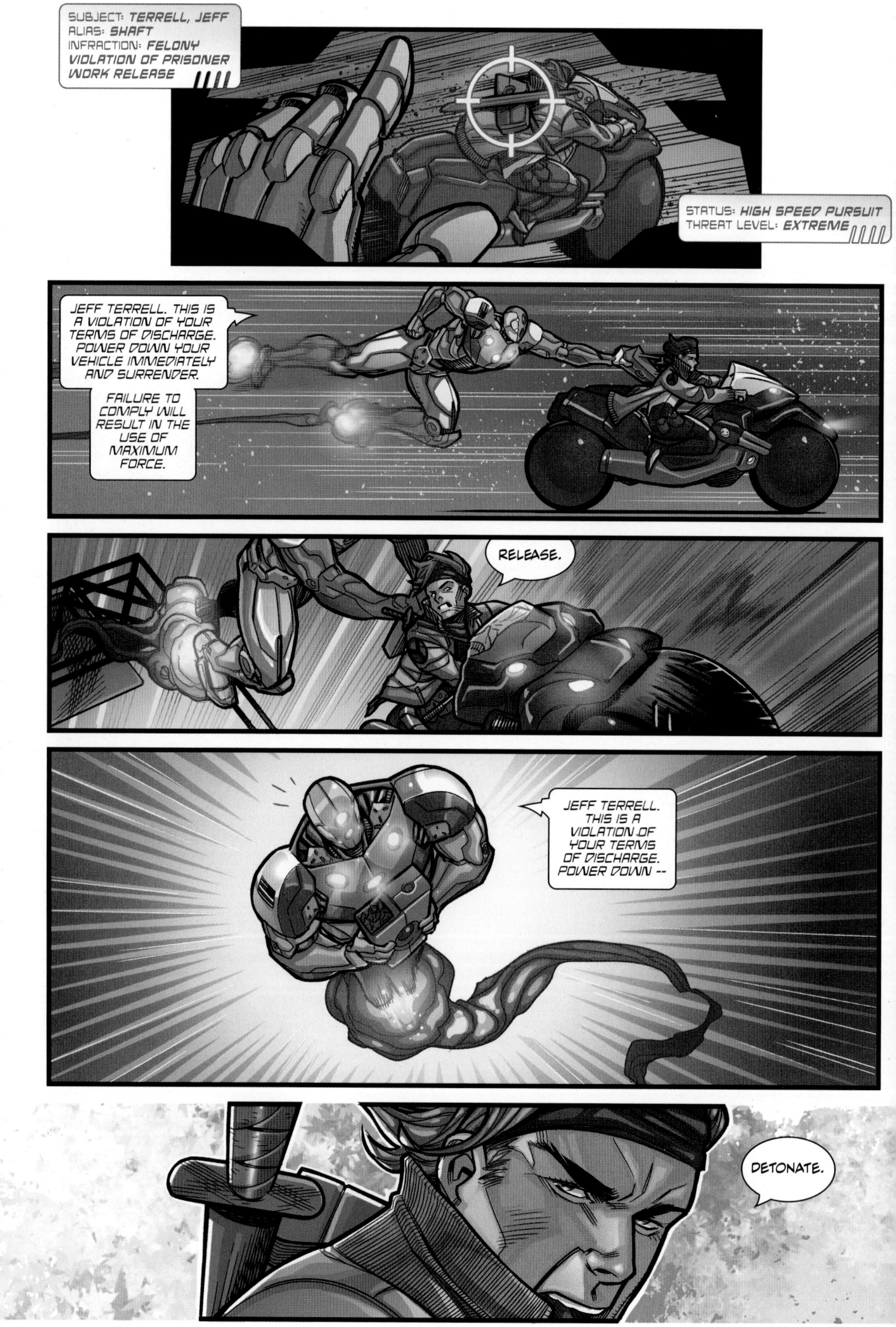
SUBJECT: TERRELL, JEFF
ALIAS: SHAFT
INFRACTION: FELONY VIOLATION OF PRISONER WORK RELEASE
STATUS: HIGH SPEED PURSUIT
THREAT LEVEL: EXTREME
JEFF TERRELL. THIS IS A VIOLATION OF YOUR TERMS OF DISCHARGE. POWER DOWN YOUR VEHICLE IMMEDIATELY AND SURRENDER.
FAILURE TO COMPLY WILL RESULT IN THE USE OF MAXIMUM FORCE.
RELEASE.
JEFF TERRELL. THIS IS A VIOLATION OF YOUR TERMS OF DISCHARGE. POWER DOWN --
DETONATE.

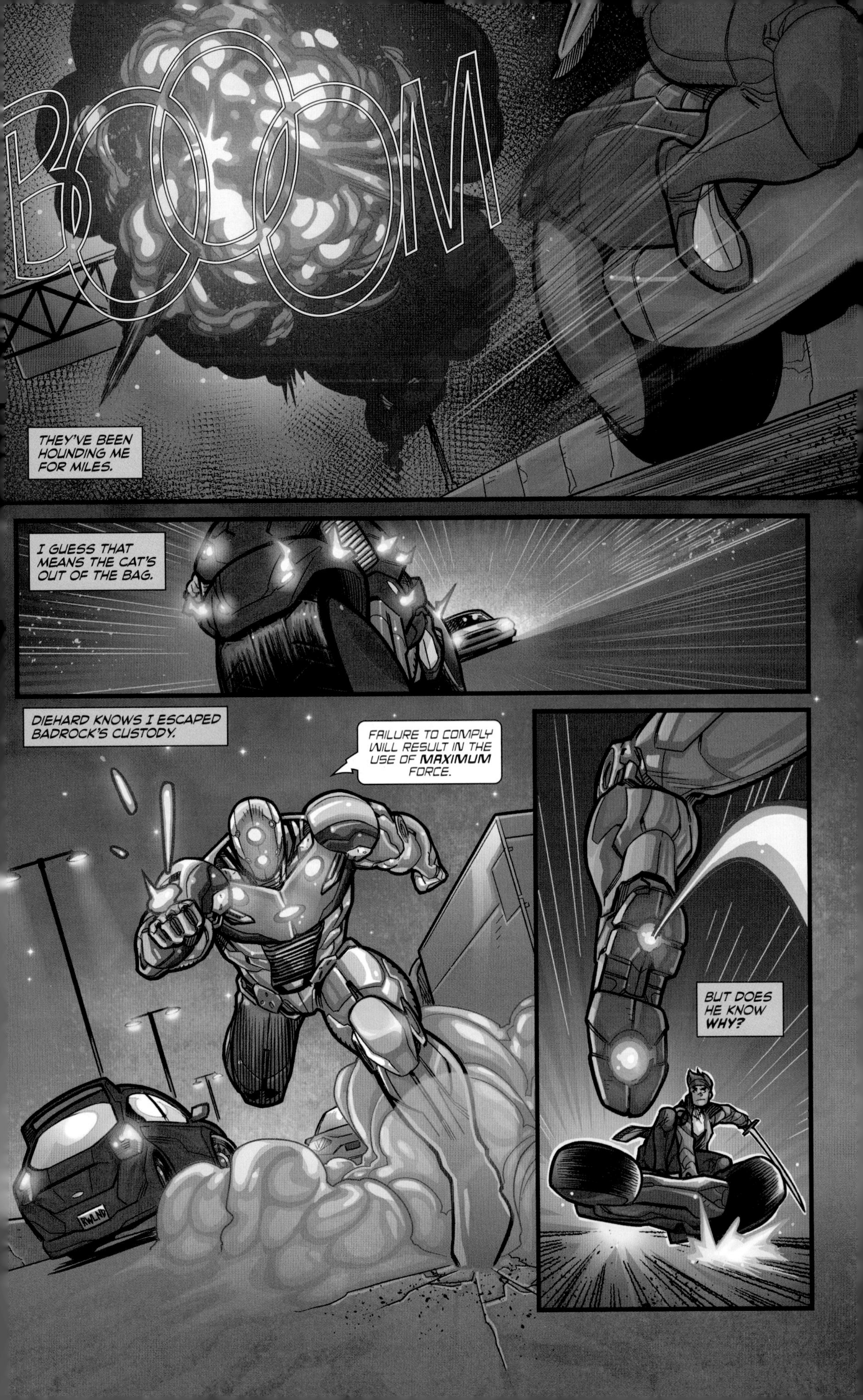
BOOOM
THEY'VE BEEN HOUNDING ME FOR MILES.
I GUESS THAT MEANS THE CAT'S OUT OF THE BAG.
DIEHARD KNOWS I ESCAPED BADROCK'S CUSTODY.
FAILURE TO COMPLY WILL RESULT IN THE USE OF MAXIMUM FORCE.
BUT DOES HE KNOW WHY?
RWLND

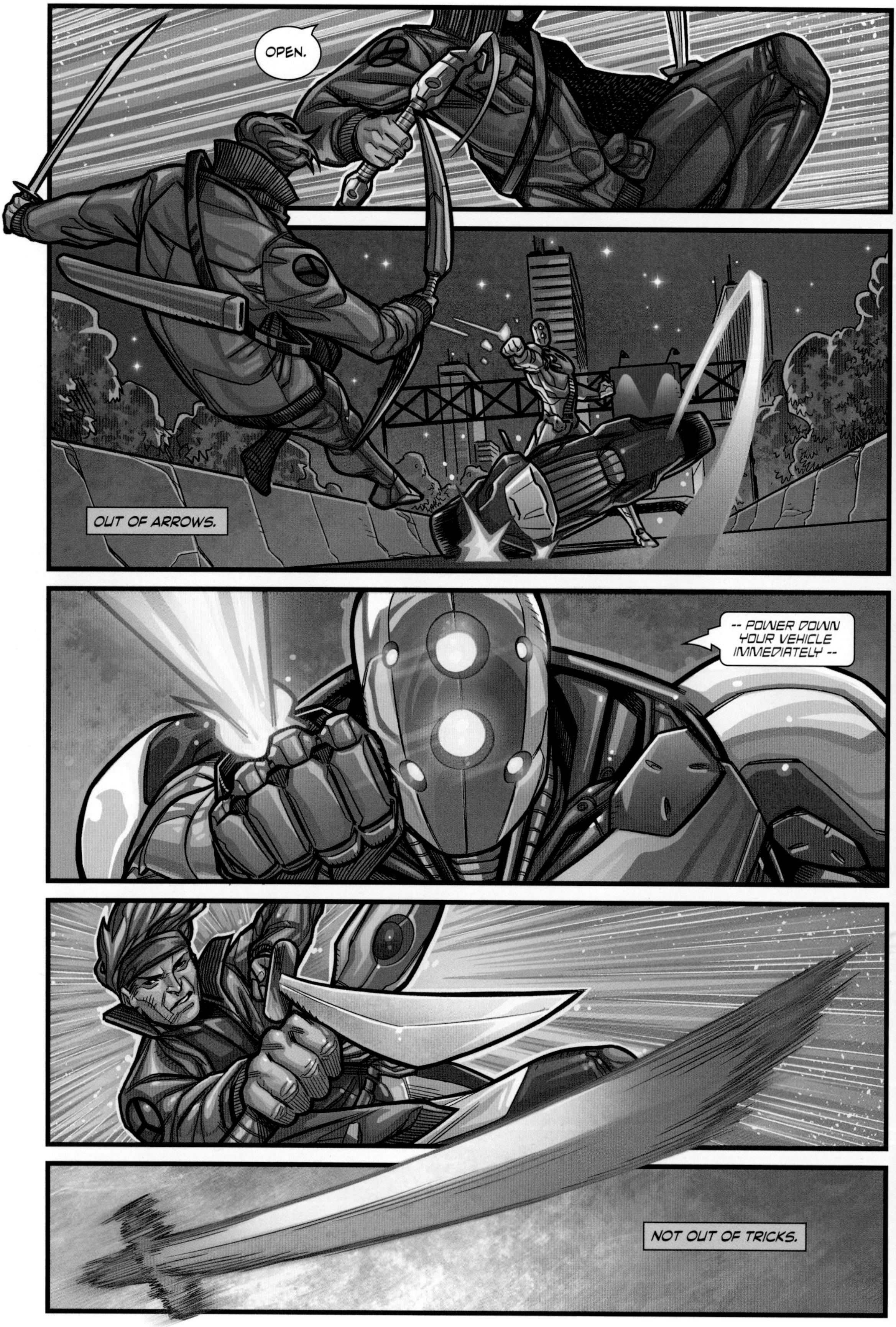
OPEN.
OUT OF ARROWS.
-- POWER DOWN YOUR VEHICLE IMMEDIATELY --
NOT OUT OF TRICKS.

ABIGGA-BOOOM

SqEEEEEE...

F - FAILURE TO COMPLY --

POWER DOWN --

DIE ALREADY!

VIOLATION OF YOUR --

DISCHARGE -- YOUR VEHICLE IMMEDIATELY --

-- JEFF TERRELL --

SURRENDER.

GO TO HELL.

MAXIMUM FORCE.

SKRNCH

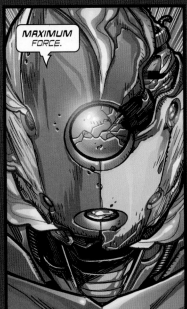

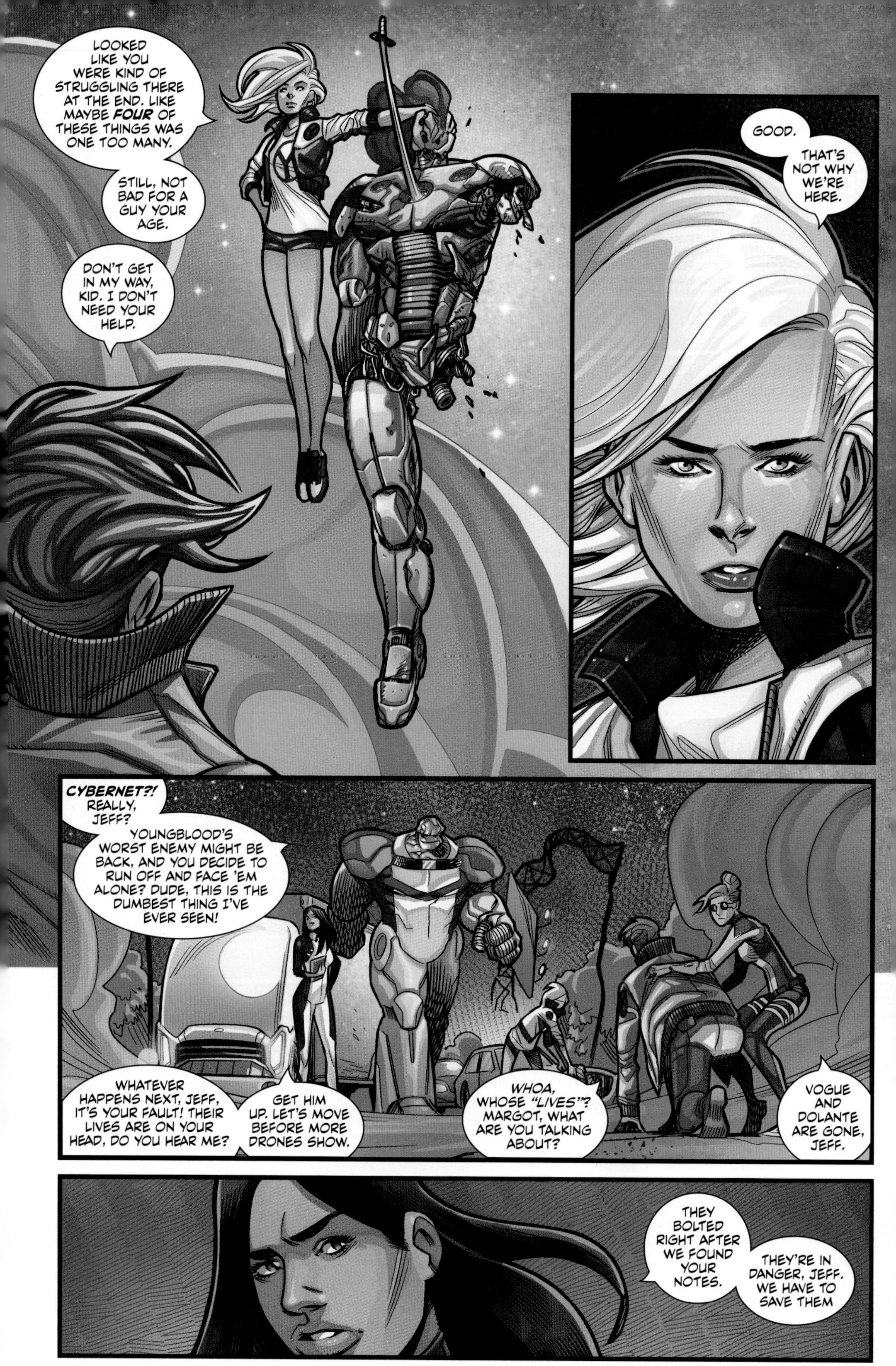
LOOKED LIKE YOU WERE KIND OF STRUGGLING THERE AT THE END. LIKE MAYBE ***FOUR*** OF THESE THINGS WAS ONE TOO MANY.
STILL, NOT BAD FOR A GUY YOUR AGE.
DON'T GET IN MY WAY, KID. I DON'T NEED YOUR HELP.
GOOD.
THAT'S NOT WHY WE'RE HERE.
CYBERNET?! REALLY, JEFF?
YOUNGBLOOD'S WORST ENEMY MIGHT BE BACK, AND YOU DECIDE TO RUN OFF AND FACE 'EM ALONE? DUDE, THIS IS THE DUMBEST THING I'VE EVER SEEN!
WHATEVER HAPPENS NEXT, JEFF, IT'S YOUR FAULT! THEIR LIVES ARE ON YOUR HEAD, DO YOU HEAR ME?
GET HIM UP. LET'S MOVE BEFORE MORE DRONES SHOW.
WHOA, WHOSE *"LIVES"*? MARGOT, WHAT ARE YOU TALKING ABOUT?
VOGUE AND DOLANTE ARE GONE, JEFF.
THEY BOLTED RIGHT AFTER WE FOUND YOUR NOTES.
THEY'RE IN DANGER, JEFF. WE HAVE TO SAVE THEM

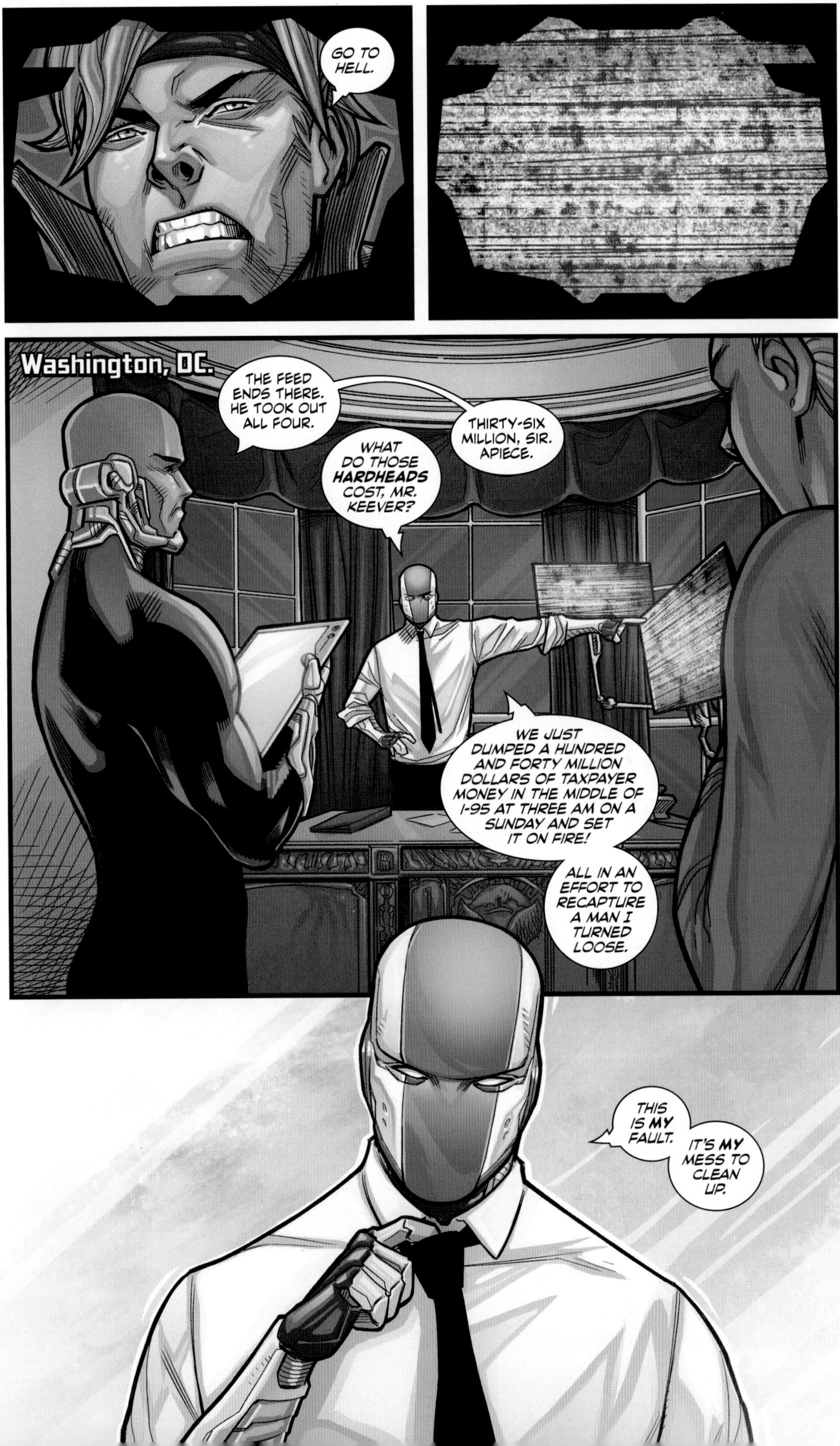
GO TO HELL.
Washington, DC.
THE FEED ENDS THERE. HE TOOK OUT ALL FOUR.
WHAT DO THOSE **HARDHEADS** COST, MR. KEEVER?
THIRTY-SIX MILLION, SIR. APIECE.
WE JUST DUMPED A HUNDRED AND FORTY MILLION DOLLARS OF TAXPAYER MONEY IN THE MIDDLE OF I-95 AT THREE AM ON A SUNDAY AND SET IT ON FIRE!
ALL IN AN EFFORT TO RECAPTURE A MAN I TURNED LOOSE.
THIS IS **MY** FAULT.
IT'S **MY** MESS TO CLEAN UP.

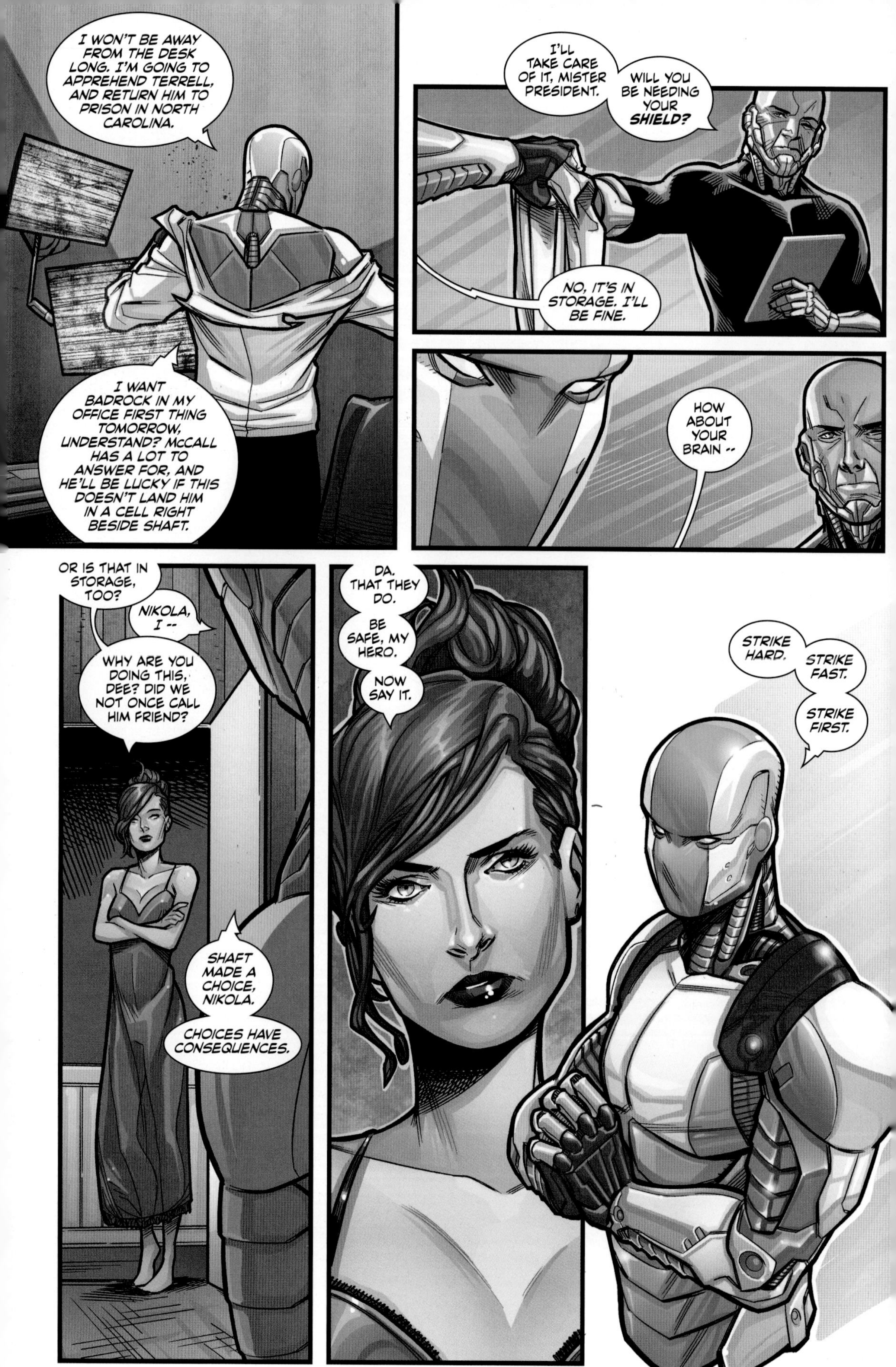
I WON'T BE AWAY FROM THE DESK LONG. I'M GOING TO APPREHEND TERRELL, AND RETURN HIM TO PRISON IN NORTH CAROLINA.
I WANT BADROCK IN MY OFFICE FIRST THING TOMORROW, UNDERSTAND? McCALL HAS A LOT TO ANSWER FOR, AND HE'LL BE LUCKY IF THIS DOESN'T LAND HIM IN A CELL RIGHT BESIDE SHAFT.
I'LL TAKE CARE OF IT, MISTER PRESIDENT.
WILL YOU BE NEEDING YOUR **SHIELD?**
NO, IT'S IN STORAGE. I'LL BE FINE.
HOW ABOUT YOUR BRAIN --
OR IS THAT IN STORAGE, TOO?
NIKOLA, I --
WHY ARE YOU DOING THIS, DEE? DID WE NOT ONCE CALL HIM FRIEND?
SHAFT MADE A CHOICE, NIKOLA.
CHOICES HAVE CONSEQUENCES.
DA. THAT THEY DO.
BE SAFE, MY HERO.
NOW SAY IT.
STRIKE HARD.
STRIKE FAST.
STRIKE FIRST.

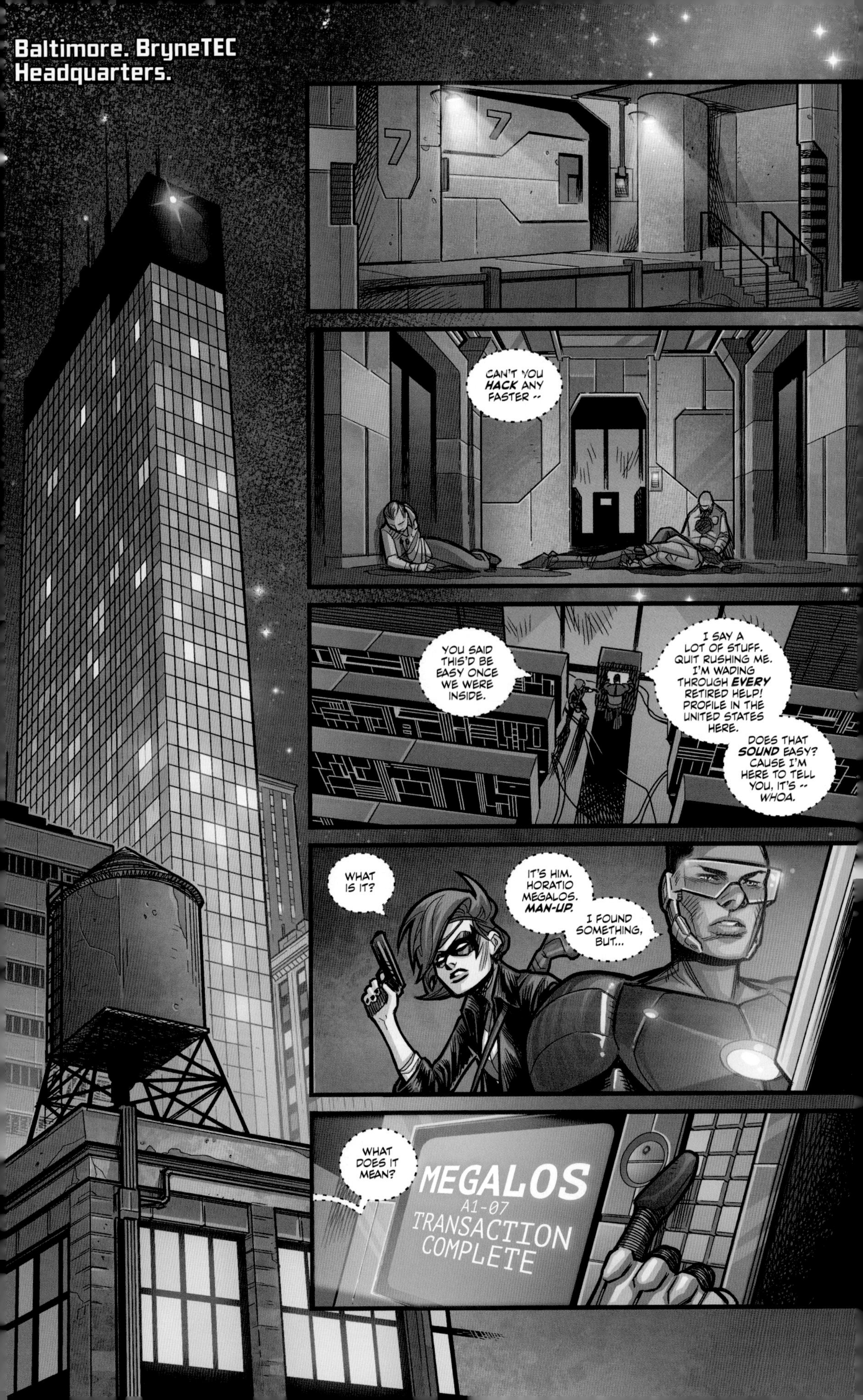
Baltimore. BryneTEC Headquarters.
CAN'T YOU HACK ANY FASTER --
YOU SAID THIS'D BE EASY ONCE WE WERE INSIDE.
I SAY A LOT OF STUFF. QUIT RUSHING ME. I'M WADING THROUGH EVERY RETIRED HELP! PROFILE IN THE UNITED STATES HERE.
DOES THAT SOUND EASY? CAUSE I'M HERE TO TELL YOU, IT'S -- WHOA.
WHAT IS IT?
IT'S HIM. HORATIO MEGALOS. MAN-UP.
I FOUND SOMETHING, BUT...
WHAT DOES IT MEAN?
MEGALOS
A1-07
TRANSACTION COMPLETE

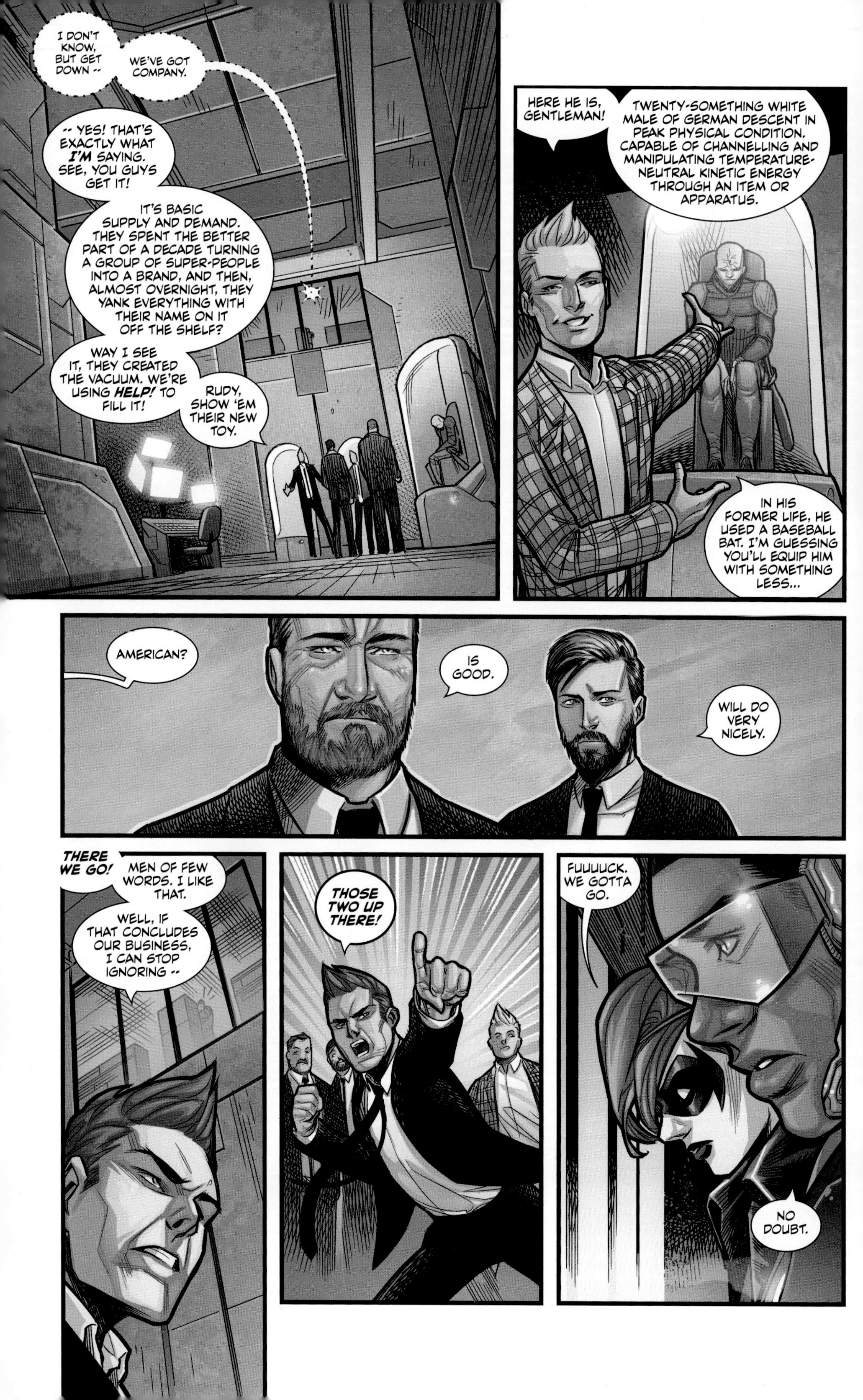
I DON'T KNOW, BUT GET DOWN --
WE'VE GOT COMPANY.
-- YES! THAT'S EXACTLY WHAT I'M SAYING. SEE, YOU GUYS GET IT!
IT'S BASIC SUPPLY AND DEMAND. THEY SPENT THE BETTER PART OF A DECADE TURNING A GROUP OF SUPER-PEOPLE INTO A BRAND, AND THEN, ALMOST OVERNIGHT, THEY YANK EVERYTHING WITH THEIR NAME ON IT OFF THE SHELF?
WAY I SEE IT, THEY CREATED THE VACUUM. WE'RE USING HELP! TO FILL IT!
RUDY, SHOW 'EM THEIR NEW TOY.
HERE HE IS, GENTLEMAN!
TWENTY-SOMETHING WHITE MALE OF GERMAN DESCENT IN PEAK PHYSICAL CONDITION. CAPABLE OF CHANNELLING AND MANIPULATING TEMPERATURE-NEUTRAL KINETIC ENERGY THROUGH AN ITEM OR APPARATUS.
IN HIS FORMER LIFE, HE USED A BASEBALL BAT. I'M GUESSING YOU'LL EQUIP HIM WITH SOMETHING LESS...
AMERICAN?
IS GOOD.
WILL DO VERY NICELY.
THERE WE GO!
MEN OF FEW WORDS. I LIKE THAT.
WELL, IF THAT CONCLUDES OUR BUSINESS, I CAN STOP IGNORING --
THOSE TWO UP THERE!
FUUUUCK. WE GOTTA GO.
NO DOUBT.

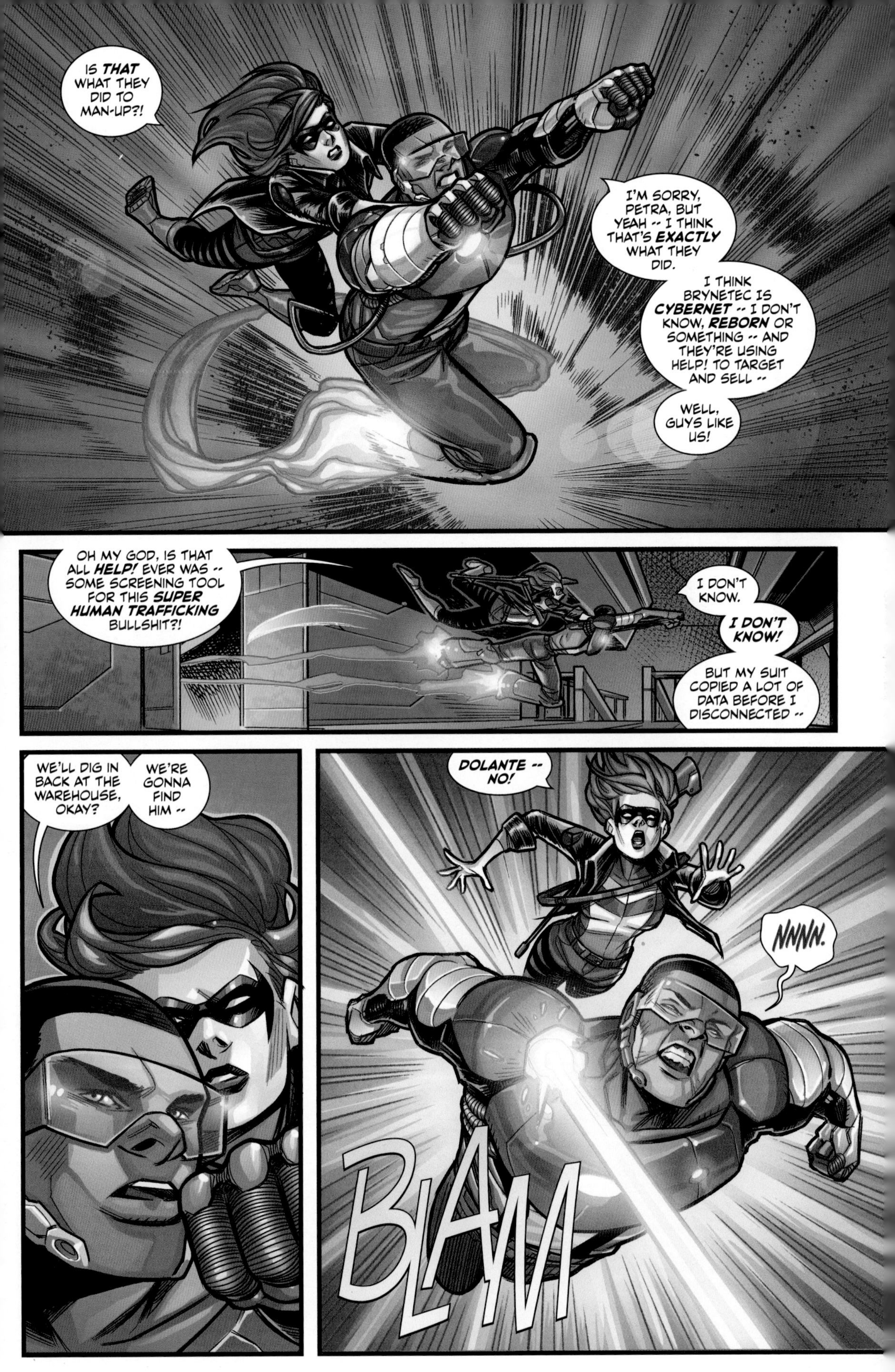

IS THAT WHAT THEY DID TO MAN-UP?!
I'M SORRY, PETRA, BUT YEAH -- I THINK THAT'S EXACTLY WHAT THEY DID.
I THINK BRYNETEC IS CYBERNET -- I DON'T KNOW, REBORN OR SOMETHING -- AND THEY'RE USING HELP! TO TARGET AND SELL --
WELL, GUYS LIKE US!
OH MY GOD, IS THAT ALL HELP! EVER WAS -- SOME SCREENING TOOL FOR THIS SUPER HUMAN TRAFFICKING BULLSHIT?!
I DON'T KNOW.
I DON'T KNOW!
BUT MY SUIT COPIED A LOT OF DATA BEFORE I DISCONNECTED --
WE'LL DIG IN BACK AT THE WAREHOUSE, OKAY?
WE'RE GONNA FIND HIM --
DOLANTE -- NO!
NNNN.
BLAM

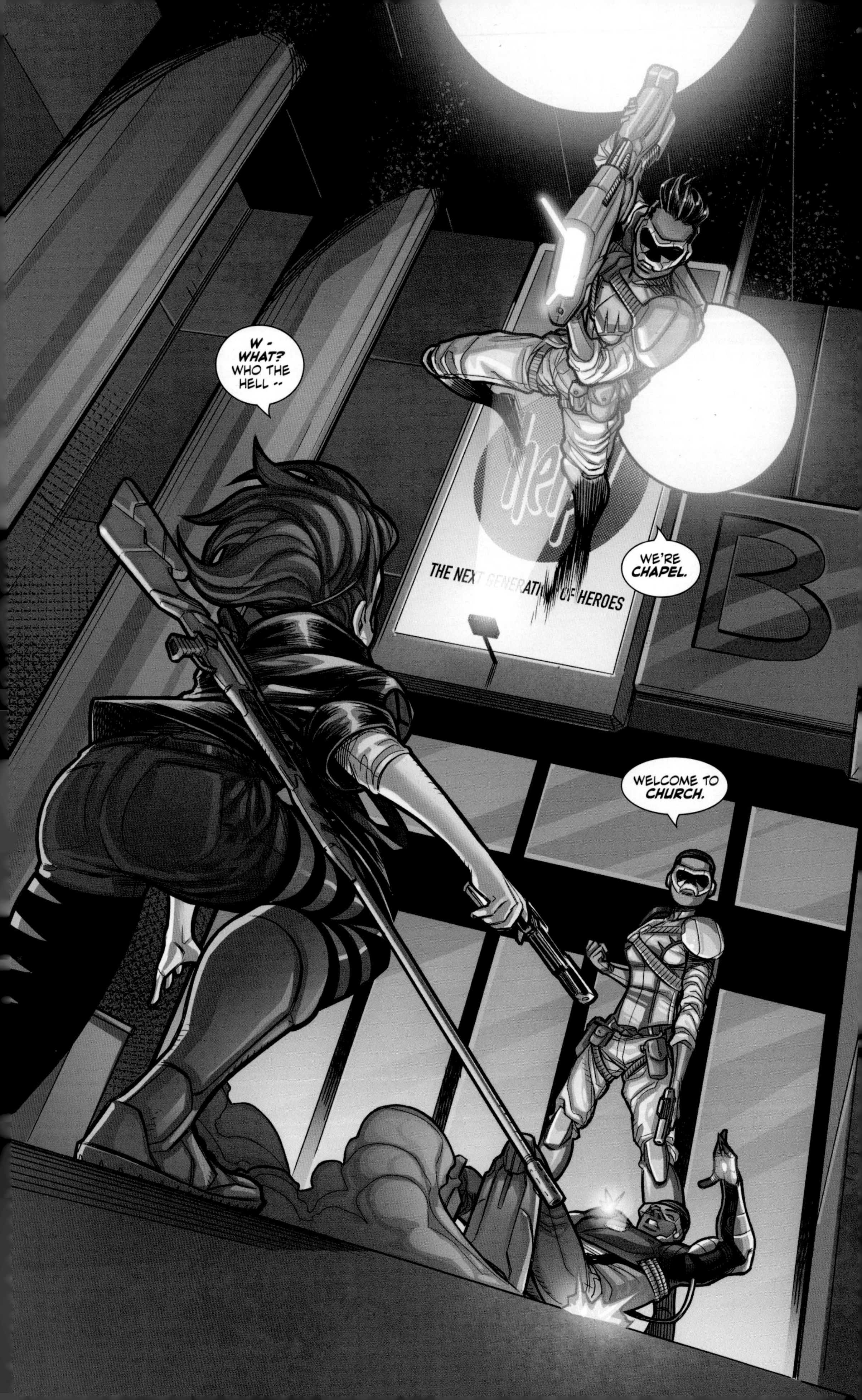
W - WHAT? WHO THE HELL --
THE NEXT GENERATION OF HEROES
WE'RE CHAPEL.
WELCOME TO CHURCH.

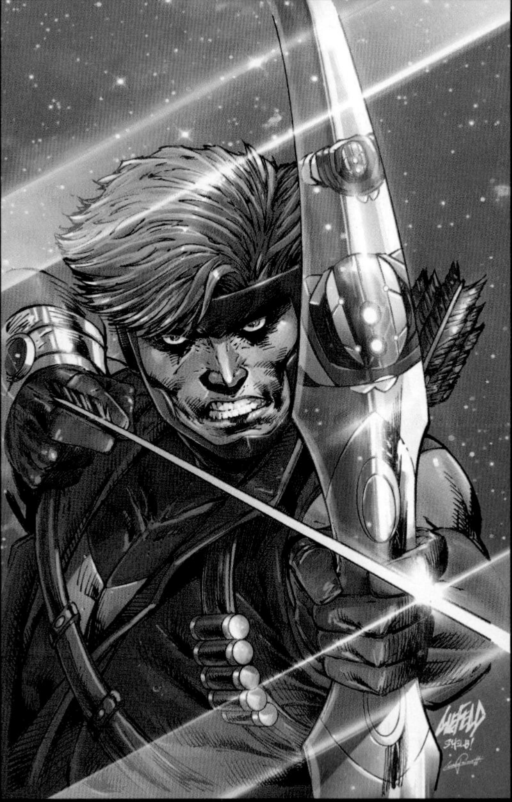

ART BY ROB LIEFELD

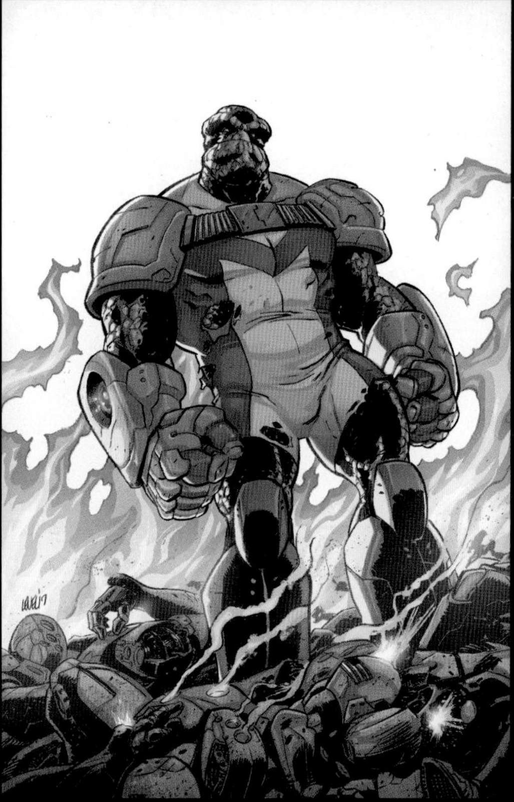

ART BY BRIAN LEVEL

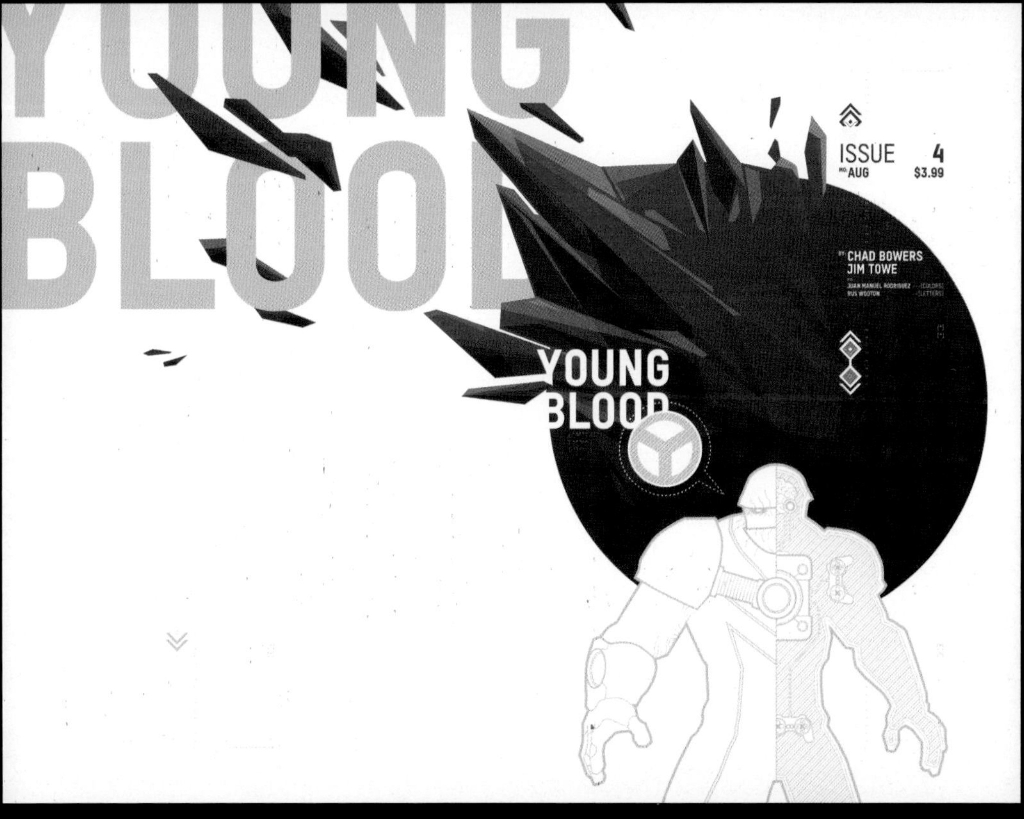
YOUNG BLOOD
ISSUE 4
AUG
$3.99
BY: CHAD BOWERS
JIM TOWE
YOUNG BLOOD

ART BY JONATHAN HICKMAN

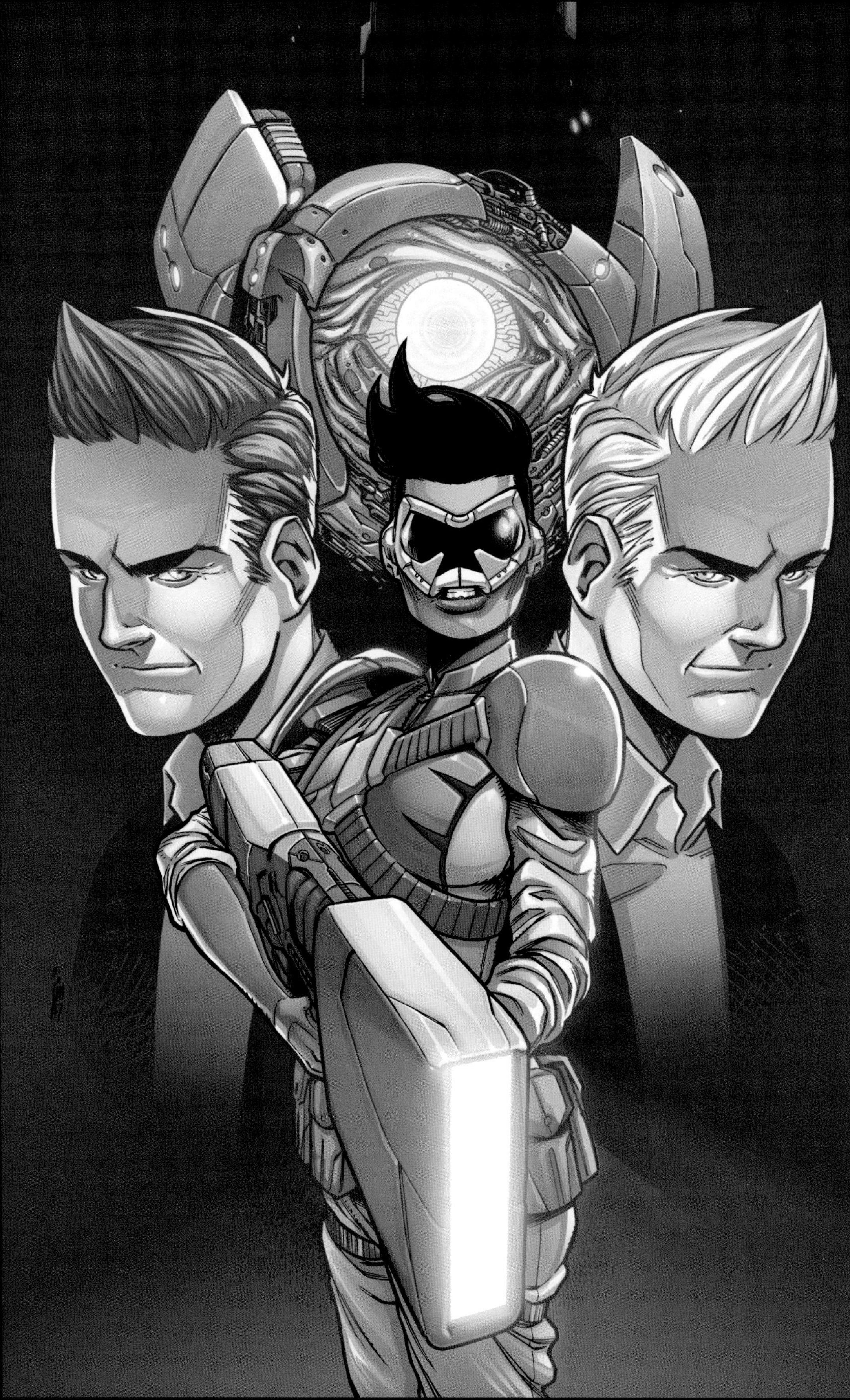

CHAPTER FIVE: EXECUTIVE DISORDER

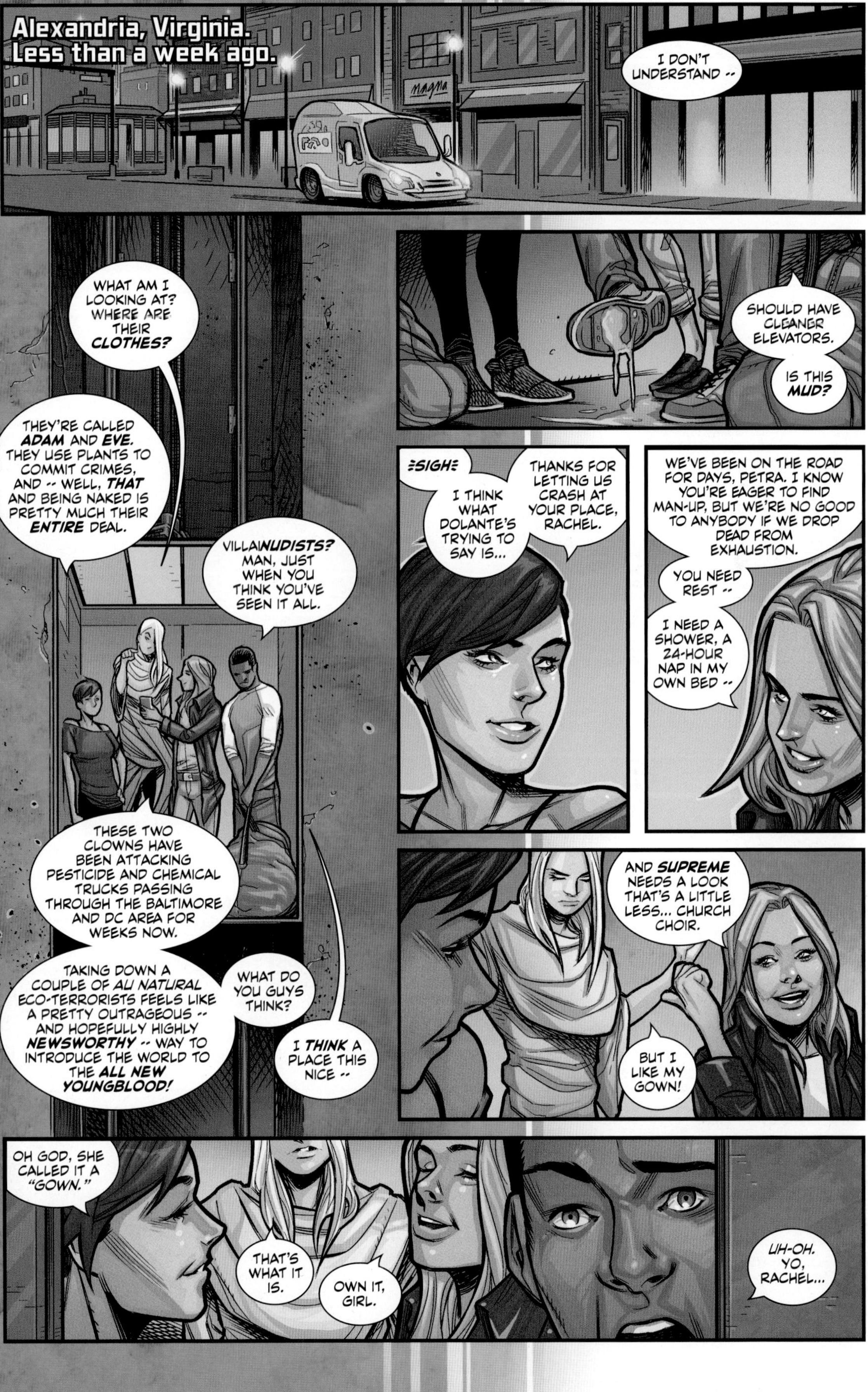
Alexandria, Virginia. Less than a week ago.
I DON'T UNDERSTAND --
WHAT AM I LOOKING AT? WHERE ARE THEIR CLOTHES?
THEY'RE CALLED ADAM AND EVE. THEY USE PLANTS TO COMMIT CRIMES, AND -- WELL, THAT AND BEING NAKED IS PRETTY MUCH THEIR ENTIRE DEAL.
VILLAINUDISTS? MAN, JUST WHEN YOU THINK YOU'VE SEEN IT ALL.
THESE TWO CLOWNS HAVE BEEN ATTACKING PESTICIDE AND CHEMICAL TRUCKS PASSING THROUGH THE BALTIMORE AND DC AREA FOR WEEKS NOW.
TAKING DOWN A COUPLE OF AU NATURAL ECO-TERRORISTS FEELS LIKE A PRETTY OUTRAGEOUS -- AND HOPEFULLY HIGHLY NEWSWORTHY -- WAY TO INTRODUCE THE WORLD TO THE ALL NEW YOUNGBLOOD!
WHAT DO YOU GUYS THINK?
I THINK A PLACE THIS NICE --
SHOULD HAVE CLEANER ELEVATORS.
IS THIS MUD?
SIGH
I THINK WHAT DOLANTE'S TRYING TO SAY IS...
THANKS FOR LETTING US CRASH AT YOUR PLACE, RACHEL.
WE'VE BEEN ON THE ROAD FOR DAYS, PETRA. I KNOW YOU'RE EAGER TO FIND MAN-UP, BUT WE'RE NO GOOD TO ANYBODY IF WE DROP DEAD FROM EXHAUSTION.
YOU NEED REST --
I NEED A SHOWER, A 24-HOUR NAP IN MY OWN BED --
AND SUPREME NEEDS A LOOK THAT'S A LITTLE LESS... CHURCH CHOIR.
BUT I LIKE MY GOWN!
OH GOD, SHE CALLED IT A "GOWN."
THAT'S WHAT IT IS.
OWN IT, GIRL.
UH-OH. YO, RACHEL...

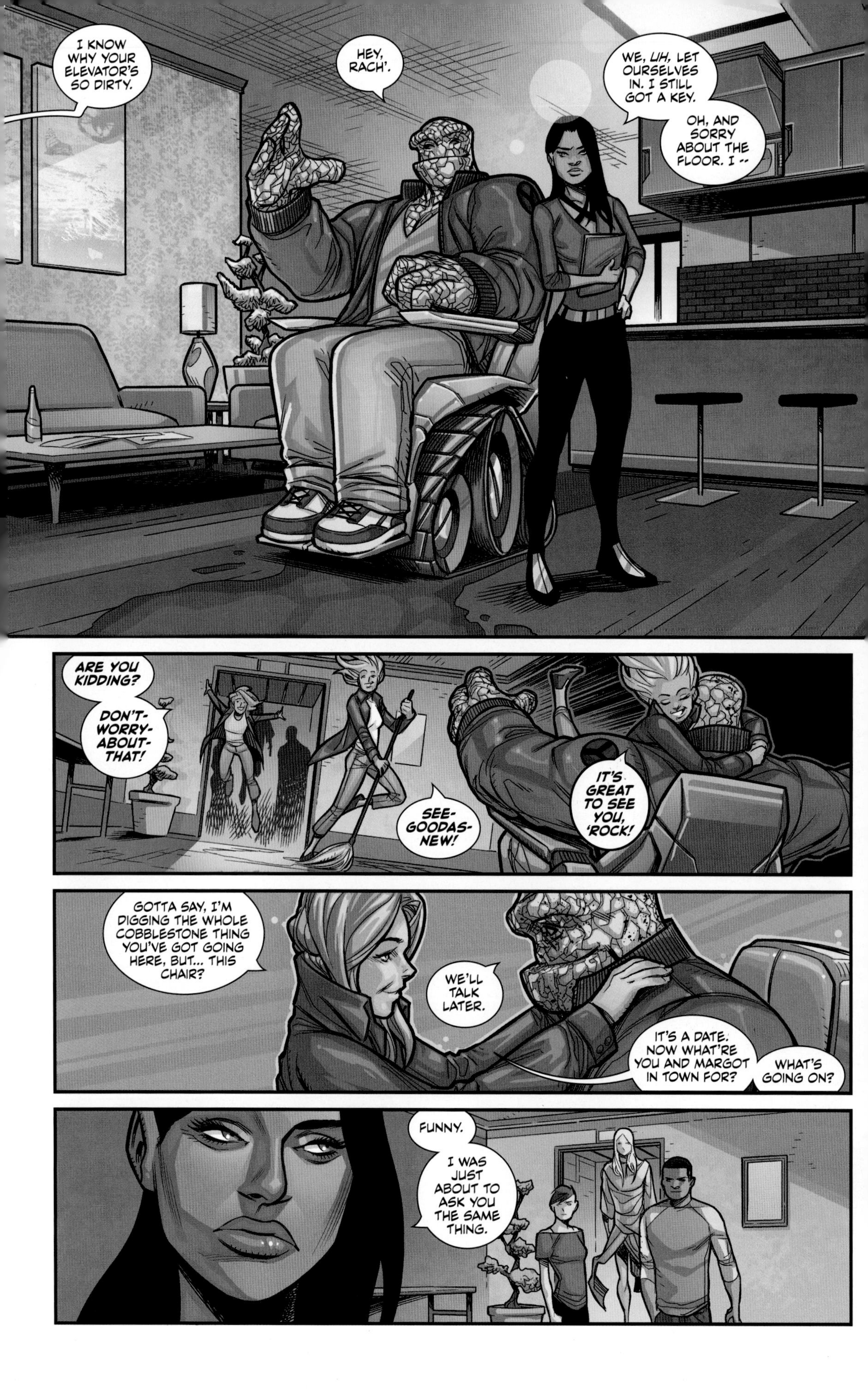
I KNOW WHY YOUR ELEVATOR'S SO DIRTY.
HEY, RACH'.
WE, UH, LET OURSELVES IN. I STILL GOT A KEY.
OH, AND SORRY ABOUT THE FLOOR. I --
ARE YOU KIDDING?
DON'T-WORRY-ABOUT-THAT!
SEE-GOODAS-NEW!
IT'S GREAT TO SEE YOU, 'ROCK!
GOTTA SAY, I'M DIGGING THE WHOLE COBBLESTONE THING YOU'VE GOT GOING HERE, BUT... THIS CHAIR?
WE'LL TALK LATER.
IT'S A DATE. NOW WHAT'RE YOU AND MARGOT IN TOWN FOR?
WHAT'S GOING ON?
FUNNY.
I WAS JUST ABOUT TO ASK YOU THE SAME THING.

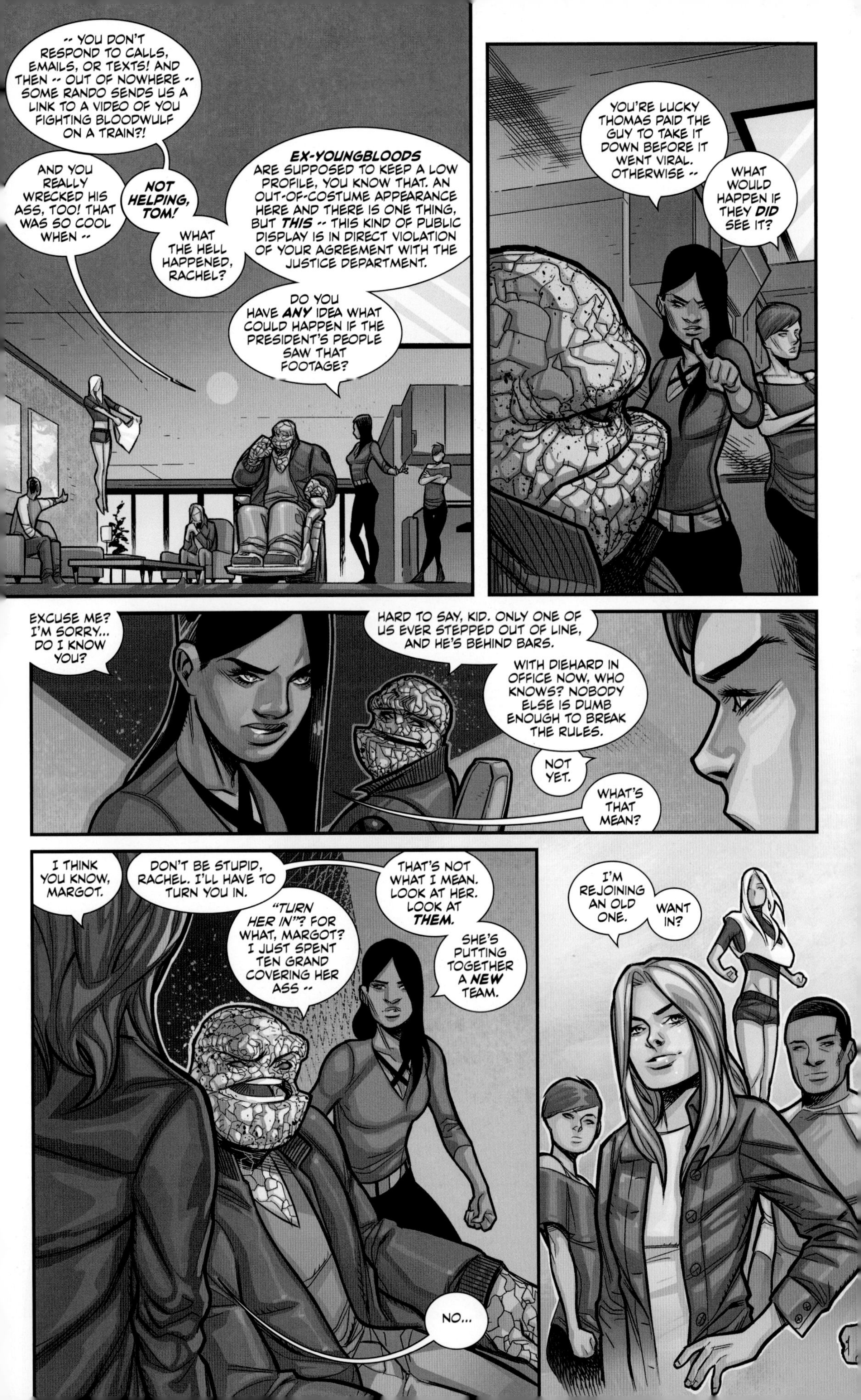

-- YOU DON'T RESPOND TO CALLS, EMAILS, OR TEXTS! AND THEN -- OUT OF NOWHERE -- SOME RANDO SENDS US A LINK TO A VIDEO OF YOU FIGHTING BLOODWULF ON A TRAIN?!
AND YOU REALLY WRECKED HIS ASS, TOO! THAT WAS SO COOL WHEN --
NOT HELPING, TOM!
WHAT THE HELL HAPPENED, RACHEL?
EX-YOUNGBLOODS ARE SUPPOSED TO KEEP A LOW PROFILE, YOU KNOW THAT. AN OUT-OF-COSTUME APPEARANCE HERE AND THERE IS ONE THING, BUT THIS -- THIS KIND OF PUBLIC DISPLAY IS IN DIRECT VIOLATION OF YOUR AGREEMENT WITH THE JUSTICE DEPARTMENT.
DO YOU HAVE ANY IDEA WHAT COULD HAPPEN IF THE PRESIDENT'S PEOPLE SAW THAT FOOTAGE?
YOU'RE LUCKY THOMAS PAID THE GUY TO TAKE IT DOWN BEFORE IT WENT VIRAL. OTHERWISE --
WHAT WOULD HAPPEN IF THEY DID SEE IT?
EXCUSE ME? I'M SORRY... DO I KNOW YOU?
HARD TO SAY, KID. ONLY ONE OF US EVER STEPPED OUT OF LINE, AND HE'S BEHIND BARS.
WITH DIEHARD IN OFFICE NOW, WHO KNOWS? NOBODY ELSE IS DUMB ENOUGH TO BREAK THE RULES.
NOT YET.
WHAT'S THAT MEAN?
I THINK YOU KNOW, MARGOT.
DON'T BE STUPID, RACHEL. I'LL HAVE TO TURN YOU IN.
"TURN HER IN"? FOR WHAT, MARGOT? I JUST SPENT TEN GRAND COVERING HER ASS --
THAT'S NOT WHAT I MEAN. LOOK AT HER. LOOK AT THEM.
SHE'S PUTTING TOGETHER A NEW TEAM.
NO...
I'M REJOINING AN OLD ONE.
WANT IN?

FOR REAL?

THE ANSWER'S *NO!* OF COURSE HE DOESN'T WANT TO BE A PART OF YOUR -- *WHATEVER THIS IS!*

I MEAN, *ARE YOU TOTALLY OUT OF YOUR MIND?!* YOU HAVE *NO* IDEA WHAT WE HAD TO DO TO KEEP YOU IDIOTS OUT OF *PRISON!*

I SACRIFICED MY REPUTATION -- MY ENTIRE CAREER TO STAND BY YOU BECAUSE I *BELIEVED* IN YOUNGBLOOD!

MARGOT.

WHAT?

SOME OF US *STILL* DO.

THOMAS?

I GAVE IT A SHOT, MARGOT. I *REALLY* DID. BUT LOOK AT US... LOOK AT *ME!* I'M NOT BUILT FOR SITTING ON THE SIDELINES.

YOU CAN BARELY STAND.

MAYBE SO...

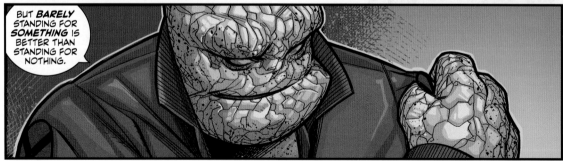

BUT *BARELY* STANDING FOR *SOMETHING* IS BETTER THAN STANDING FOR NOTHING.

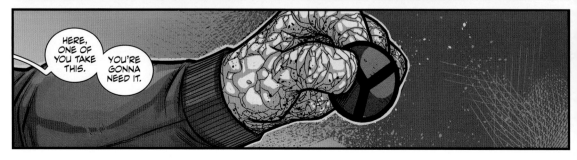

HERE, ONE OF YOU TAKE THIS.

YOU'RE GONNA NEED IT.

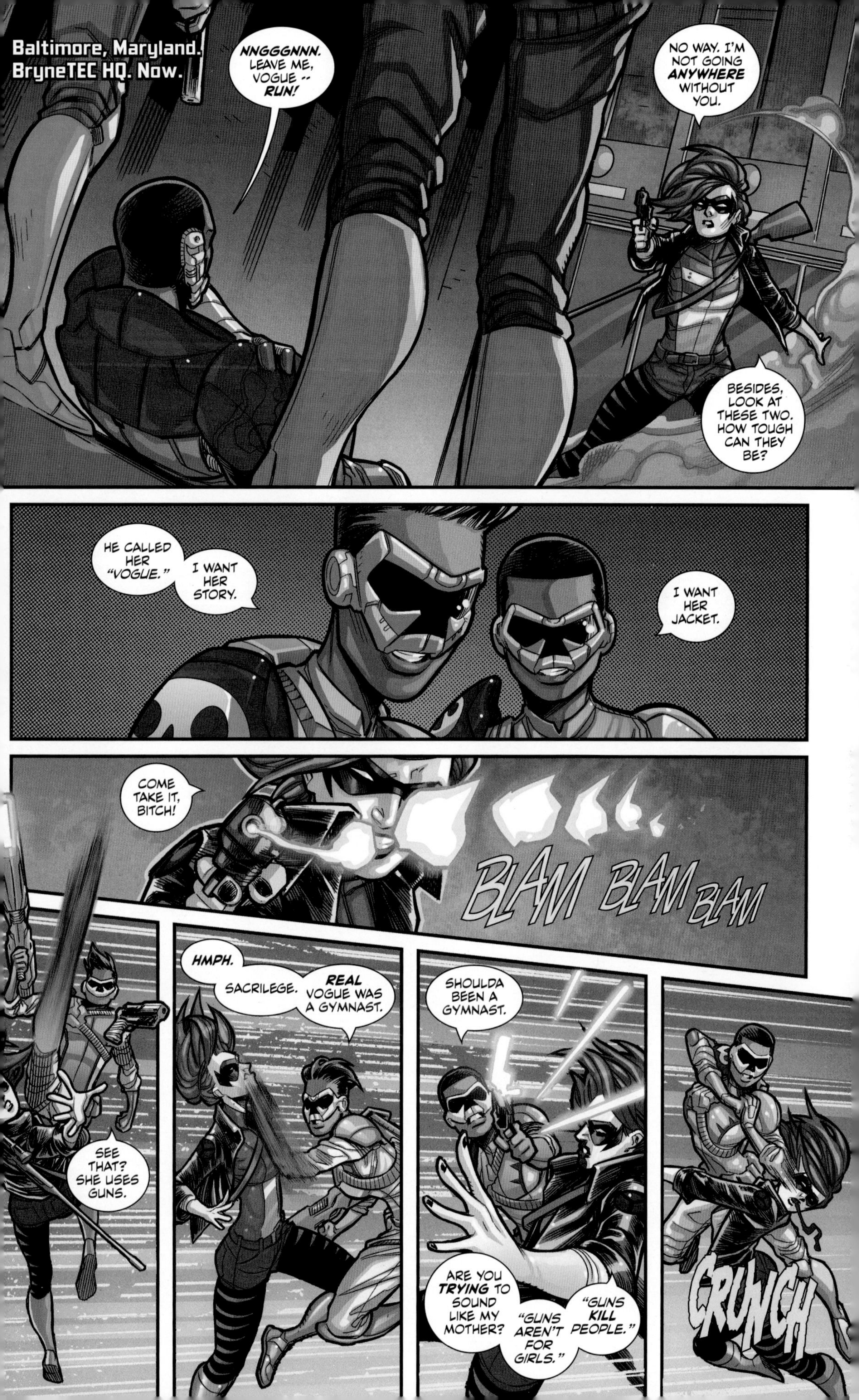
Baltimore, Maryland. BryneTEC HQ. Now.
NNGGGNNN. LEAVE ME, VOGUE -- RUN!
NO WAY. I'M NOT GOING ANYWHERE WITHOUT YOU.
BESIDES, LOOK AT THESE TWO. HOW TOUGH CAN THEY BE?
HE CALLED HER "VOGUE."
I WANT HER STORY.
I WANT HER JACKET.
COME TAKE IT, BITCH!
BLAM BLAM BLAM
SEE THAT? SHE USES GUNS.
HMPH.
SACRILEGE.
REAL VOGUE WAS A GYMNAST.
SHOULDA BEEN A GYMNAST.
ARE YOU TRYING TO SOUND LIKE MY MOTHER?
"GUNS AREN'T FOR GIRLS."
"GUNS KILL PEOPLE."
CRUNCH

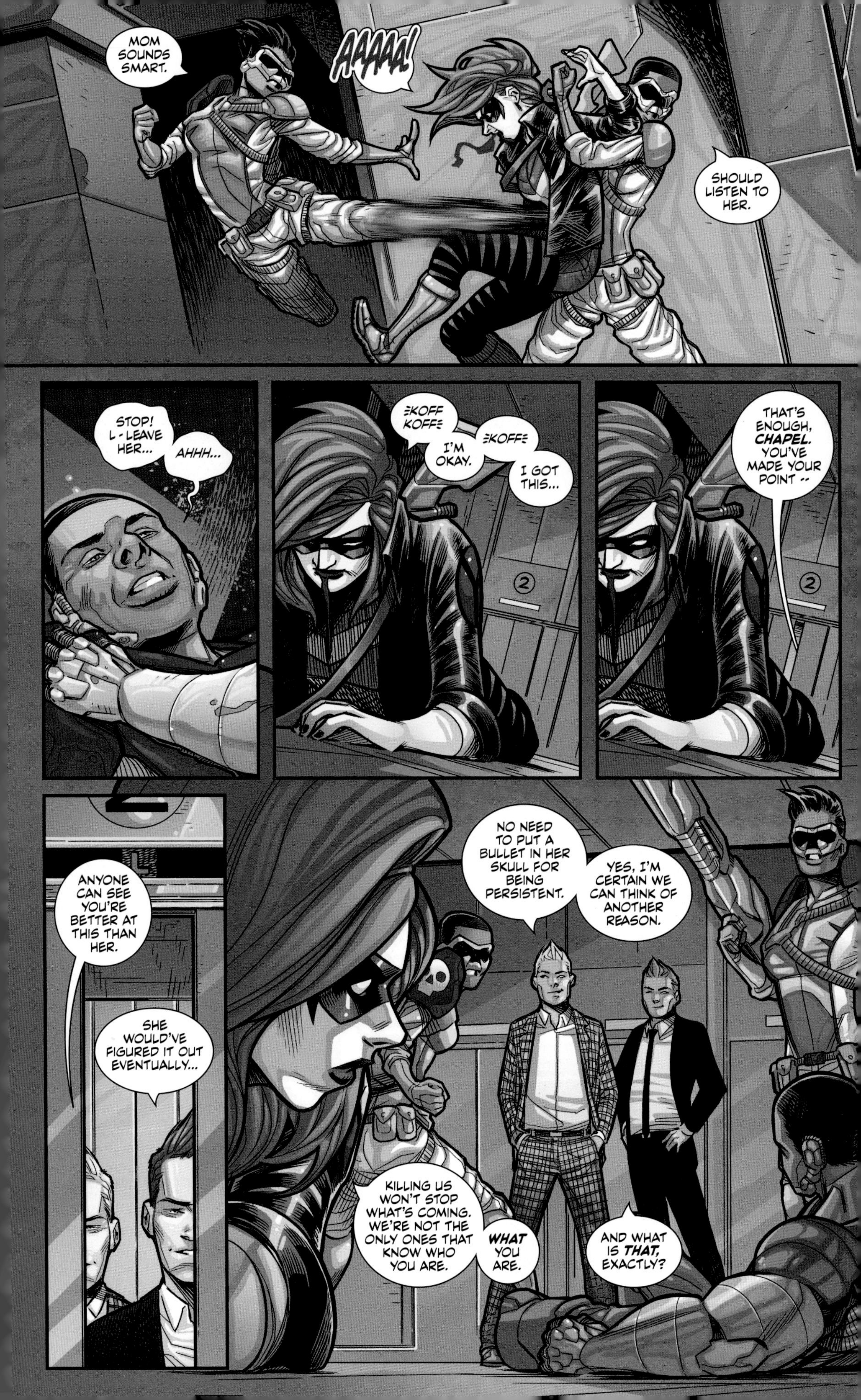
MOM SOUNDS SMART.
AAAAA!
SHOULD LISTEN TO HER.
STOP! L-LEAVE HER...
AHHH...
KOFF KOFF
I'M OKAY.
KOFF
I GOT THIS...
THAT'S ENOUGH, CHAPEL. YOU'VE MADE YOUR POINT --
ANYONE CAN SEE YOU'RE BETTER AT THIS THAN HER.
SHE WOULD'VE FIGURED IT OUT EVENTUALLY...
NO NEED TO PUT A BULLET IN HER SKULL FOR BEING PERSISTENT.
YES, I'M CERTAIN WE CAN THINK OF ANOTHER REASON.
KILLING US WON'T STOP WHAT'S COMING. WE'RE NOT THE ONLY ONES THAT KNOW WHO YOU ARE.
WHAT YOU ARE.
AND WHAT IS THAT, EXACTLY?

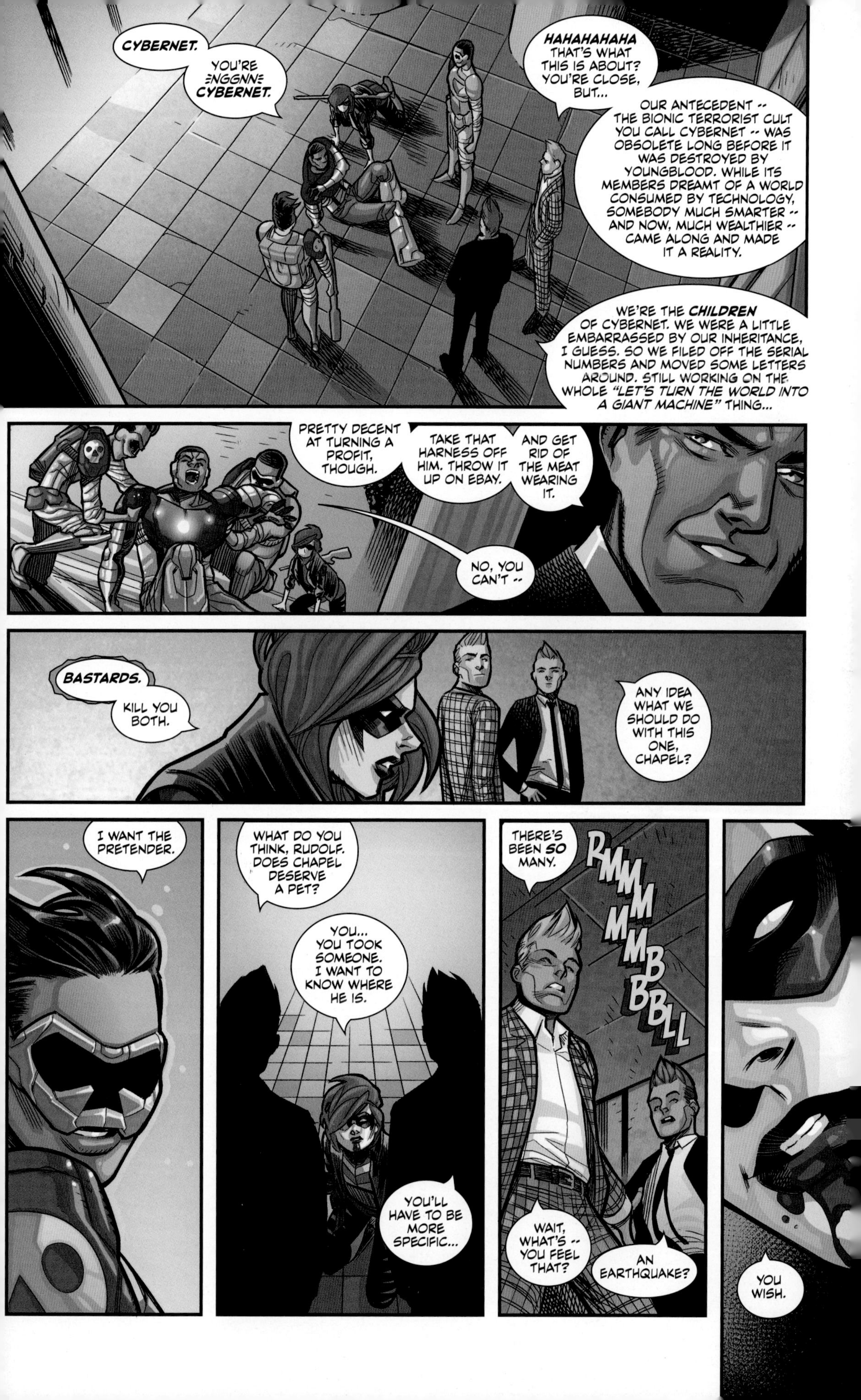

CYBERNET.
YOU'RE ENGGNN CYBERNET.
HAHAHAHAHA THAT'S WHAT THIS IS ABOUT? YOU'RE CLOSE, BUT...
OUR ANTECEDENT -- THE BIONIC TERRORIST CULT YOU CALL CYBERNET -- WAS OBSOLETE LONG BEFORE IT WAS DESTROYED BY YOUNGBLOOD. WHILE ITS MEMBERS DREAMT OF A WORLD CONSUMED BY TECHNOLOGY, SOMEBODY MUCH SMARTER -- AND NOW, MUCH WEALTHIER -- CAME ALONG AND MADE IT A REALITY.
WE'RE THE CHILDREN OF CYBERNET. WE WERE A LITTLE EMBARRASSED BY OUR INHERITANCE, I GUESS. SO WE FILED OFF THE SERIAL NUMBERS AND MOVED SOME LETTERS AROUND. STILL WORKING ON THE WHOLE "LET'S TURN THE WORLD INTO A GIANT MACHINE" THING...
PRETTY DECENT AT TURNING A PROFIT, THOUGH.
TAKE THAT HARNESS OFF HIM. THROW IT UP ON EBAY.
AND GET RID OF THE MEAT WEARING IT.
NO, YOU CAN'T --
BASTARDS.
KILL YOU BOTH.
ANY IDEA WHAT WE SHOULD DO WITH THIS ONE, CHAPEL?
I WANT THE PRETENDER.
WHAT DO YOU THINK, RUDOLF. DOES CHAPEL DESERVE A PET?
YOU... YOU TOOK SOMEONE. I WANT TO KNOW WHERE HE IS.
YOU'LL HAVE TO BE MORE SPECIFIC...
THERE'S BEEN SO MANY.
RMMMMMBBBLL
WAIT, WHAT'S -- YOU FEEL THAT?
AN EARTHQUAKE?
YOU WISH.

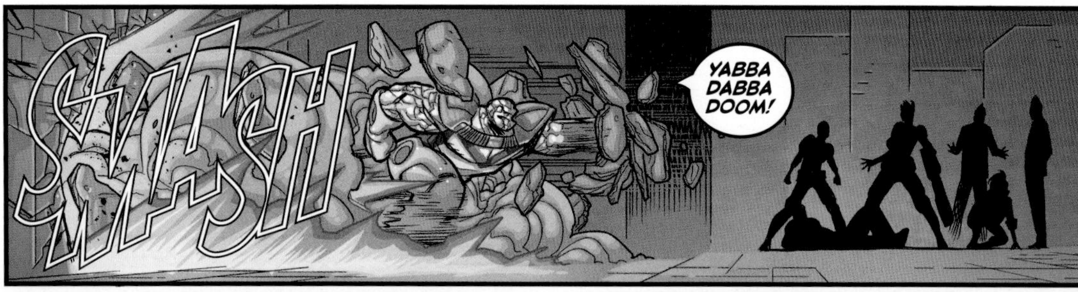
SMASH
YABBA DABBA DOOM!

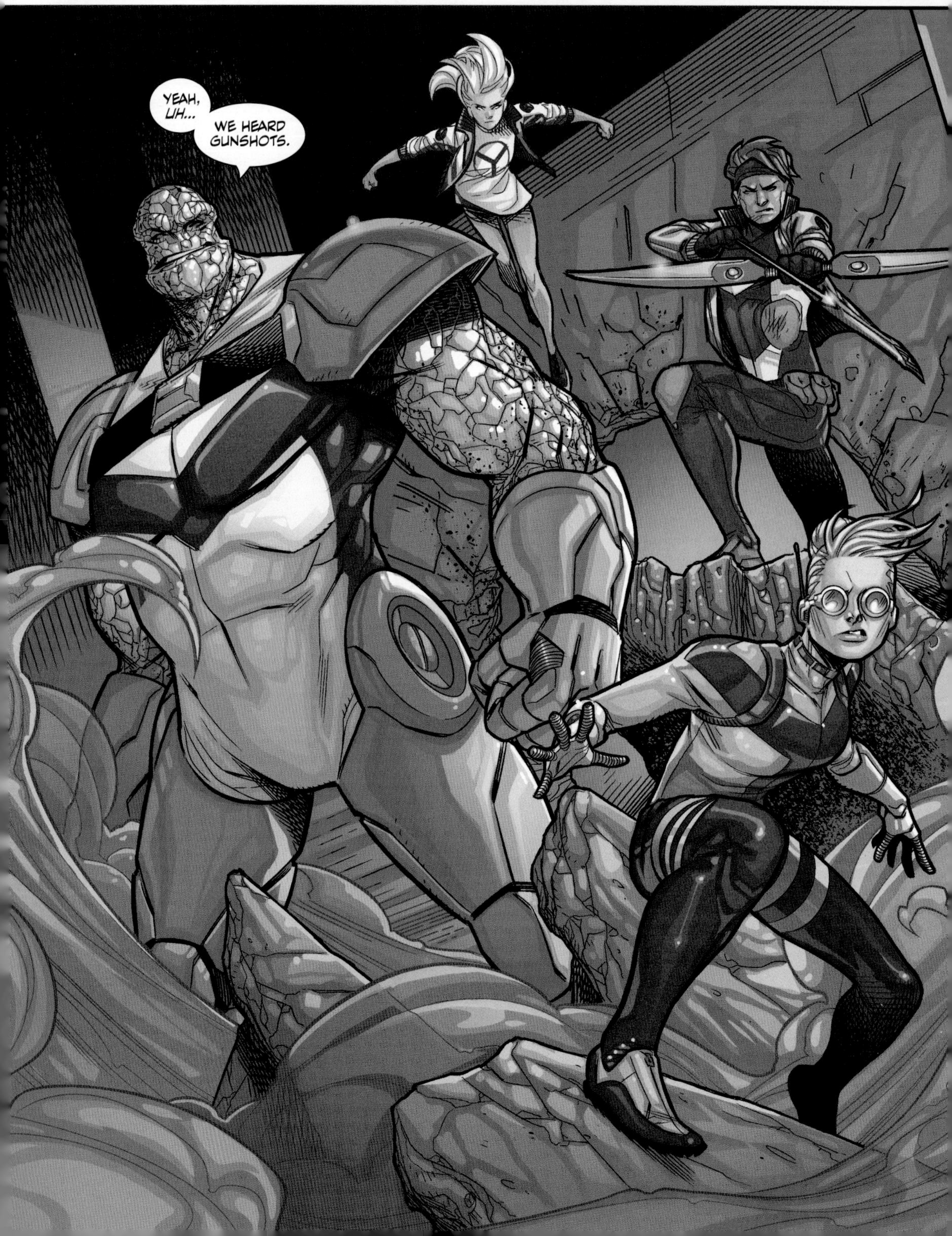
YEAH, UH...
WE HEARD GUNSHOTS.

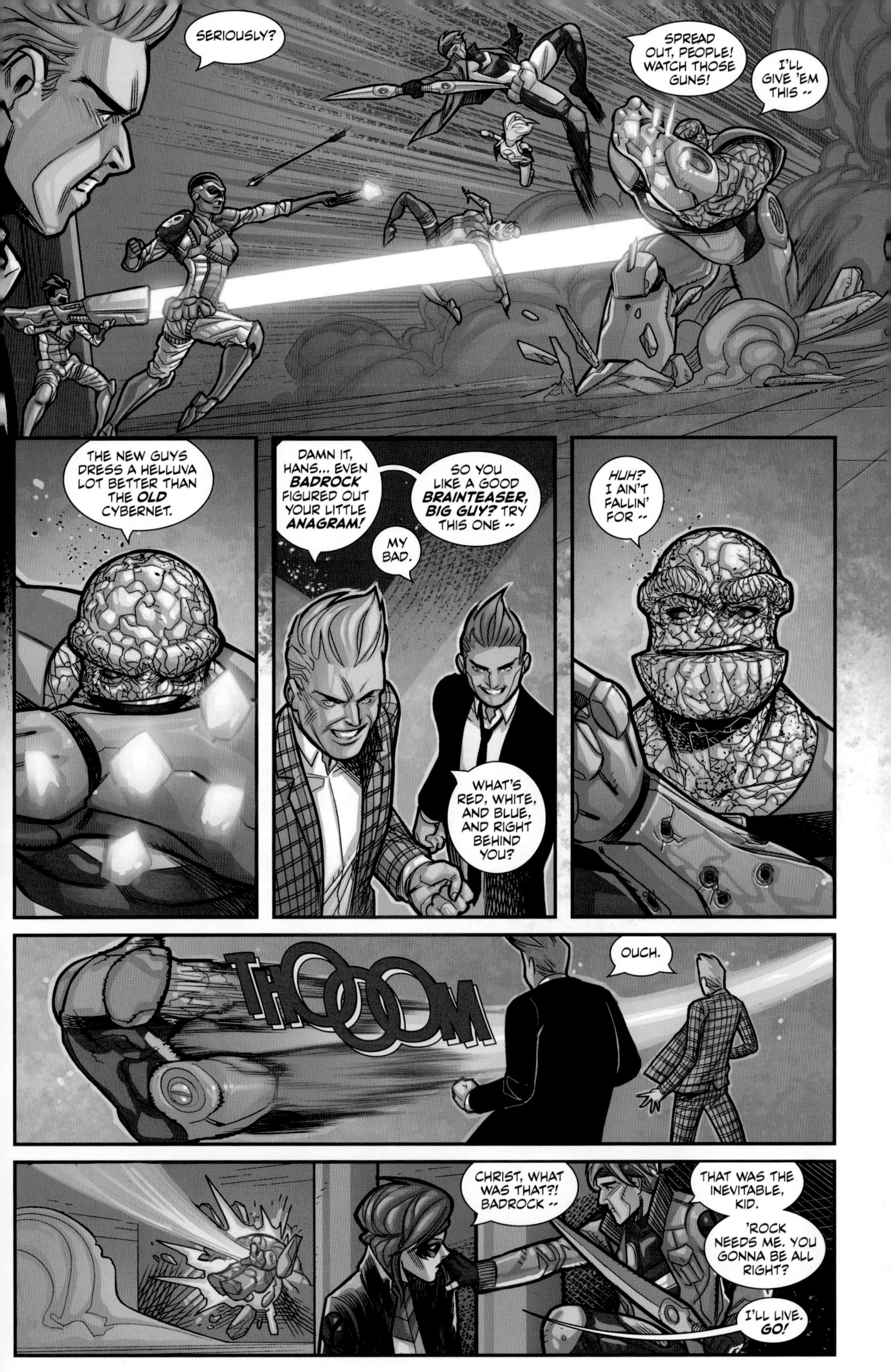
SERIOUSLY?
SPREAD OUT, PEOPLE! WATCH THOSE GUNS!
I'LL GIVE 'EM THIS --
THE NEW GUYS DRESS A HELLUVA LOT BETTER THAN THE OLD CYBERNET.
DAMN IT, HANS... EVEN BADROCK FIGURED OUT YOUR LITTLE ANAGRAM!
MY BAD.
SO YOU LIKE A GOOD BRAINTEASER, BIG GUY? TRY THIS ONE --
WHAT'S RED, WHITE, AND BLUE, AND RIGHT BEHIND YOU?
HUH? I AIN'T FALLIN' FOR --
THOOOM
OUCH.
CHRIST, WHAT WAS THAT?! BADROCK --
THAT WAS THE INEVITABLE, KID.
'ROCK NEEDS ME. YOU GONNA BE ALL RIGHT?
I'LL LIVE. GO!

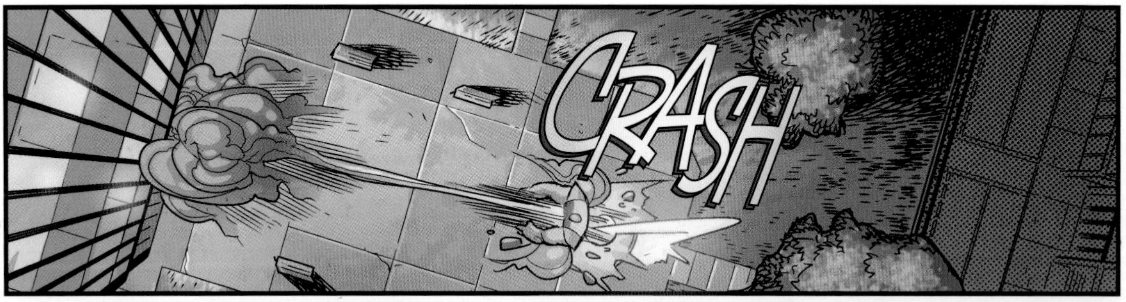
CRASH

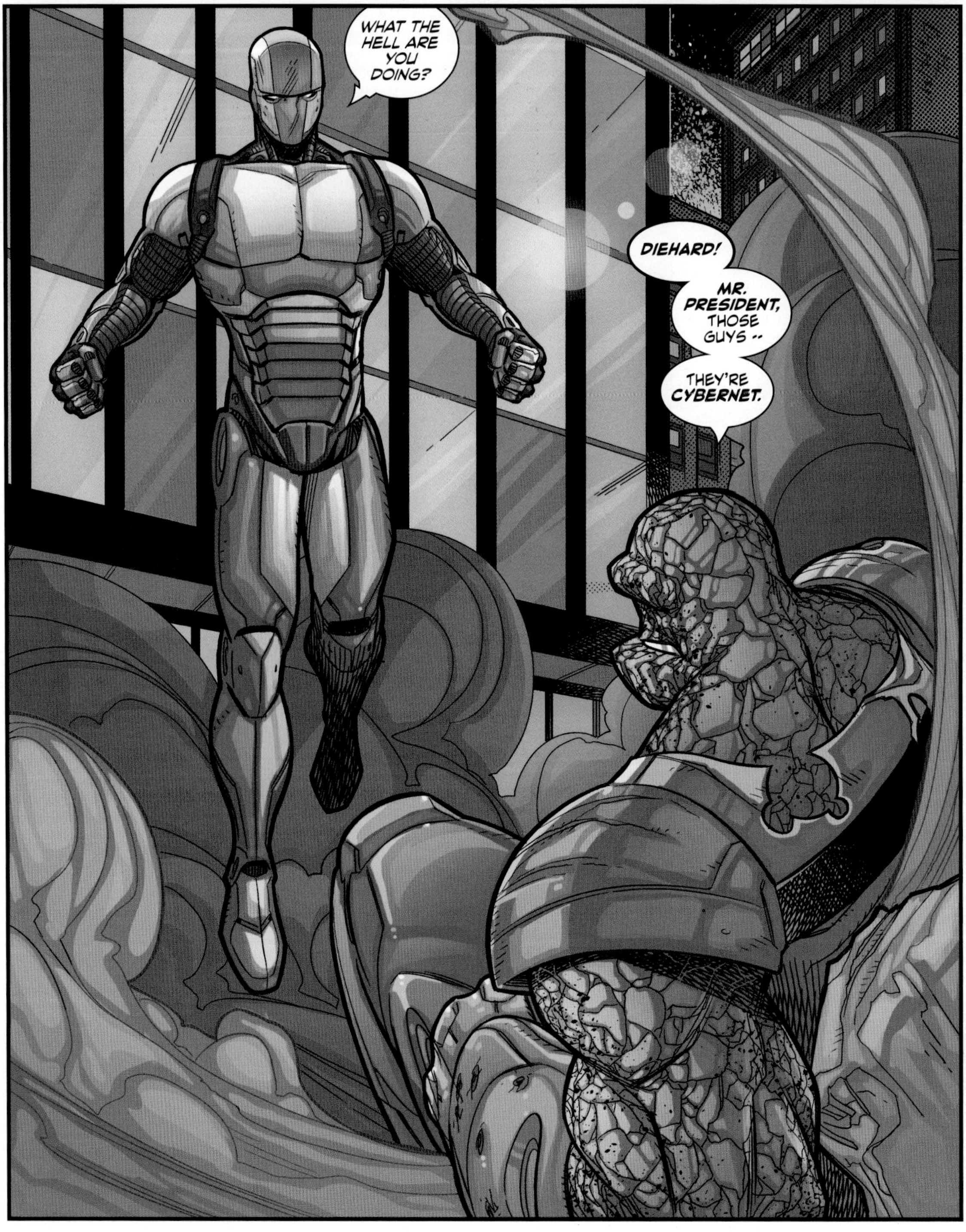
WHAT THE HELL ARE YOU DOING?
DIEHARD!
MR. PRESIDENT, THOSE GUYS --
THEY'RE CYBERNET.

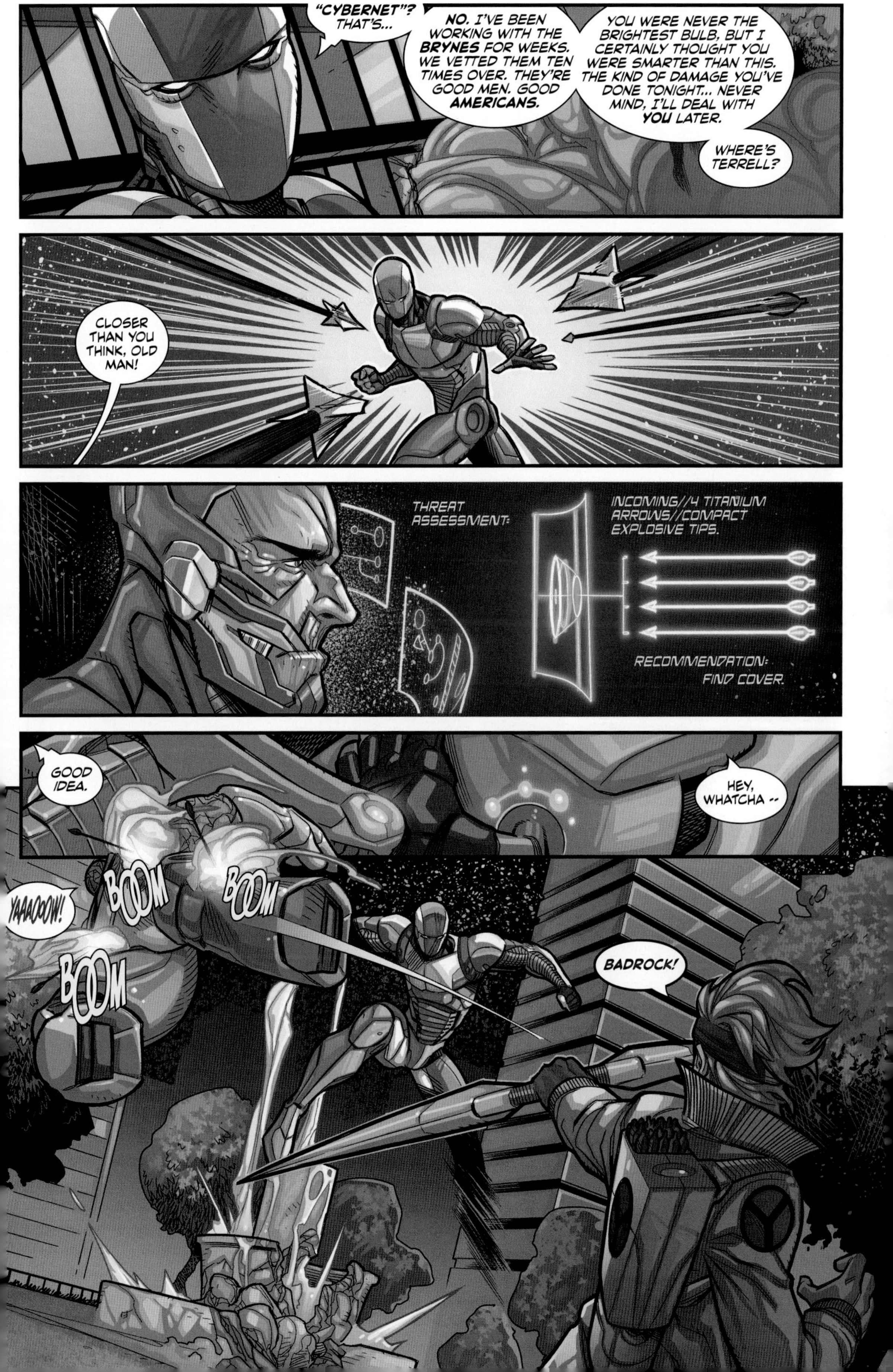
"CYBERNET"? THAT'S...
NO. I'VE BEEN WORKING WITH THE BRYNES FOR WEEKS. WE VETTED THEM TEN TIMES OVER. THEY'RE GOOD MEN. GOOD AMERICANS.
YOU WERE NEVER THE BRIGHTEST BULB, BUT I CERTAINLY THOUGHT YOU WERE SMARTER THAN THIS. THE KIND OF DAMAGE YOU'VE DONE TONIGHT... NEVER MIND, I'LL DEAL WITH YOU LATER.
WHERE'S TERRELL?
CLOSER THAN YOU THINK, OLD MAN!
THREAT ASSESSMENT:
INCOMING//4 TITANIUM ARROWS//COMPACT EXPLOSIVE TIPS.
RECOMMENDATION: FIND COVER.
GOOD IDEA.
HEY, WHATCHA --
YAAAOOOW!
BOOM
BOOM
BOOM
BADROCK!

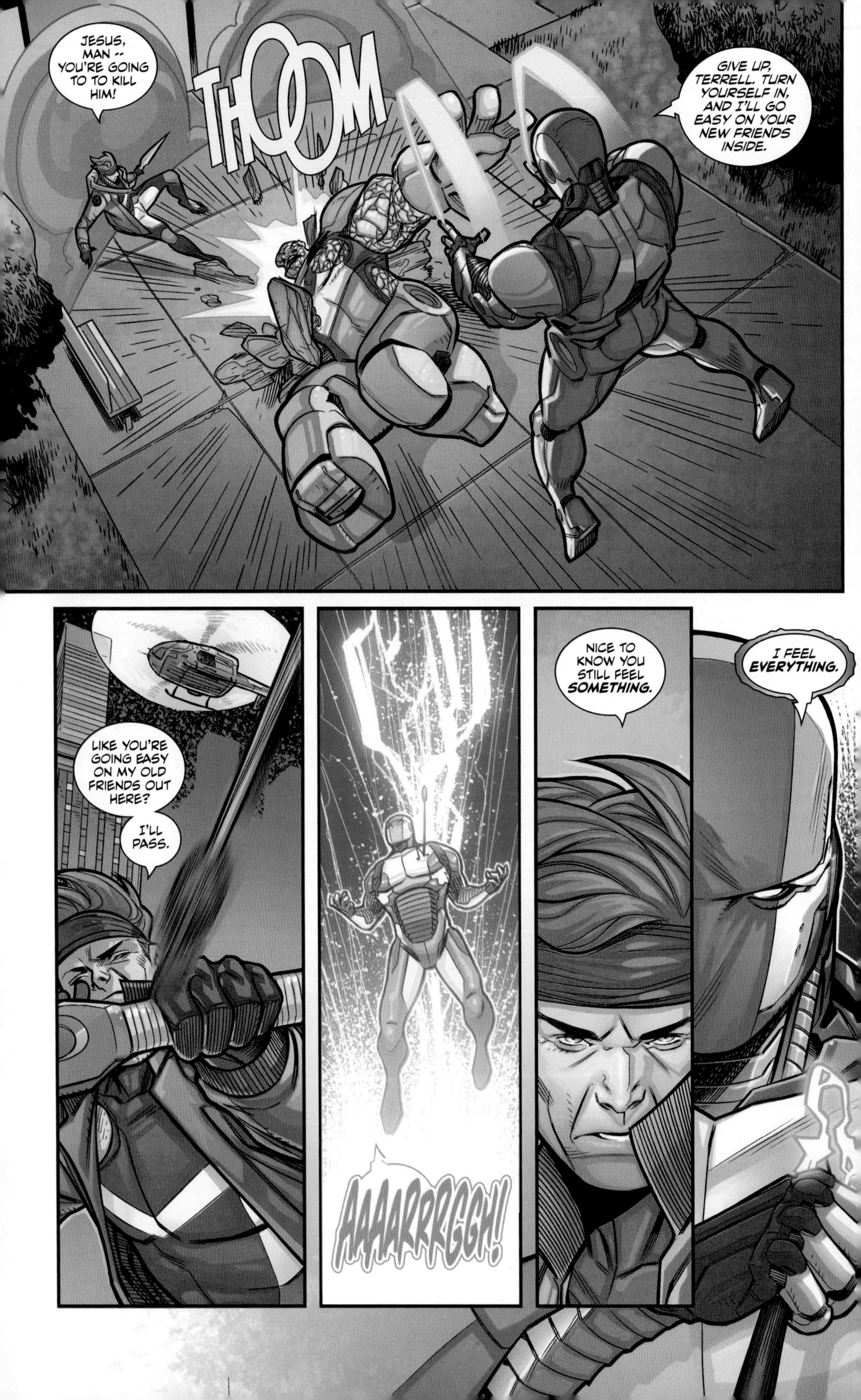
JESUS, MAN -- YOU'RE GOING TO TO KILL HIM!
THOOM
GIVE UP, TERRELL. TURN YOURSELF IN, AND I'LL GO EASY ON YOUR NEW FRIENDS INSIDE.
LIKE YOU'RE GOING EASY ON MY OLD FRIENDS OUT HERE?
I'LL PASS.
AAAARRRGGH!
NICE TO KNOW YOU STILL FEEL SOMETHING.
I FEEL EVERYTHING.

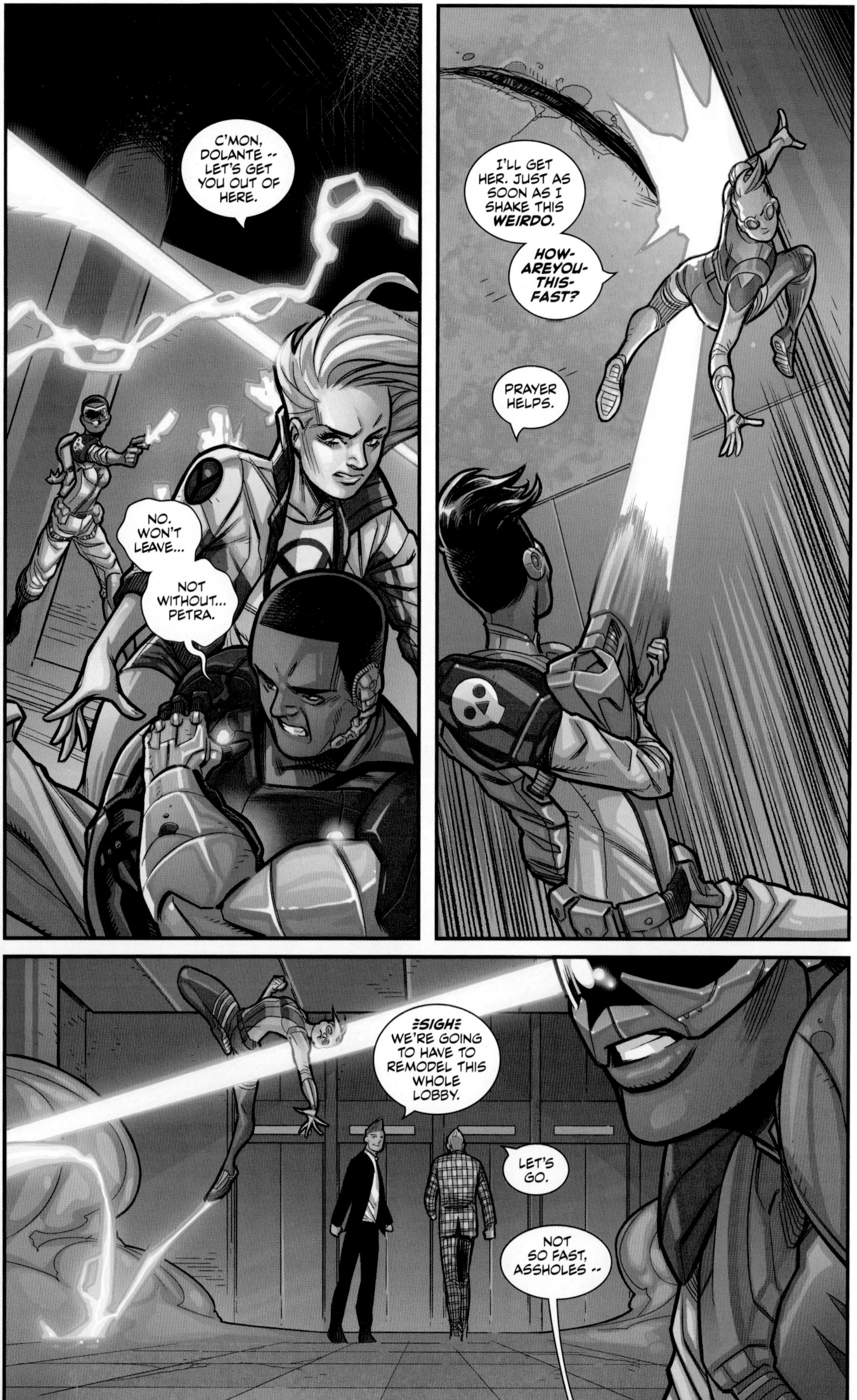
C'MON, DOLANTE -- LET'S GET YOU OUT OF HERE.
NO. WON'T LEAVE...
NOT WITHOUT... PETRA.
I'LL GET HER. JUST AS SOON AS I SHAKE THIS *WEIRDO.*
HOW-AREYOU-THIS-FAST?
PRAYER HELPS.
SIGH WE'RE GOING TO HAVE TO REMODEL THIS WHOLE LOBBY.
LET'S GO.
NOT SO FAST, ASSHOLES --

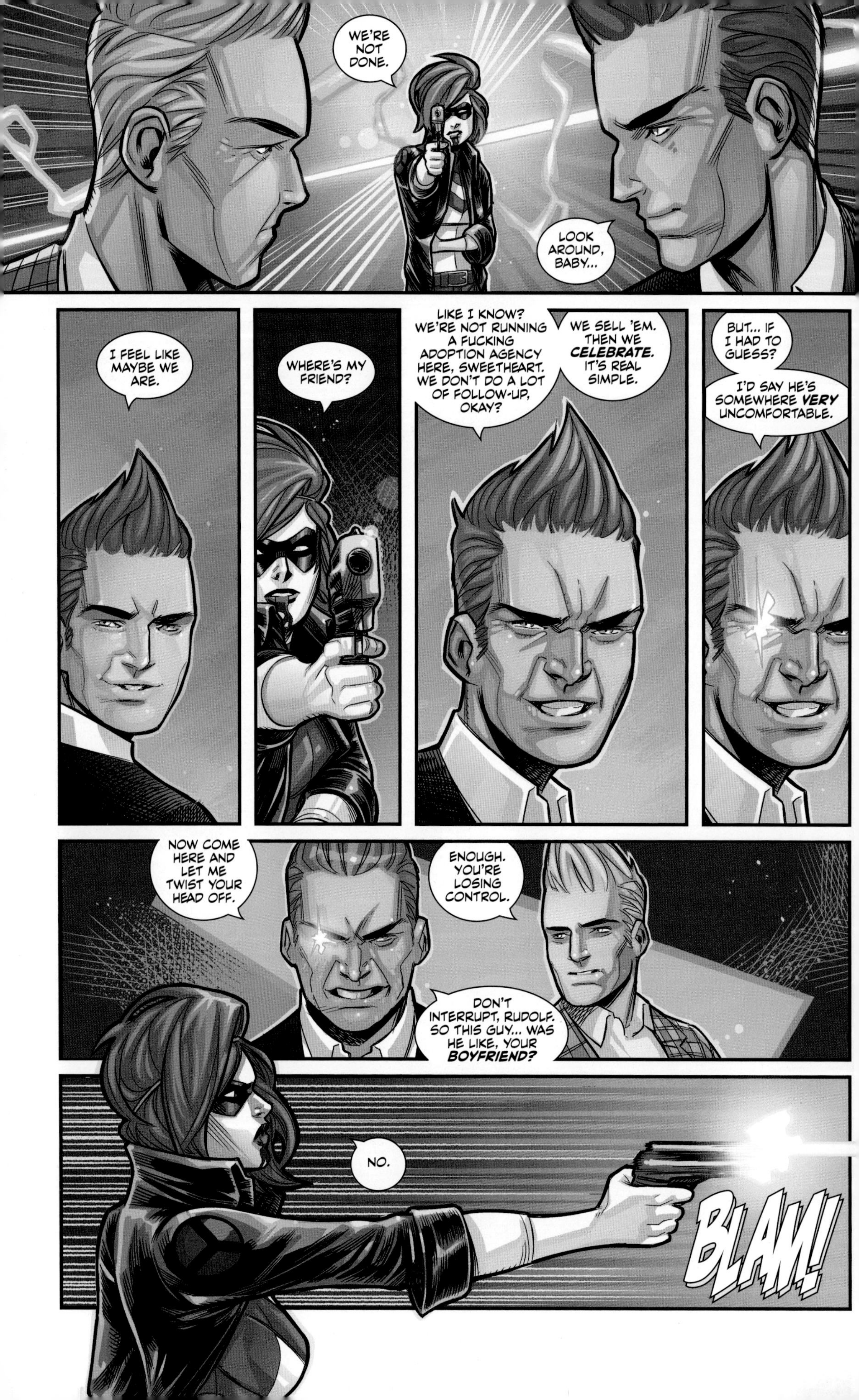
WE'RE NOT DONE.
LOOK AROUND, BABY...
I FEEL LIKE MAYBE WE ARE.
WHERE'S MY FRIEND?
LIKE I KNOW? WE'RE NOT RUNNING A FUCKING ADOPTION AGENCY HERE, SWEETHEART. WE DON'T DO A LOT OF FOLLOW-UP, OKAY?
WE SELL 'EM. THEN WE CELEBRATE. IT'S REAL SIMPLE.
BUT... IF I HAD TO GUESS?
I'D SAY HE'S SOMEWHERE VERY UNCOMFORTABLE.
NOW COME HERE AND LET ME TWIST YOUR HEAD OFF.
ENOUGH. YOU'RE LOSING CONTROL.
DON'T INTERRUPT, RUDOLF. SO THIS GUY... WAS HE LIKE, YOUR BOYFRIEND?
NO.
BLAM!

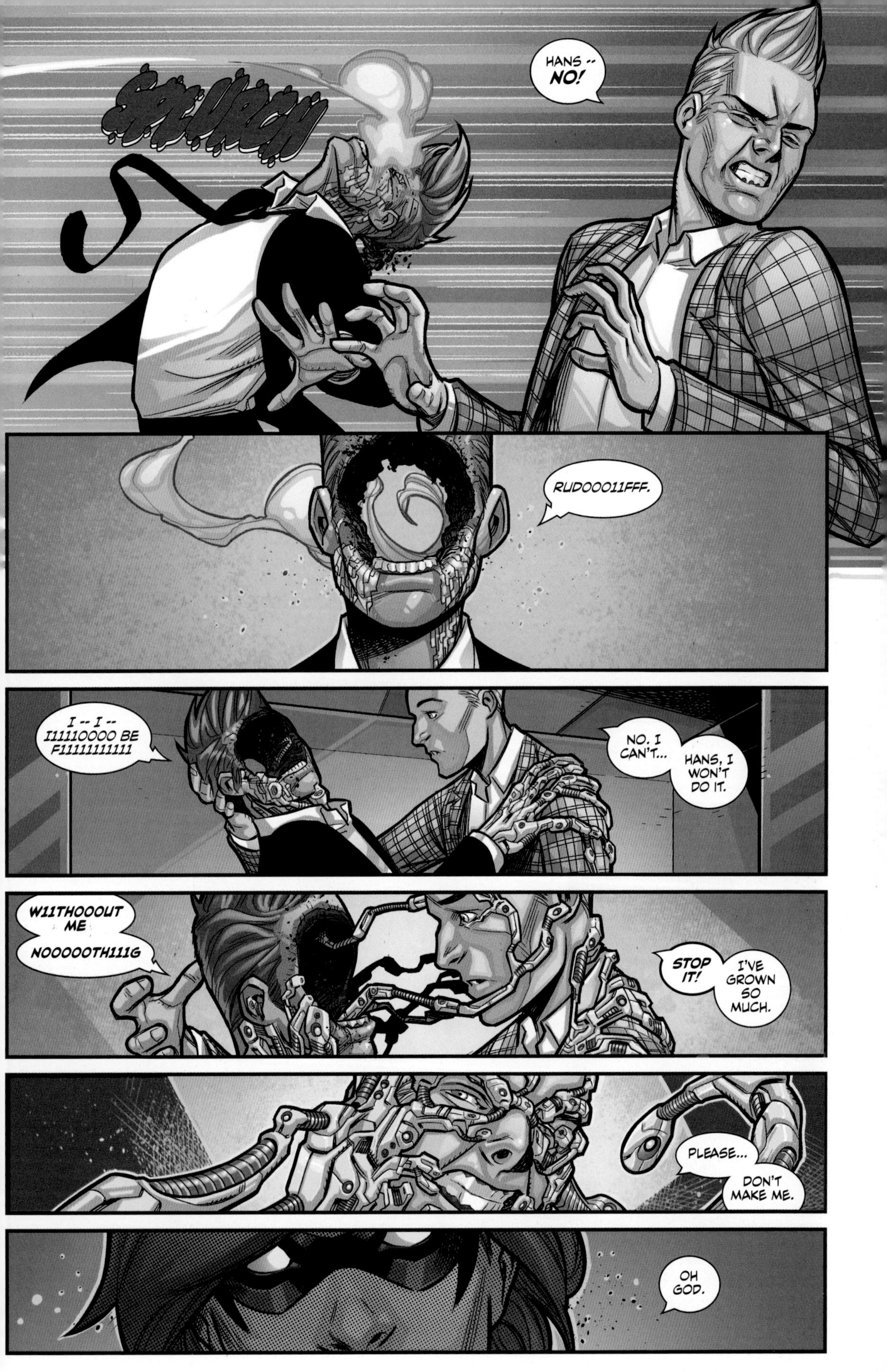

SPLURCH
HANS -- NO!
RUDOOO11FFF.
I -- I -- I11110000 BE F11111111111
NO. I CAN'T...
HANS, I WON'T DO IT.
W11THOOOUT ME
NOOOOOTH111G
STOP IT!
I'VE GROWN SO MUCH.
PLEASE...
DON'T MAKE ME.
OH GOD.

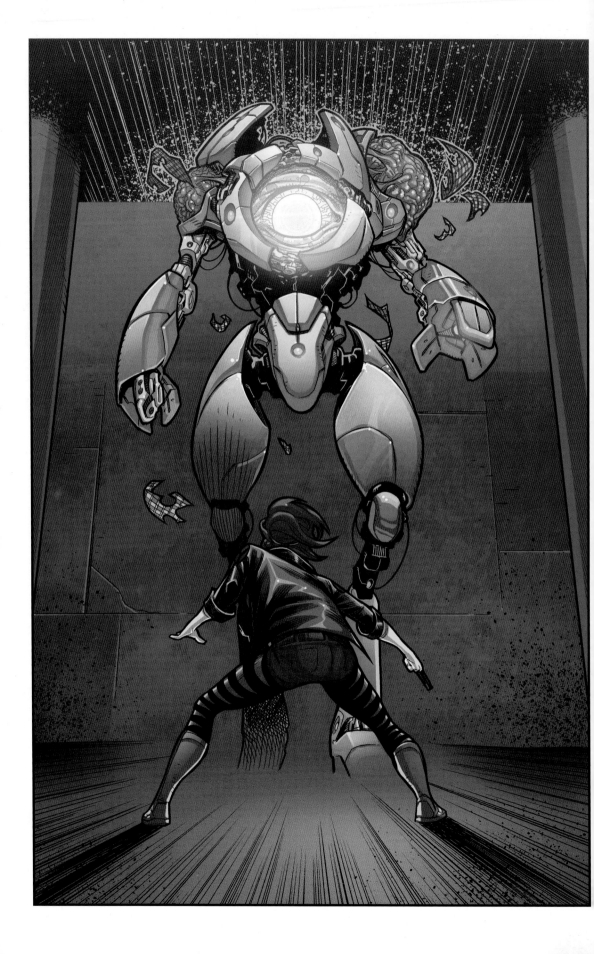

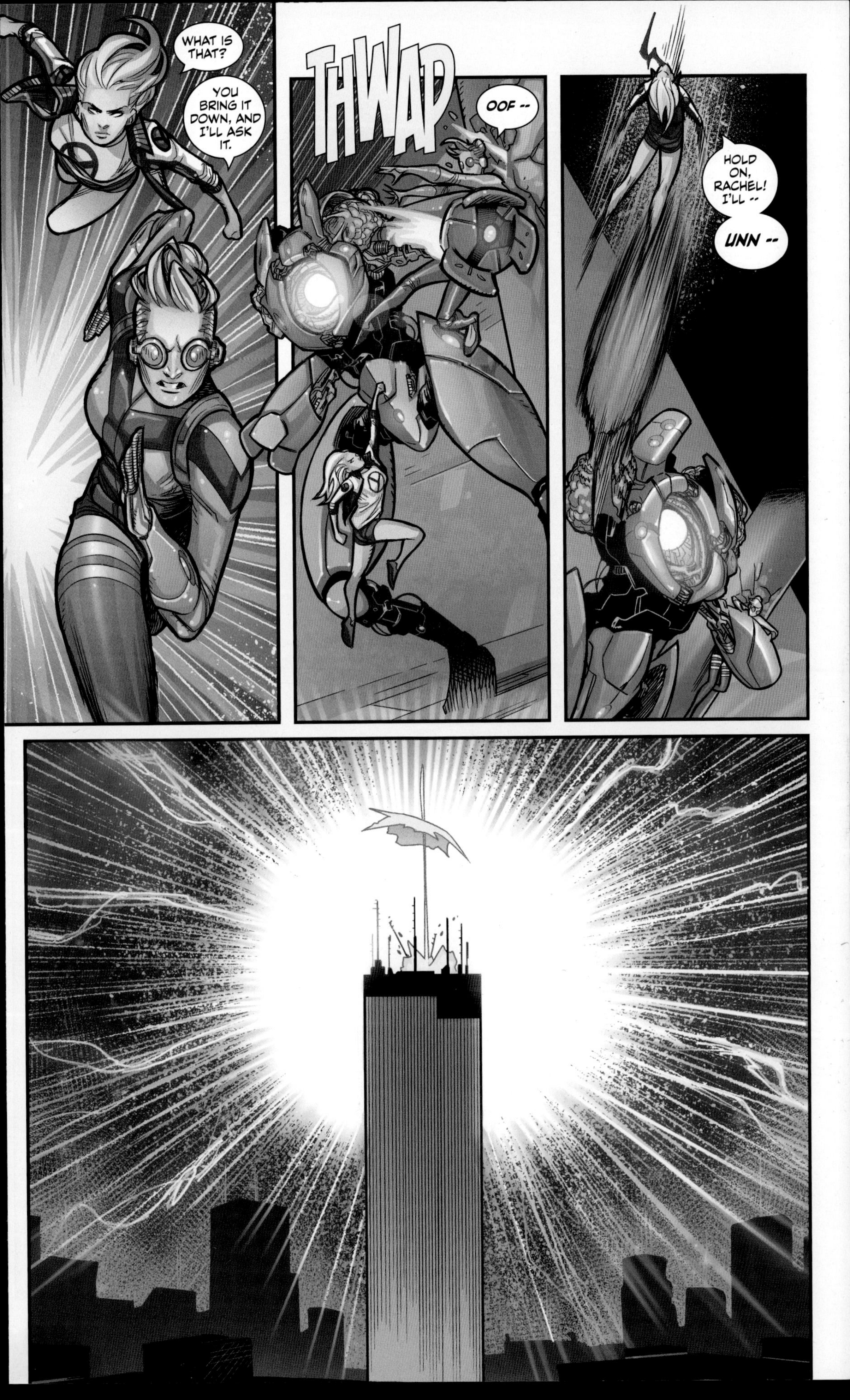
WHAT IS THAT?
YOU BRING IT DOWN, AND I'LL ASK IT.
THWAP
OOF --
HOLD ON, RACHEL! I'LL --
UNN --

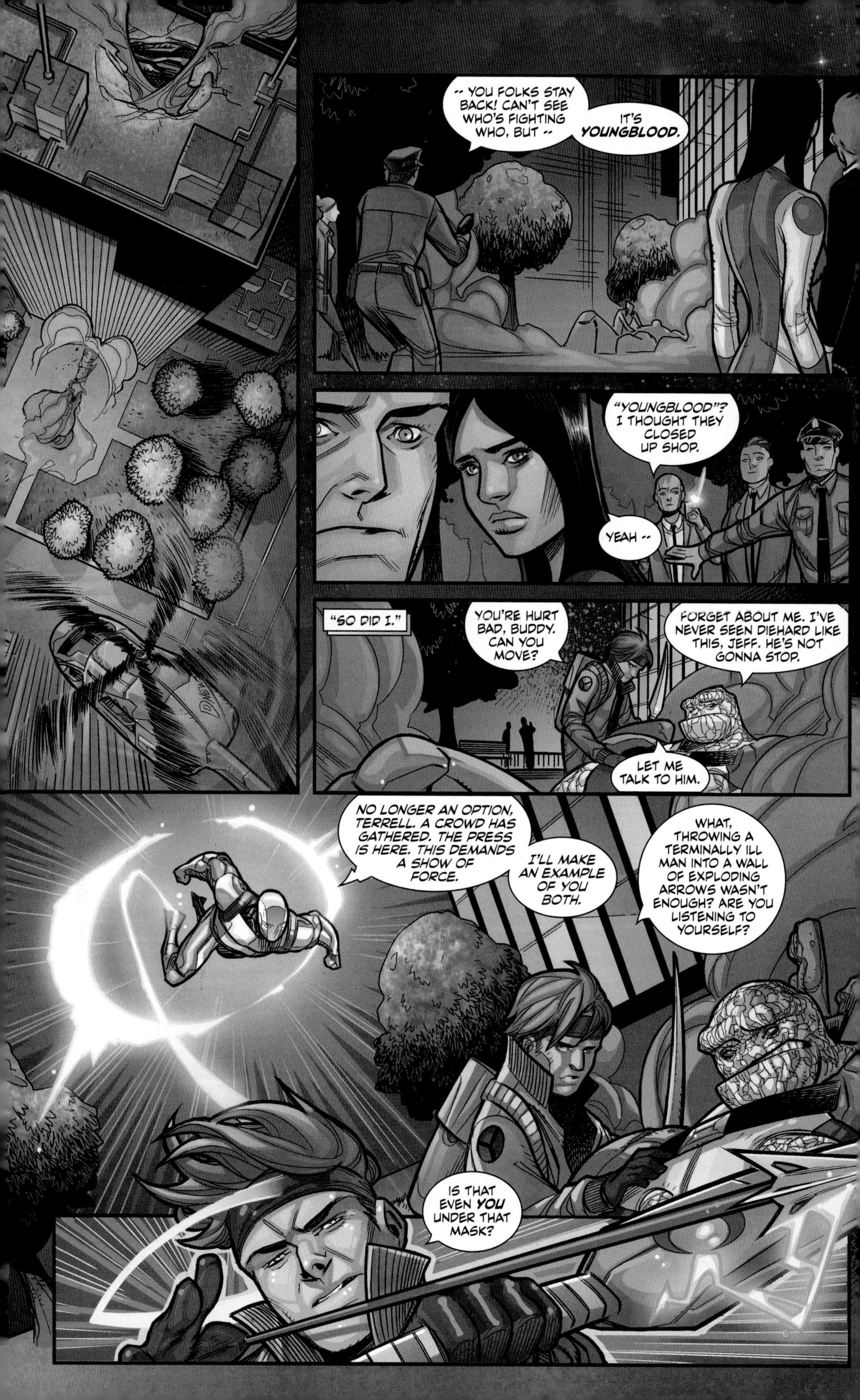
-- YOU FOLKS STAY BACK! CAN'T SEE WHO'S FIGHTING WHO, BUT --
IT'S YOUNGBLOOD.
"YOUNGBLOOD"? I THOUGHT THEY CLOSED UP SHOP.
YEAH --
"SO DID I."
YOU'RE HURT BAD, BUDDY. CAN YOU MOVE?
FORGET ABOUT ME. I'VE NEVER SEEN DIEHARD LIKE THIS, JEFF. HE'S NOT GONNA STOP.
LET ME TALK TO HIM.
NO LONGER AN OPTION, TERRELL. A CROWD HAS GATHERED. THE PRESS IS HERE. THIS DEMANDS A SHOW OF FORCE.
I'LL MAKE AN EXAMPLE OF YOU BOTH.
WHAT, THROWING A TERMINALLY ILL MAN INTO A WALL OF EXPLODING ARROWS WASN'T ENOUGH? ARE YOU LISTENING TO YOURSELF?
IS THAT EVEN YOU UNDER THAT MASK?

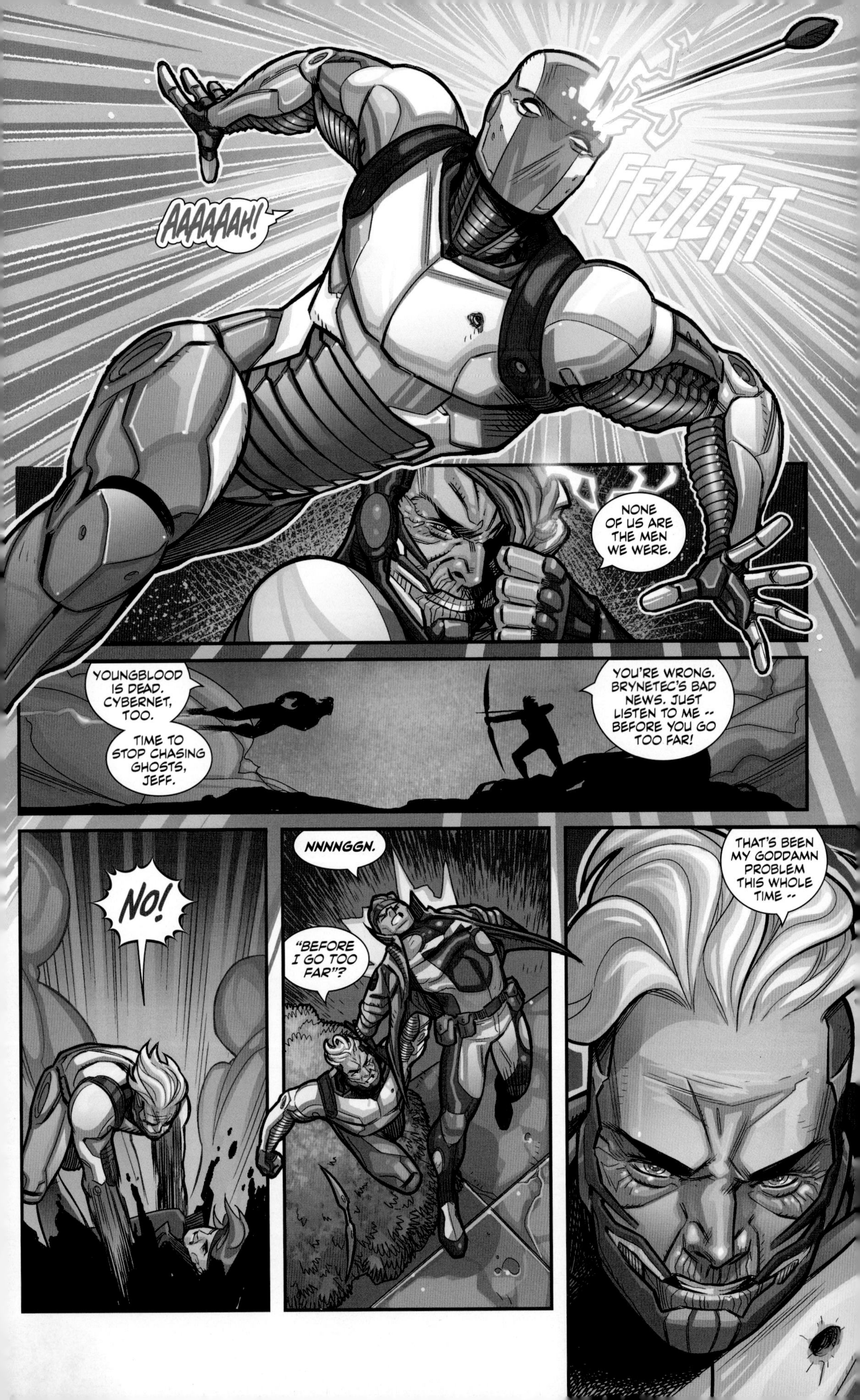

AAAAAAH!
FFZZZTTT
NONE OF US ARE THE MEN WE WERE.
YOUNGBLOOD IS DEAD. CYBERNET, TOO.
TIME TO STOP CHASING GHOSTS, JEFF.
YOU'RE WRONG. BRYNETEC'S BAD NEWS. JUST LISTEN TO ME -- BEFORE YOU GO TOO FAR!
NO!
NNNNGGN.
"BEFORE I GO TOO FAR"?
THAT'S BEEN MY GODDAMN PROBLEM THIS WHOLE TIME --

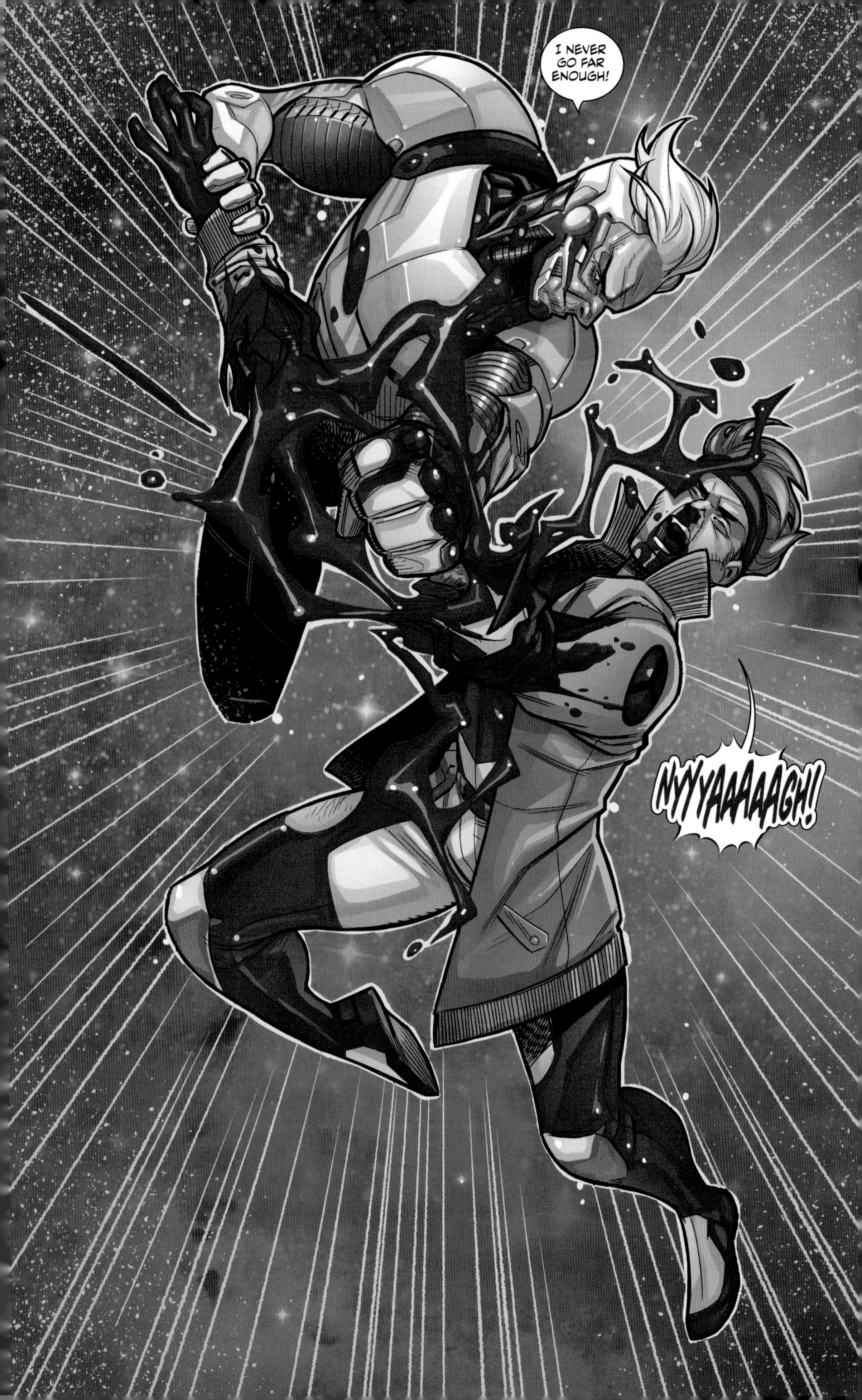
I NEVER GO FAR ENOUGH!
NYYAAAAAGH!

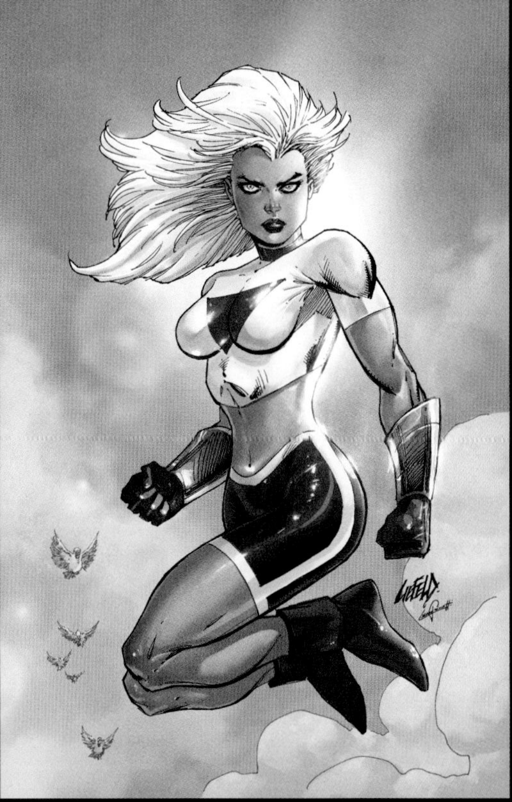

ART BY ROB LIEFELD

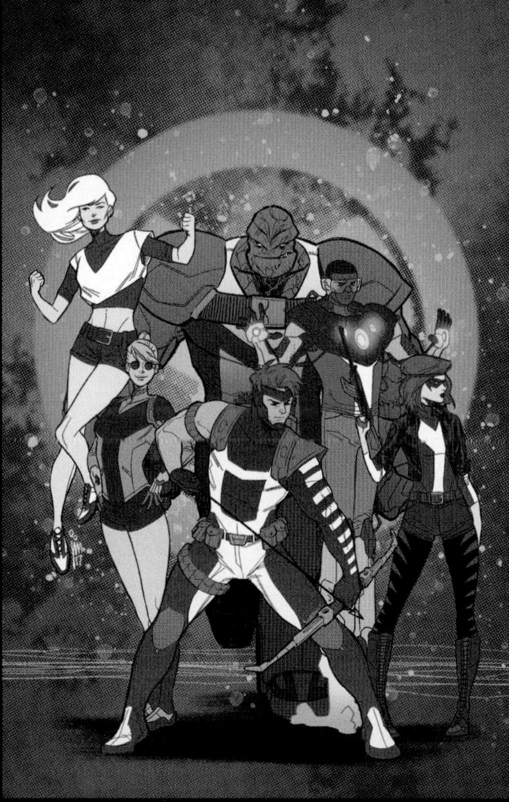

ART BY JIM TOWE

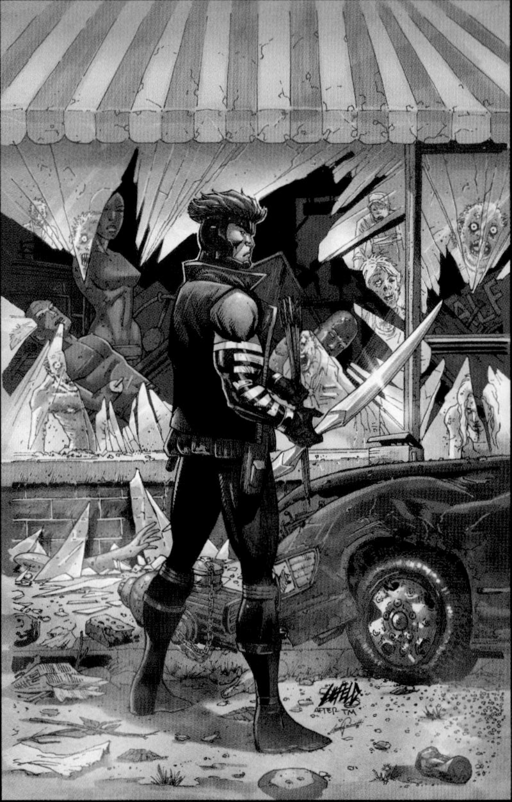

ART BY ROB LIEFELD

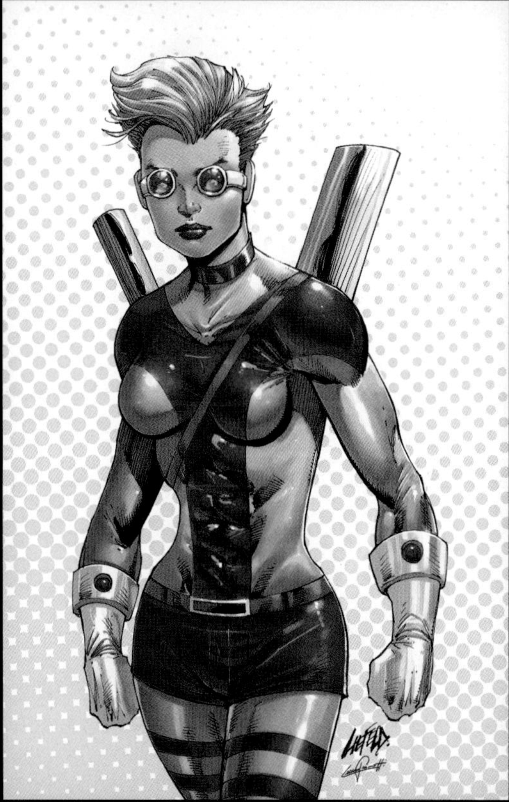

ART BY ROB LIEFELD

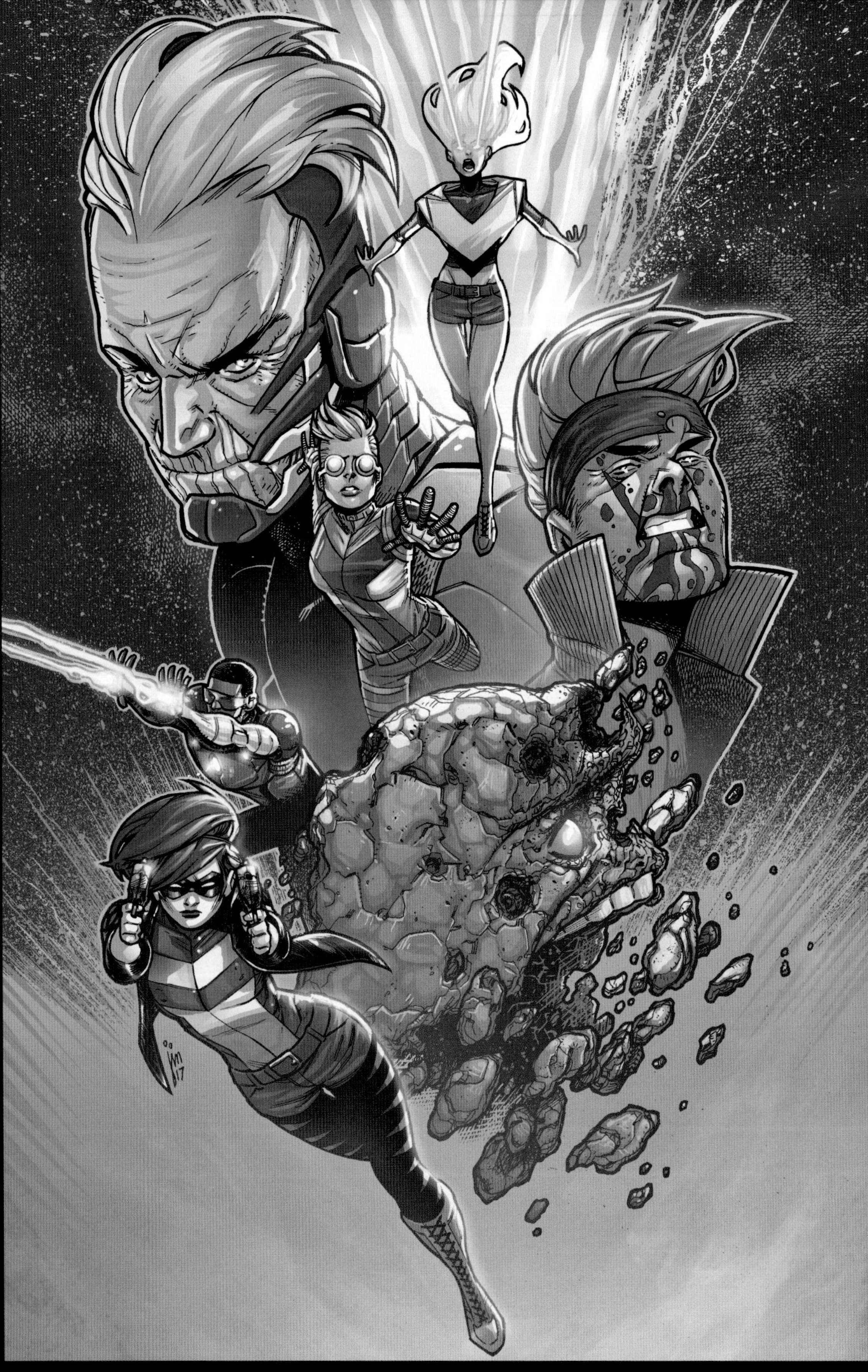

CHAPTER SIX: BLOOD FROM A STONE

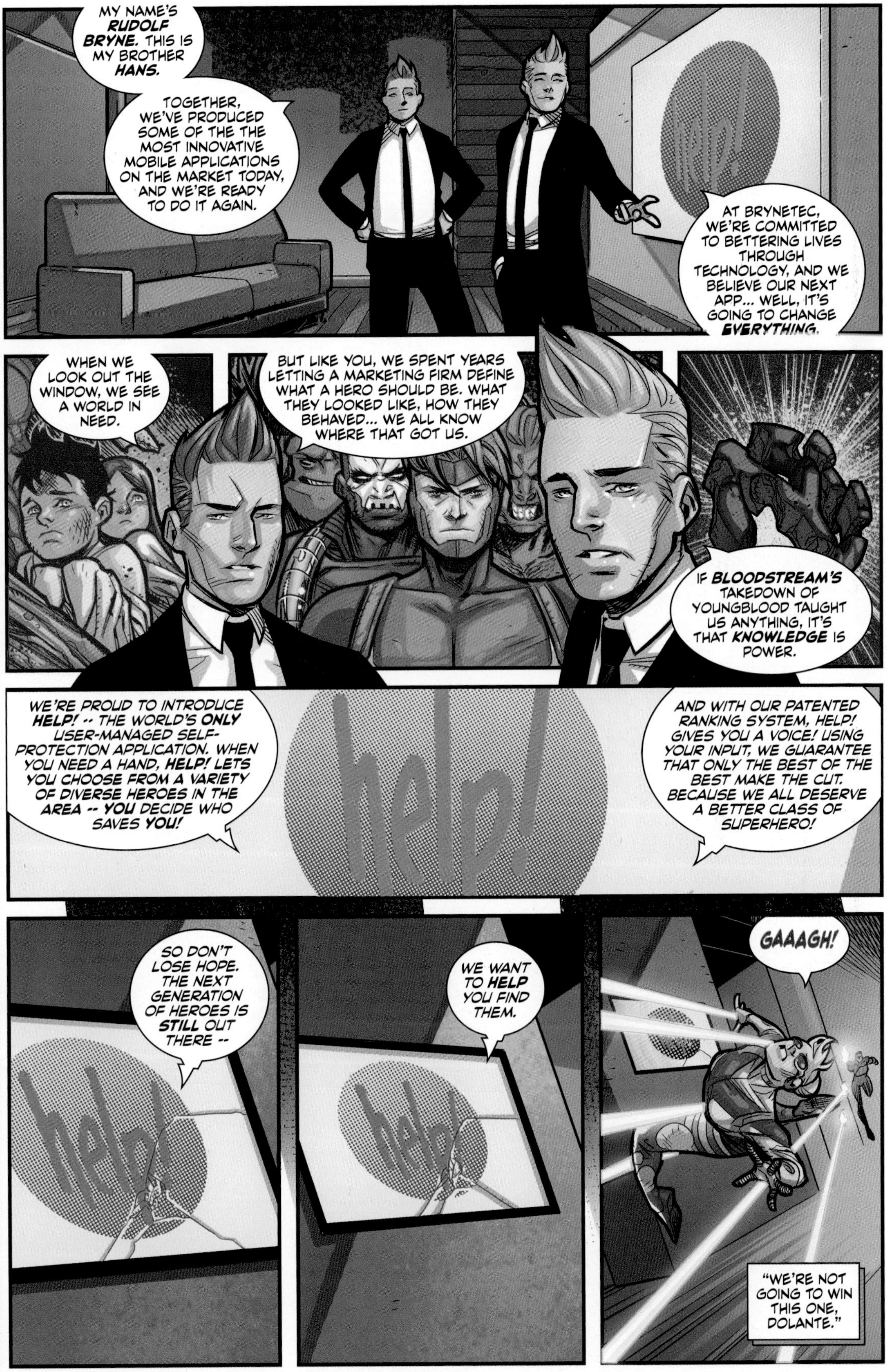
MY NAME'S RUDOLF BRYNE. THIS IS MY BROTHER HANS.
TOGETHER, WE'VE PRODUCED SOME OF THE THE MOST INNOVATIVE MOBILE APPLICATIONS ON THE MARKET TODAY, AND WE'RE READY TO DO IT AGAIN.
AT BRYNETEC, WE'RE COMMITTED TO BETTERING LIVES THROUGH TECHNOLOGY, AND WE BELIEVE OUR NEXT APP... WELL, IT'S GOING TO CHANGE EVERYTHING.
WHEN WE LOOK OUT THE WINDOW, WE SEE A WORLD IN NEED.
BUT LIKE YOU, WE SPENT YEARS LETTING A MARKETING FIRM DEFINE WHAT A HERO SHOULD BE. WHAT THEY LOOKED LIKE, HOW THEY BEHAVED... WE ALL KNOW WHERE THAT GOT US.
IF BLOODSTREAM'S TAKEDOWN OF YOUNGBLOOD TAUGHT US ANYTHING, IT'S THAT KNOWLEDGE IS POWER.
WE'RE PROUD TO INTRODUCE HELP! -- THE WORLD'S ONLY USER-MANAGED SELF-PROTECTION APPLICATION. WHEN YOU NEED A HAND, HELP! LETS YOU CHOOSE FROM A VARIETY OF DIVERSE HEROES IN THE AREA -- YOU DECIDE WHO SAVES YOU!
help!
AND WITH OUR PATENTED RANKING SYSTEM, HELP! GIVES YOU A VOICE! USING YOUR INPUT, WE GUARANTEE THAT ONLY THE BEST OF THE BEST MAKE THE CUT. BECAUSE WE ALL DESERVE A BETTER CLASS OF SUPERHERO!
SO DON'T LOSE HOPE. THE NEXT GENERATION OF HEROES IS STILL OUT THERE --
WE WANT TO HELP YOU FIND THEM.
GAAAGH!
"WE'RE NOT GOING TO WIN THIS ONE, DOLANTE."

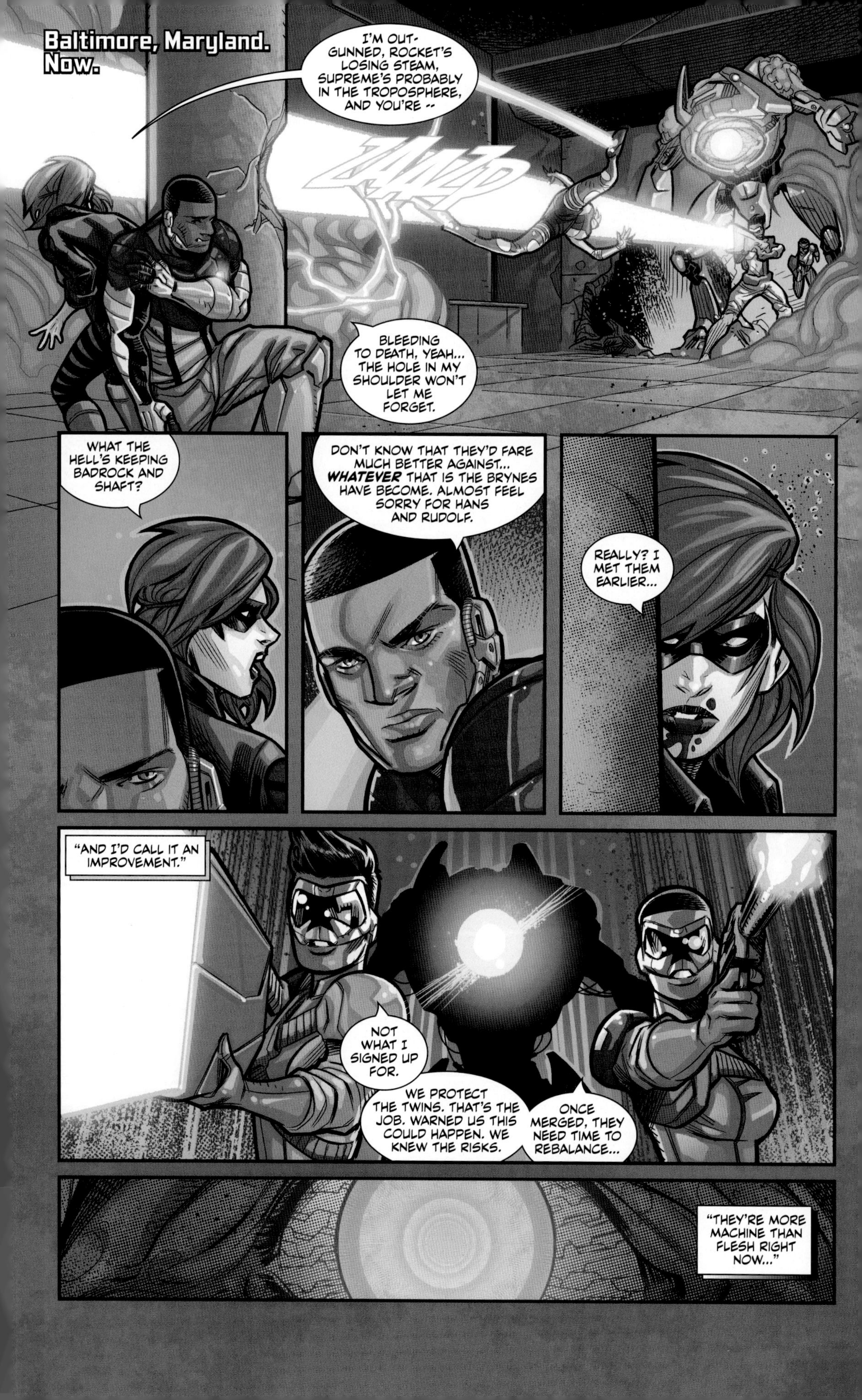

Baltimore, Maryland. Now.
I'M OUT-GUNNED, ROCKET'S LOSING STEAM, SUPREME'S PROBABLY IN THE TROPOSPHERE, AND YOU'RE --
ZAAAZZP
BLEEDING TO DEATH, YEAH... THE HOLE IN MY SHOULDER WON'T LET ME FORGET.
WHAT THE HELL'S KEEPING BADROCK AND SHAFT?
DON'T KNOW THAT THEY'D FARE MUCH BETTER AGAINST... WHATEVER THAT IS THE BRYNES HAVE BECOME. ALMOST FEEL SORRY FOR HANS AND RUDOLF.
REALLY? I MET THEM EARLIER...
"AND I'D CALL IT AN IMPROVEMENT."
NOT WHAT I SIGNED UP FOR.
WE PROTECT THE TWINS. THAT'S THE JOB. WARNED US THIS COULD HAPPEN. WE KNEW THE RISKS.
ONCE MERGED, THEY NEED TIME TO REBALANCE...
"THEY'RE MORE MACHINE THAN FLESH RIGHT NOW..."

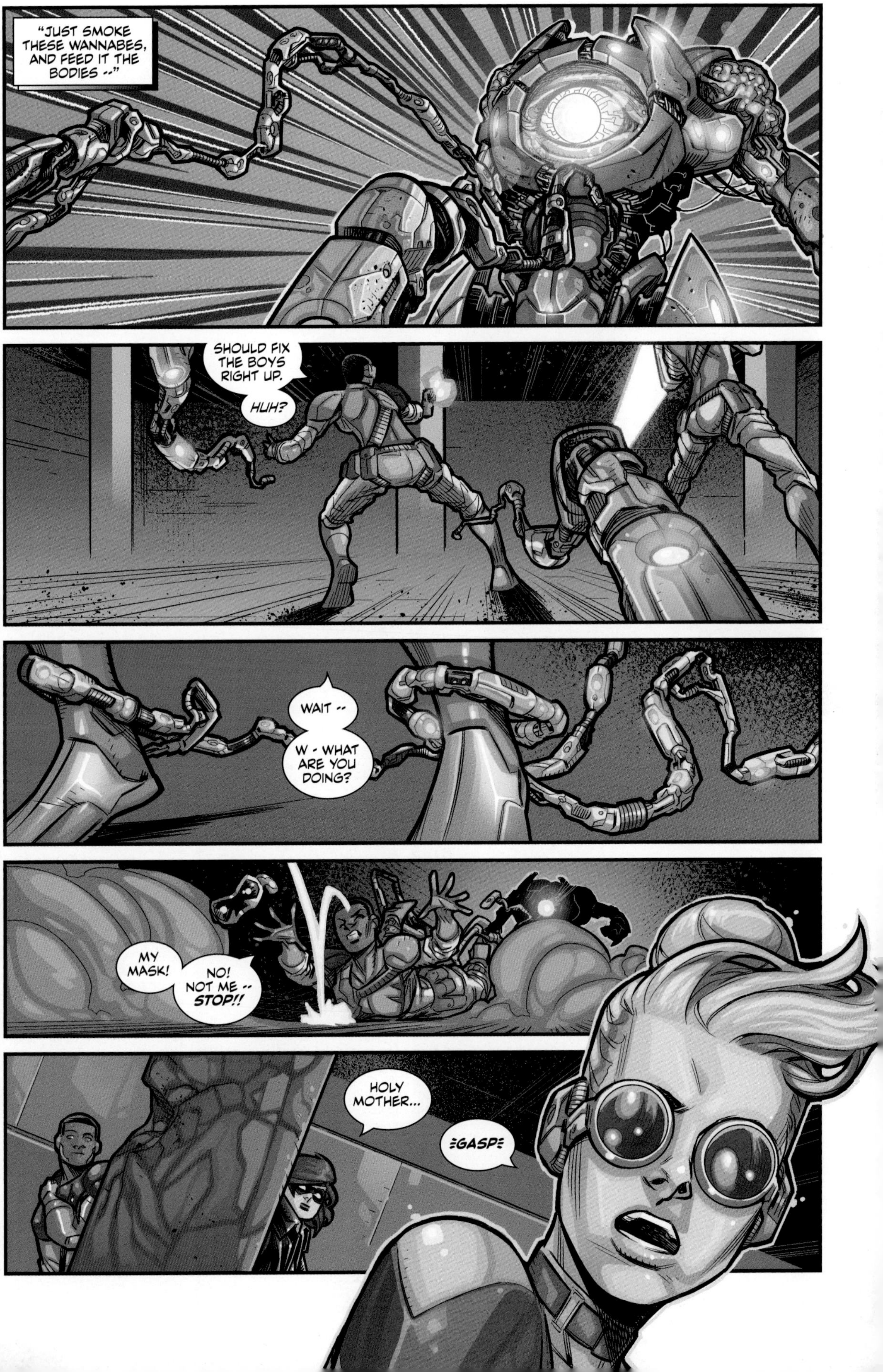
"JUST SMOKE THESE WANNABES, AND FEED IT THE BODIES --"
SHOULD FIX THE BOYS RIGHT UP.
HUH?
WAIT --
W - WHAT ARE YOU DOING?
MY MASK!
NO! NOT ME -- STOP!!
HOLY MOTHER...
GASP

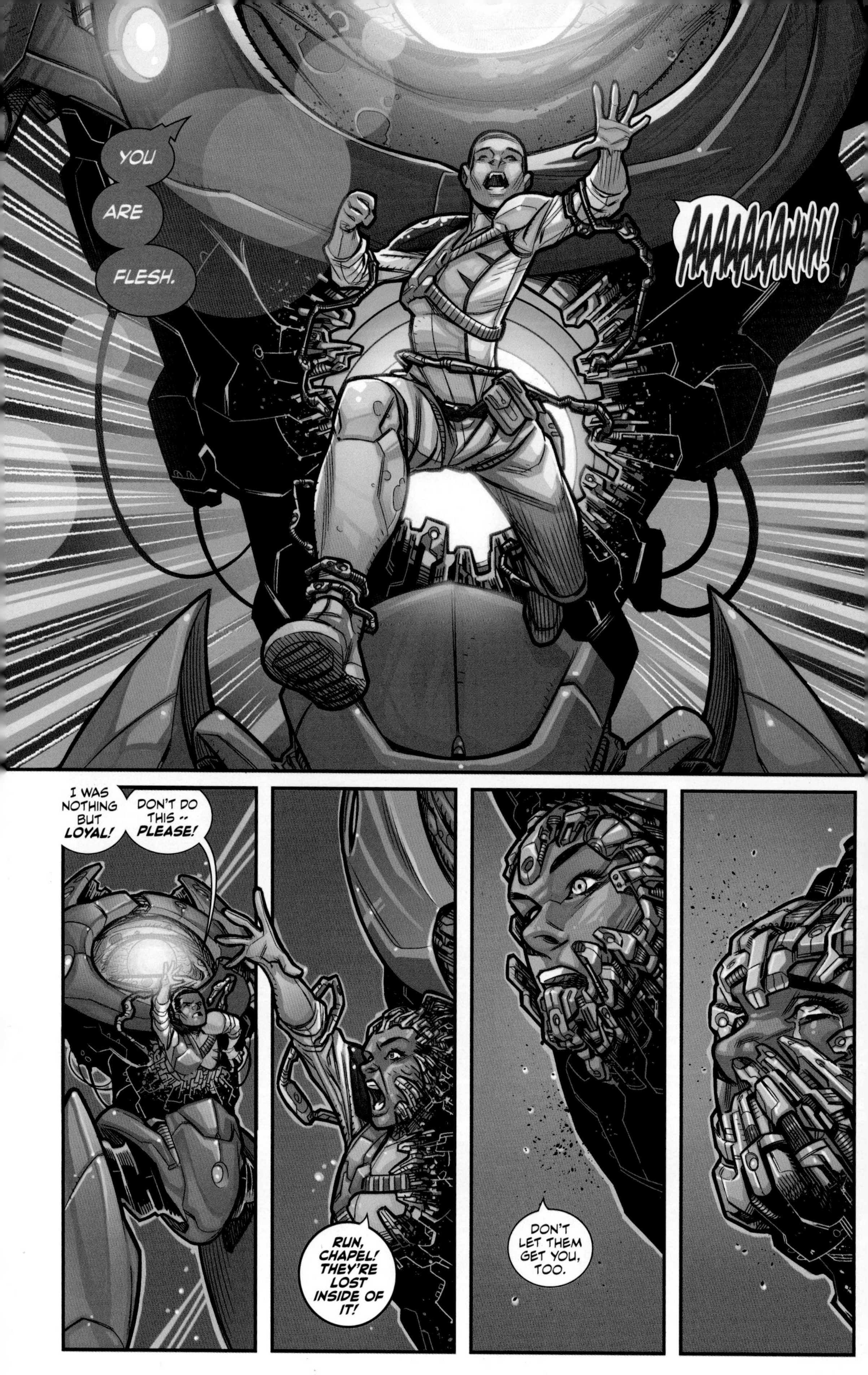
YOU
ARE
FLESH.
AAAAAAAHHH!
I WAS NOTHING BUT LOYAL!
DON'T DO THIS -- PLEASE!
RUN, CHAPEL! THEY'RE LOST INSIDE OF IT!
DON'T LET THEM GET YOU, TOO.

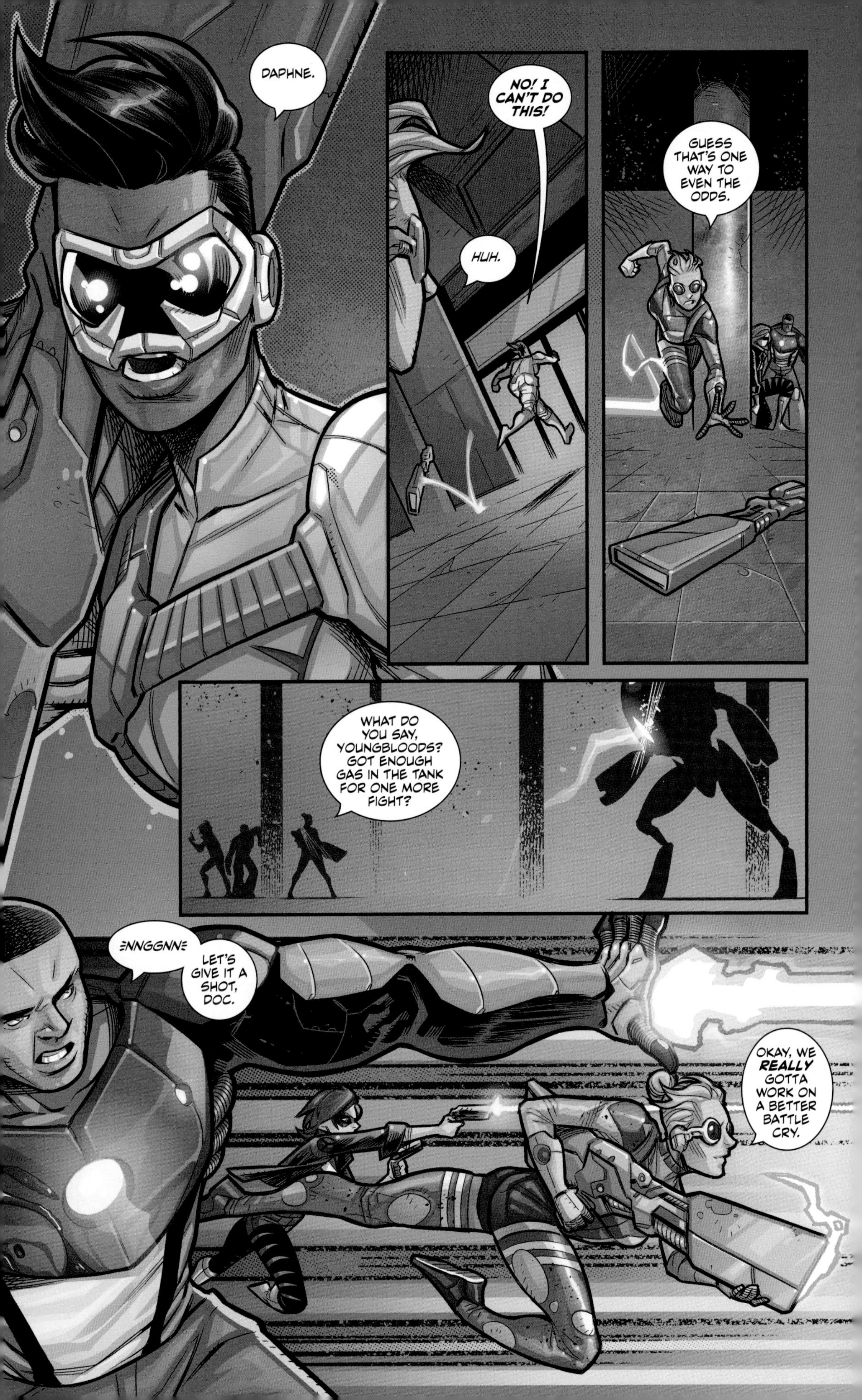
DAPHNE.
NO! I CAN'T DO THIS!
HUH.
GUESS THAT'S ONE WAY TO EVEN THE ODDS.
WHAT DO YOU SAY, YOUNGBLOODS? GOT ENOUGH GAS IN THE TANK FOR ONE MORE FIGHT?
ᴇNNGGNNᴇ
LET'S GIVE IT A SHOT, DOC.
OKAY, WE *REALLY* GOTTA WORK ON A BETTER BATTLE CRY.

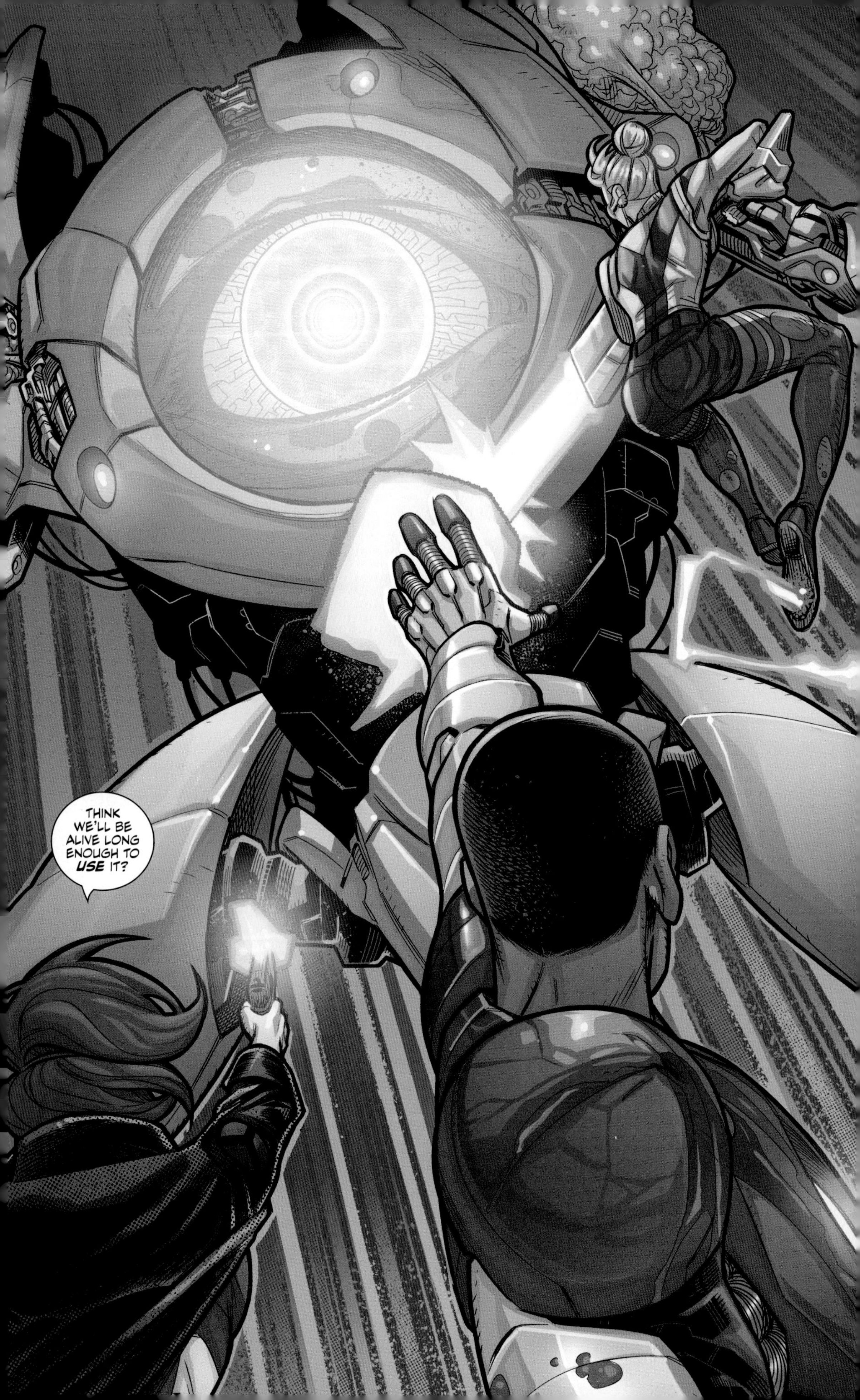
THINK WE'LL BE ALIVE LONG ENOUGH TO USE IT?

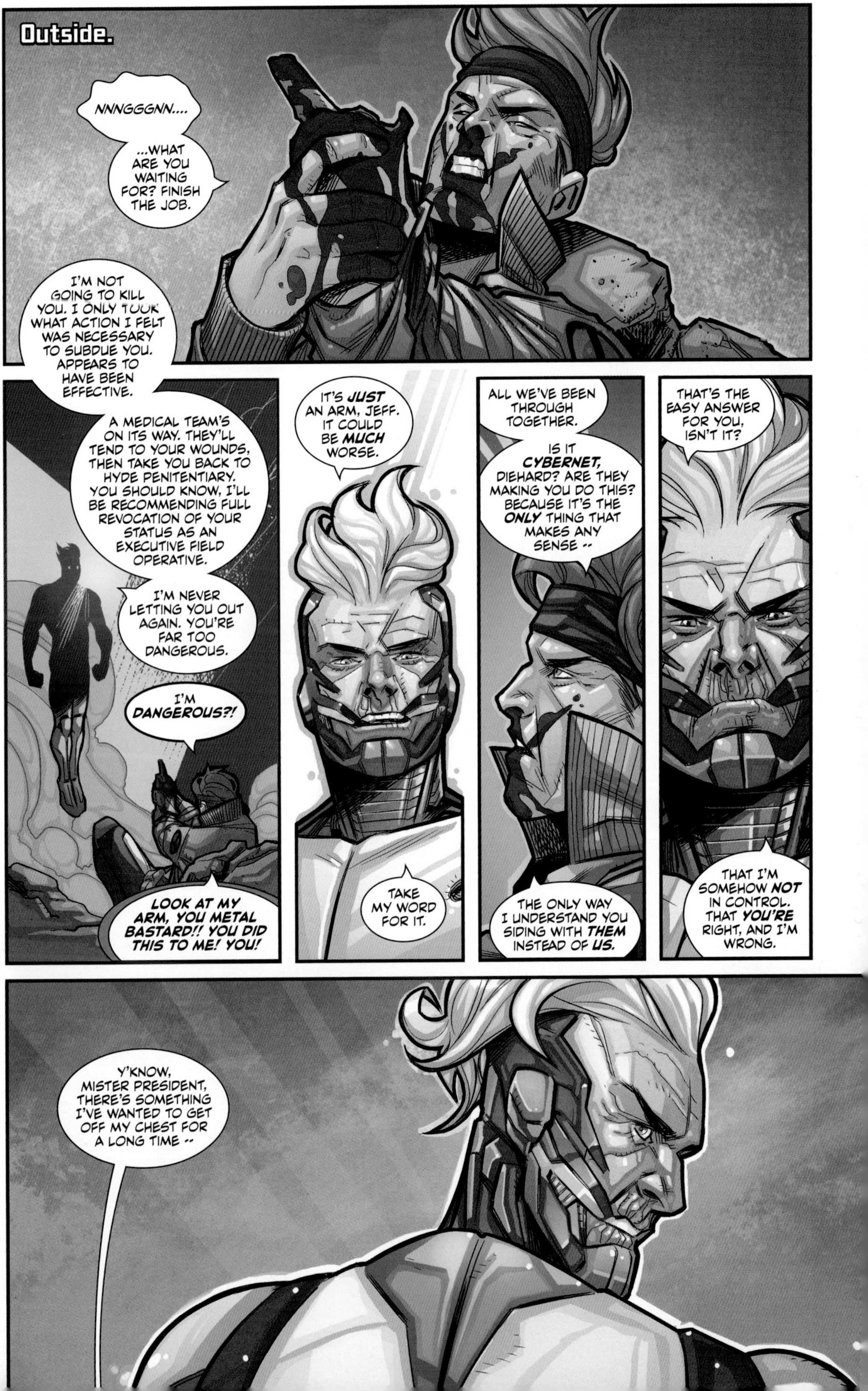
Outside.
NNNGGGNN....
...WHAT ARE YOU WAITING FOR? FINISH THE JOB.
I'M NOT GOING TO KILL YOU. I ONLY TOOK WHAT ACTION I FELT WAS NECESSARY TO SUBDUE YOU. APPEARS TO HAVE BEEN EFFECTIVE.
A MEDICAL TEAM'S ON ITS WAY. THEY'LL TEND TO YOUR WOUNDS, THEN TAKE YOU BACK TO HYDE PENITENTIARY. YOU SHOULD KNOW, I'LL BE RECOMMENDING FULL REVOCATION OF YOUR STATUS AS AN EXECUTIVE FIELD OPERATIVE.
I'M NEVER LETTING YOU OUT AGAIN. YOU'RE FAR TOO DANGEROUS.
I'M DANGEROUS?!
LOOK AT MY ARM, YOU METAL BASTARD!! YOU DID THIS TO ME! YOU!
IT'S JUST AN ARM, JEFF. IT COULD BE MUCH WORSE.
TAKE MY WORD FOR IT.
ALL WE'VE BEEN THROUGH TOGETHER.
IS IT CYBERNET, DIEHARD? ARE THEY MAKING YOU DO THIS? BECAUSE IT'S THE ONLY THING THAT MAKES ANY SENSE --
THE ONLY WAY I UNDERSTAND YOU SIDING WITH THEM INSTEAD OF US.
THAT'S THE EASY ANSWER FOR YOU, ISN'T IT?
THAT I'M SOMEHOW NOT IN CONTROL. THAT YOU'RE RIGHT, AND I'M WRONG.
Y'KNOW, MISTER PRESIDENT, THERE'S SOMETHING I'VE WANTED TO GET OFF MY CHEST FOR A LONG TIME --

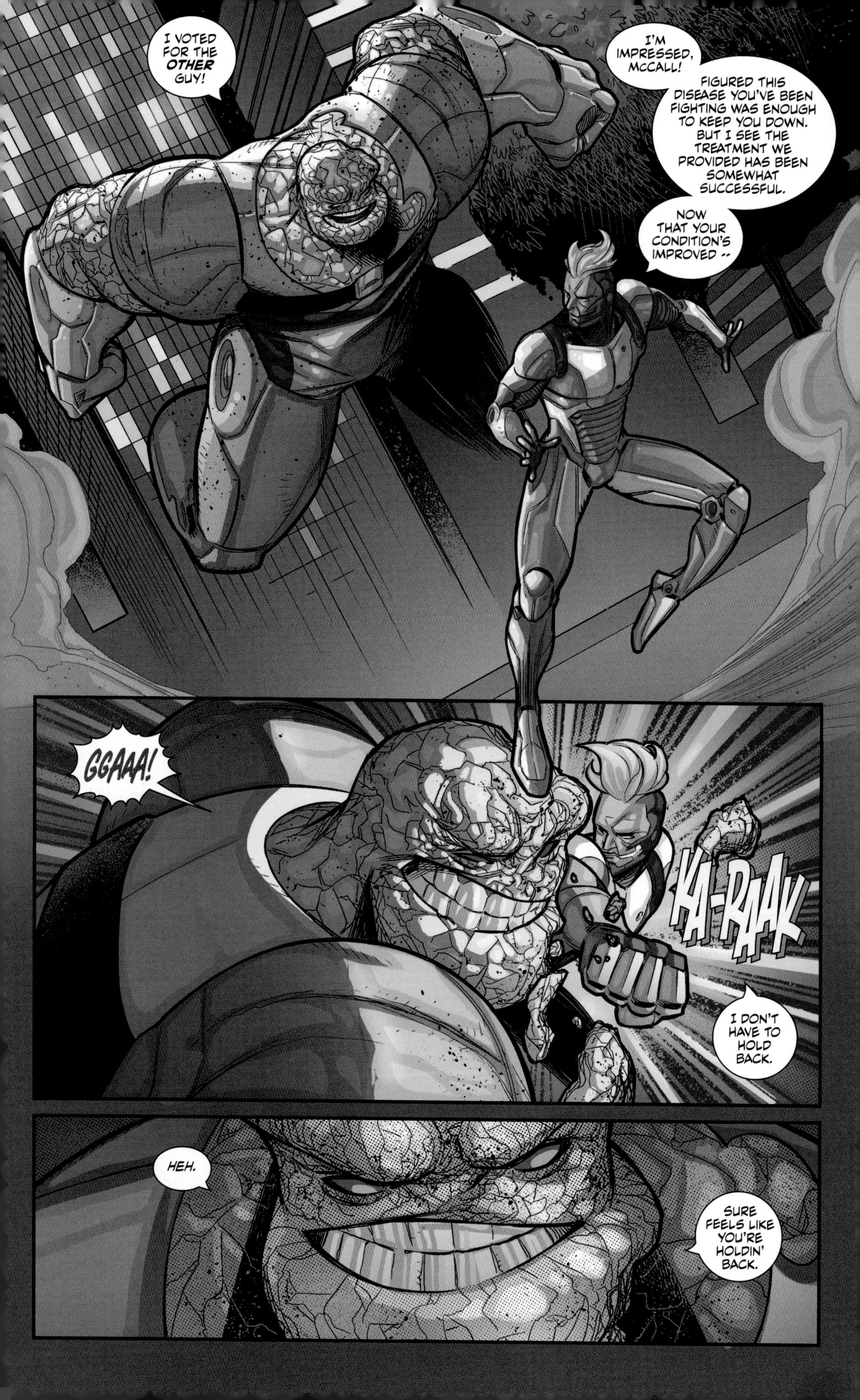
I VOTED FOR THE OTHER GUY!
I'M IMPRESSED, MCCALL!
FIGURED THIS DISEASE YOU'VE BEEN FIGHTING WAS ENOUGH TO KEEP YOU DOWN. BUT I SEE THE TREATMENT WE PROVIDED HAS BEEN SOMEWHAT SUCCESSFUL.
NOW THAT YOUR CONDITION'S IMPROVED --
GGAAA!
KA-RAAK
I DON'T HAVE TO HOLD BACK.
HEH.
SURE FEELS LIKE YOU'RE HOLDIN' BACK.

THWOOOM

NNNNGG --

YOU HAD ONE JOB --

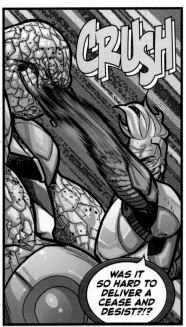

CRUSH

WAS IT SO HARD TO DELIVER A CEASE AND DESIST?!?

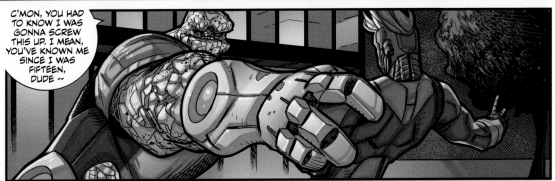

C'MON, YOU HAD TO KNOW I WAS GONNA SCREW THIS UP. I MEAN, YOU'VE KNOWN ME SINCE I WAS FIFTEEN, DUDE --

HAVE I EVER BEEN GOOD AT ANYTHING BESIDES KICKIN' ASS?

BRAAAKKSH

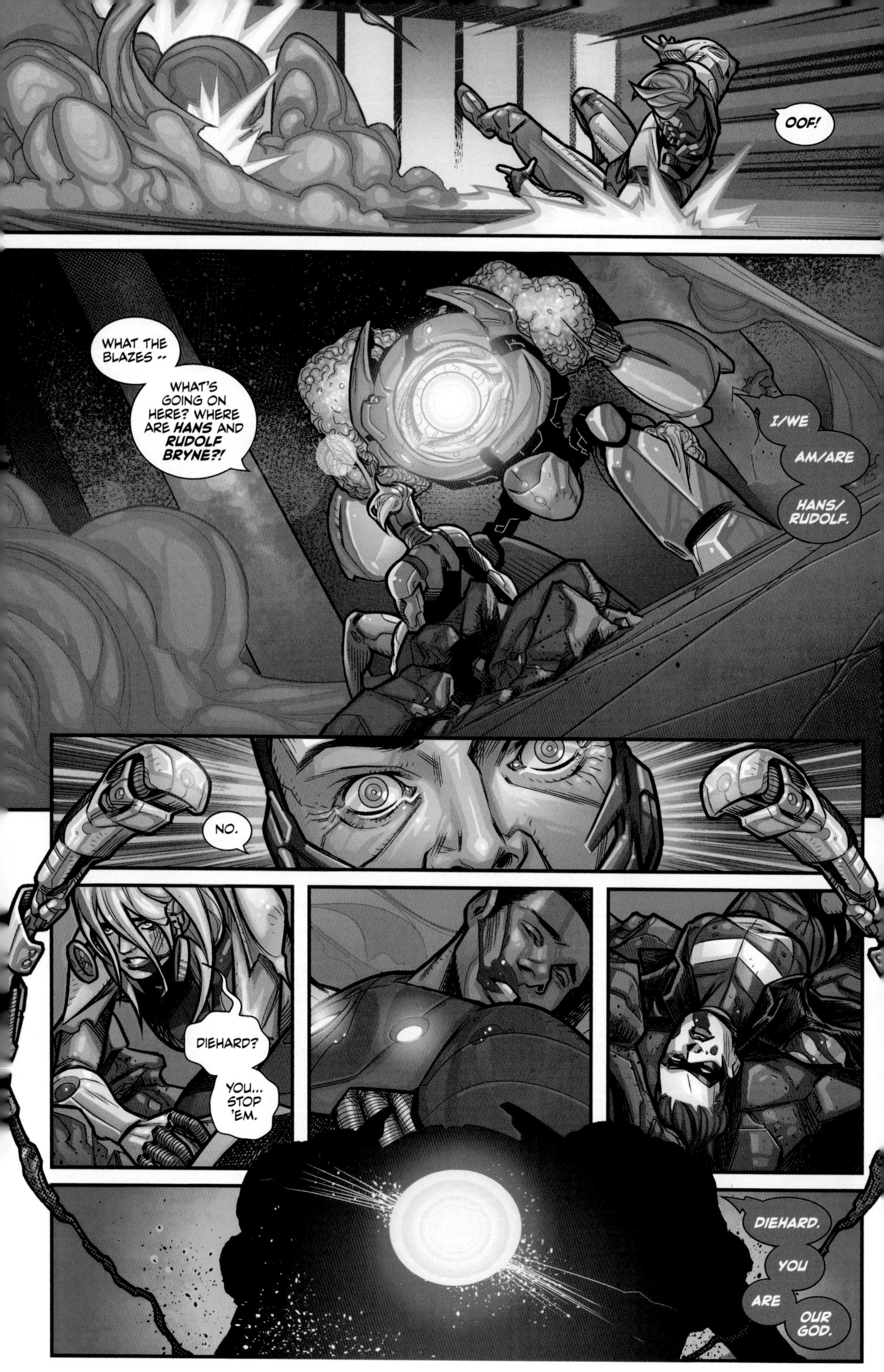
OOF!
WHAT THE BLAZES --
WHAT'S GOING ON HERE? WHERE ARE HANS AND RUDOLF BRYNE?!
I/WE
AM/ARE
HANS/ RUDOLF.
NO.
DIEHARD?
YOU... STOP 'EM.
DIEHARD.
YOU
ARE
OUR GOD.

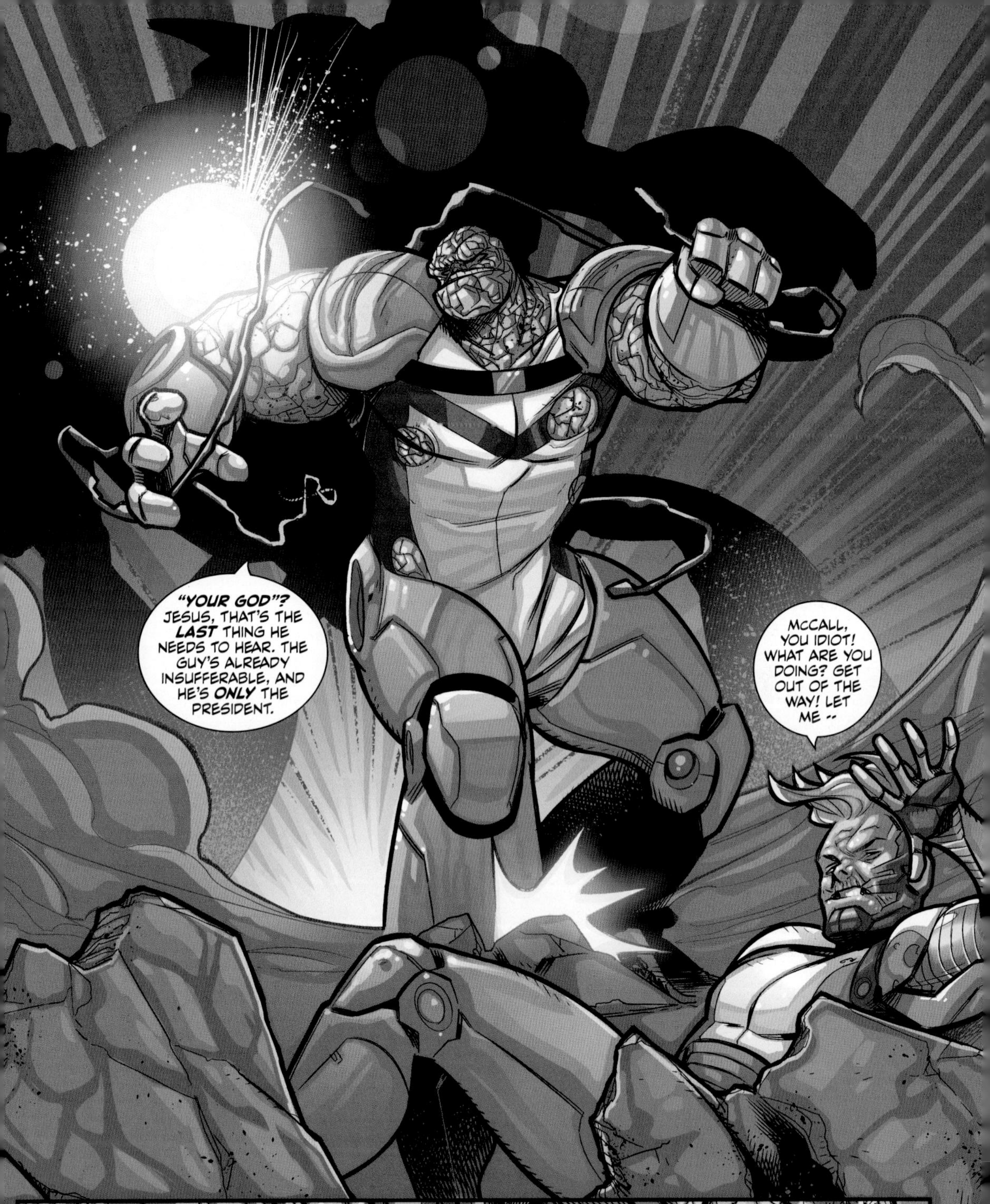
"YOUR GOD"? JESUS, THAT'S THE LAST THING HE NEEDS TO HEAR. THE GUY'S ALREADY INSUFFERABLE, AND HE'S ONLY THE PRESIDENT.
McCALL, YOU IDIOT! WHAT ARE YOU DOING? GET OUT OF THE WAY! LET ME --

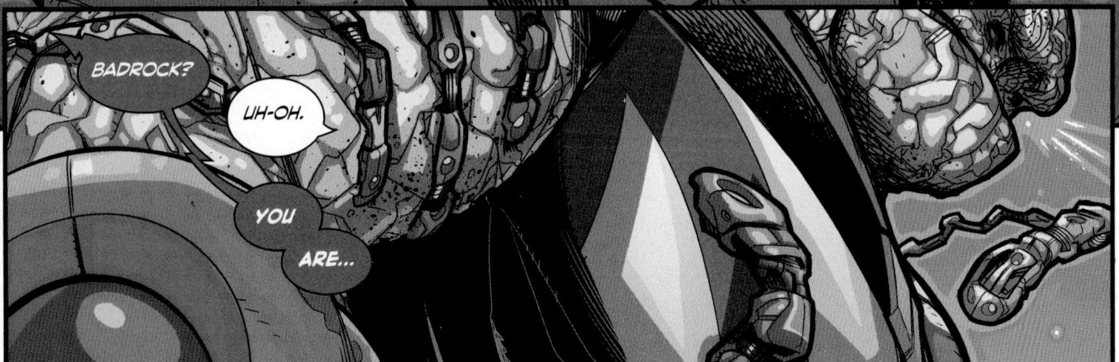
BADROCK?
UH-OH.
YOU
ARE...

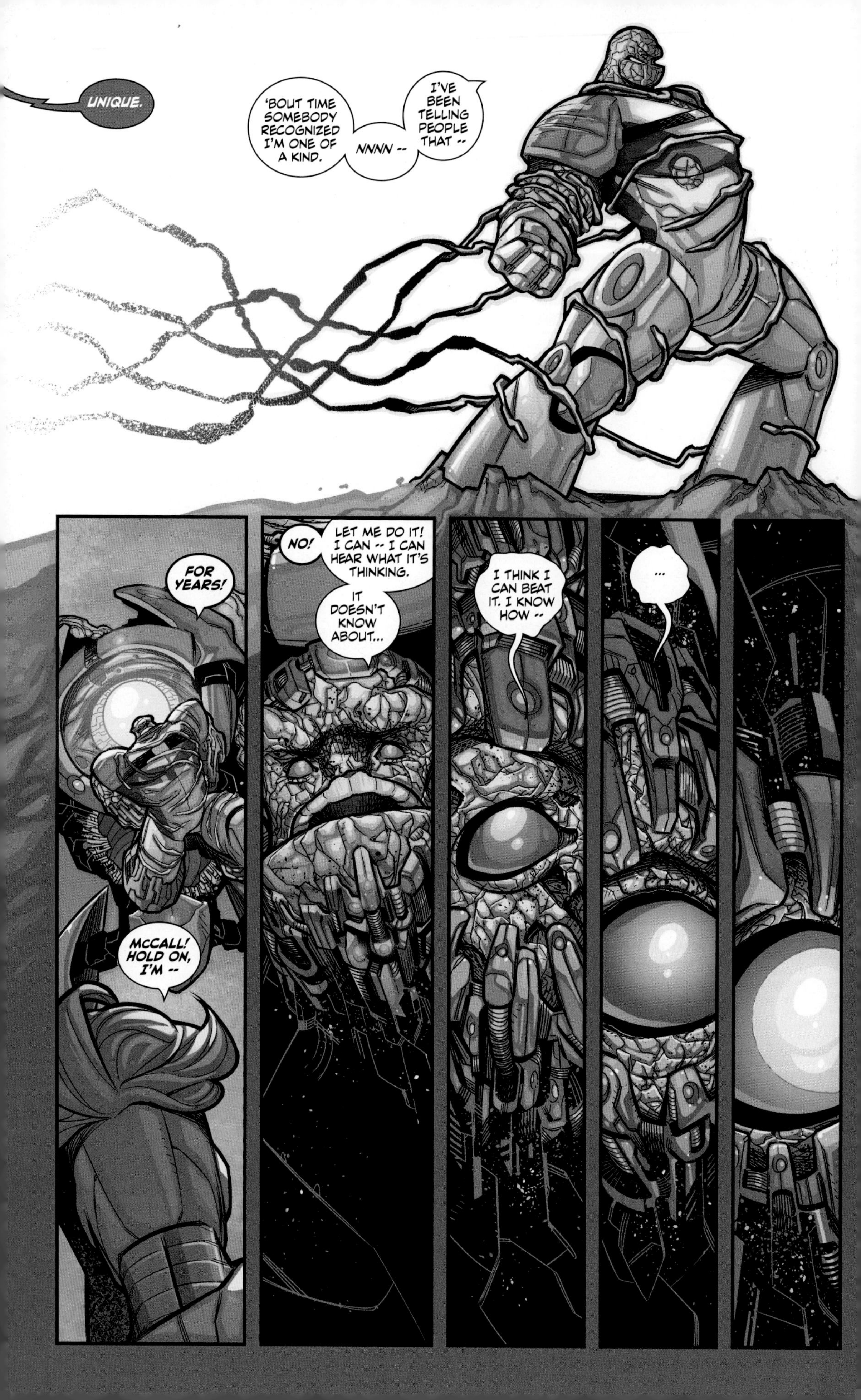
UNIQUE.
'BOUT TIME SOMEBODY RECOGNIZED I'M ONE OF A KIND.
NNNN --
I'VE BEEN TELLING PEOPLE THAT --
FOR YEARS!
McCALL! HOLD ON, I'M --
NO!
LET ME DO IT! I CAN -- I CAN HEAR WHAT IT'S THINKING.
IT DOESN'T KNOW ABOUT...
I THINK I CAN BEAT IT. I KNOW HOW --
...

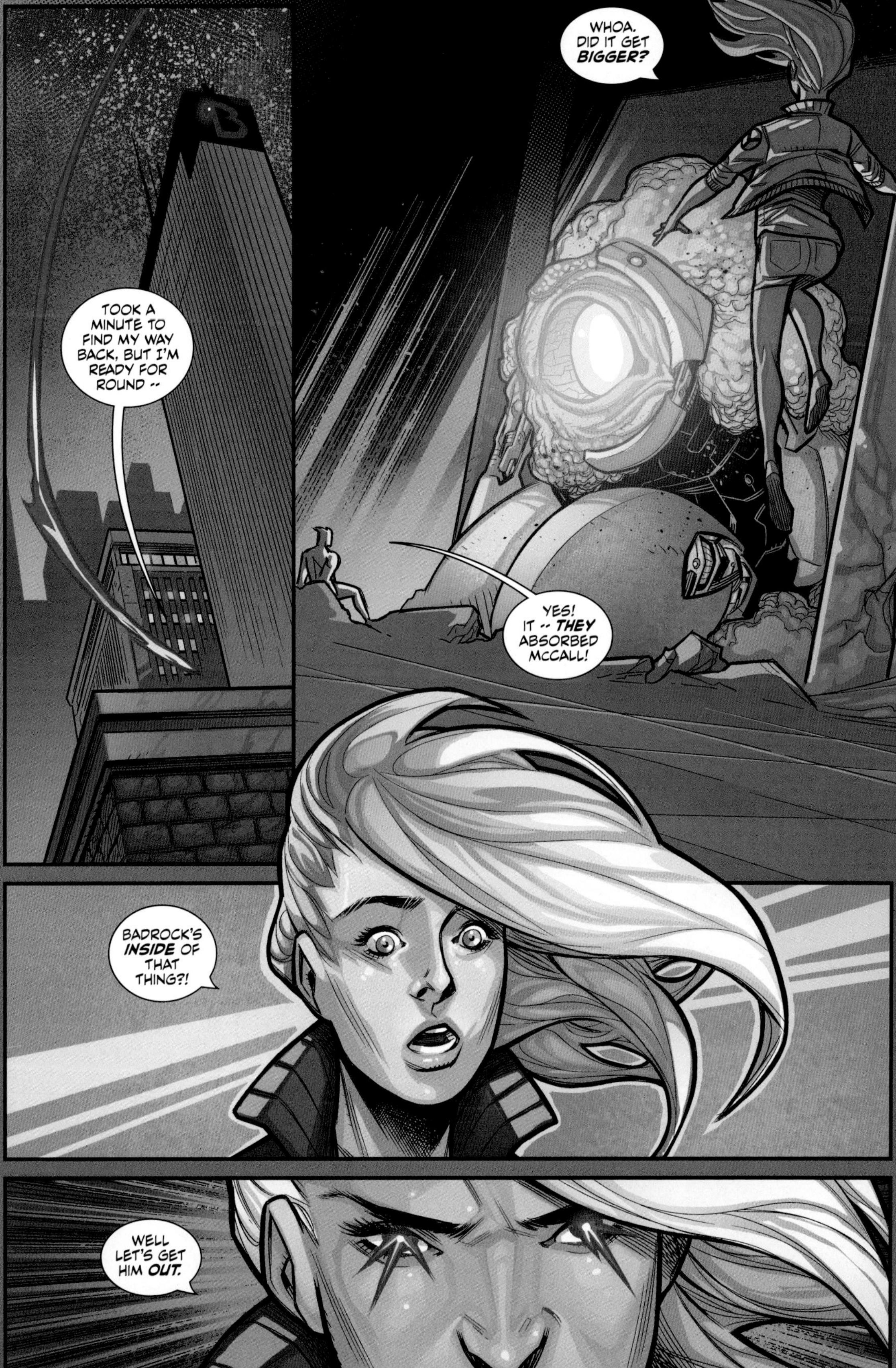
TOOK A MINUTE TO FIND MY WAY BACK, BUT I'M READY FOR ROUND --
WHOA. DID IT GET **BIGGER?**
YES! IT -- **THEY** ABSORBED McCALL!
BADROCK'S **INSIDE** OF THAT THING?!
WELL LET'S GET HIM **OUT.**

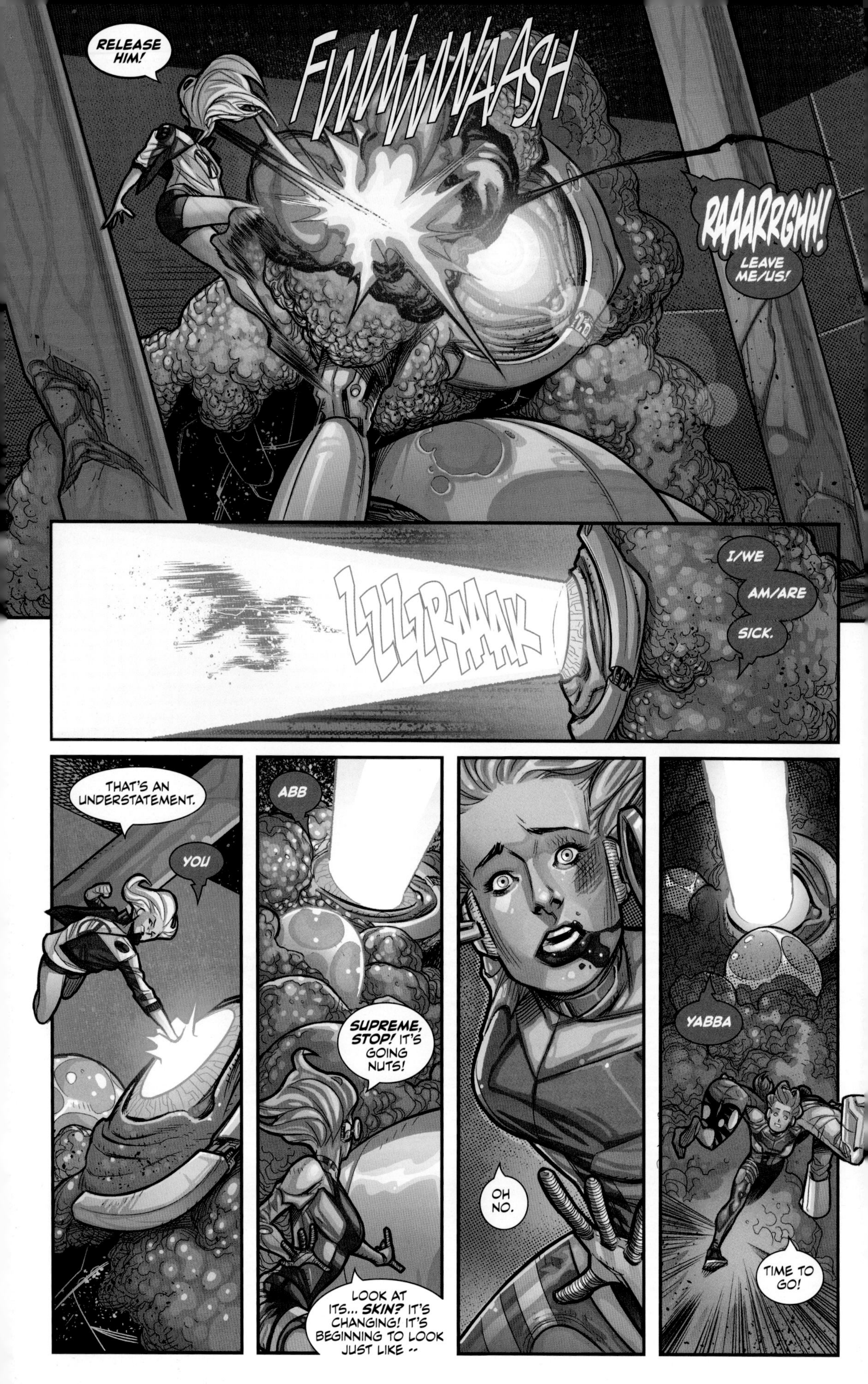
RELEASE HIM!
FWMMWAASH
RAAARRGHH!
LEAVE ME/US!
ZZZZRAAAK
I/WE
AM/ARE
SICK.
THAT'S AN UNDERSTATEMENT.
YOU
ABB
SUPREME, STOP! IT'S GOING NUTS!
LOOK AT ITS... SKIN? IT'S CHANGING! IT'S BEGINNING TO LOOK JUST LIKE --
OH NO.
YABBA
TIME TO GO!

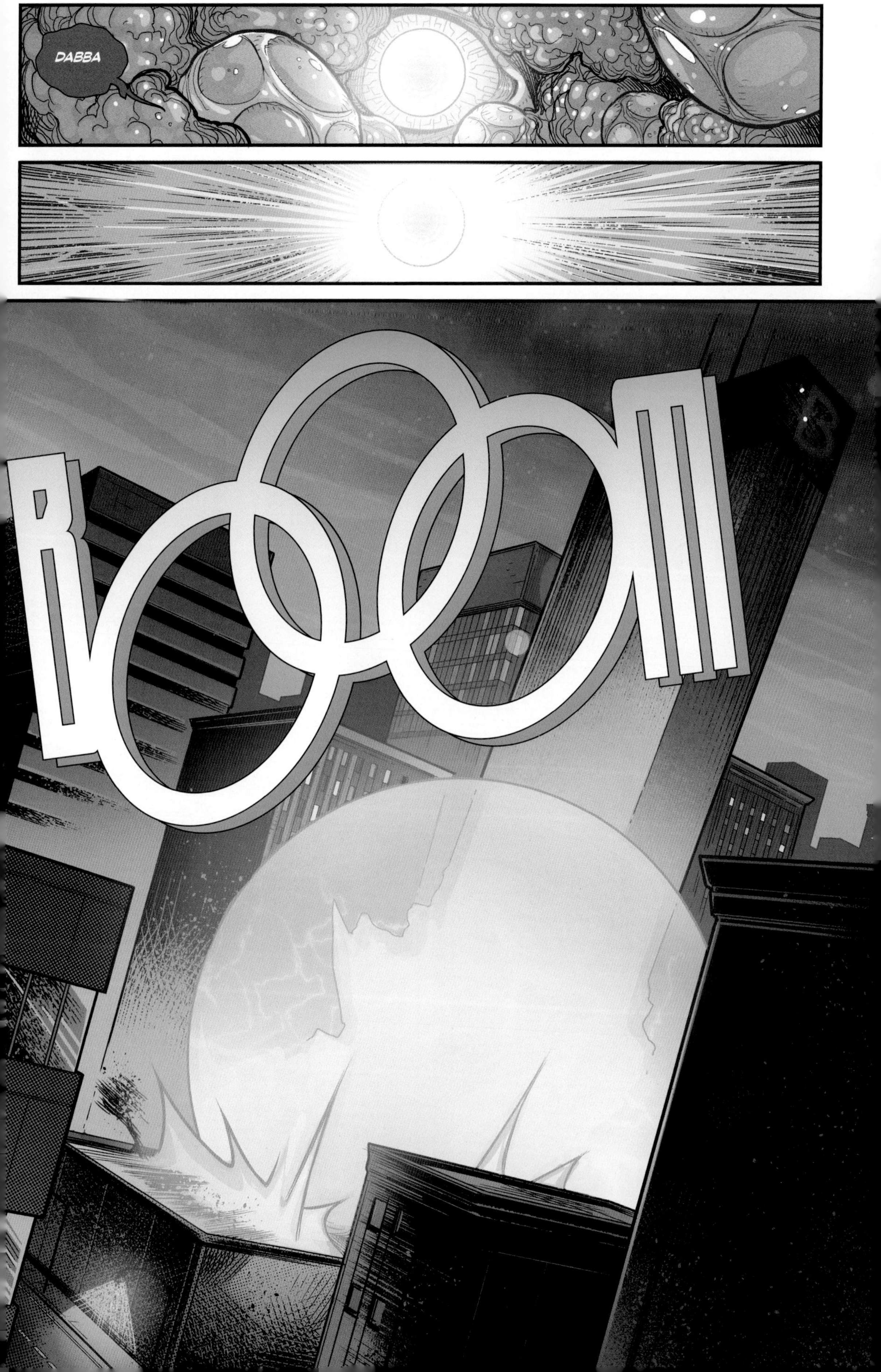
DABBA
BOOOM

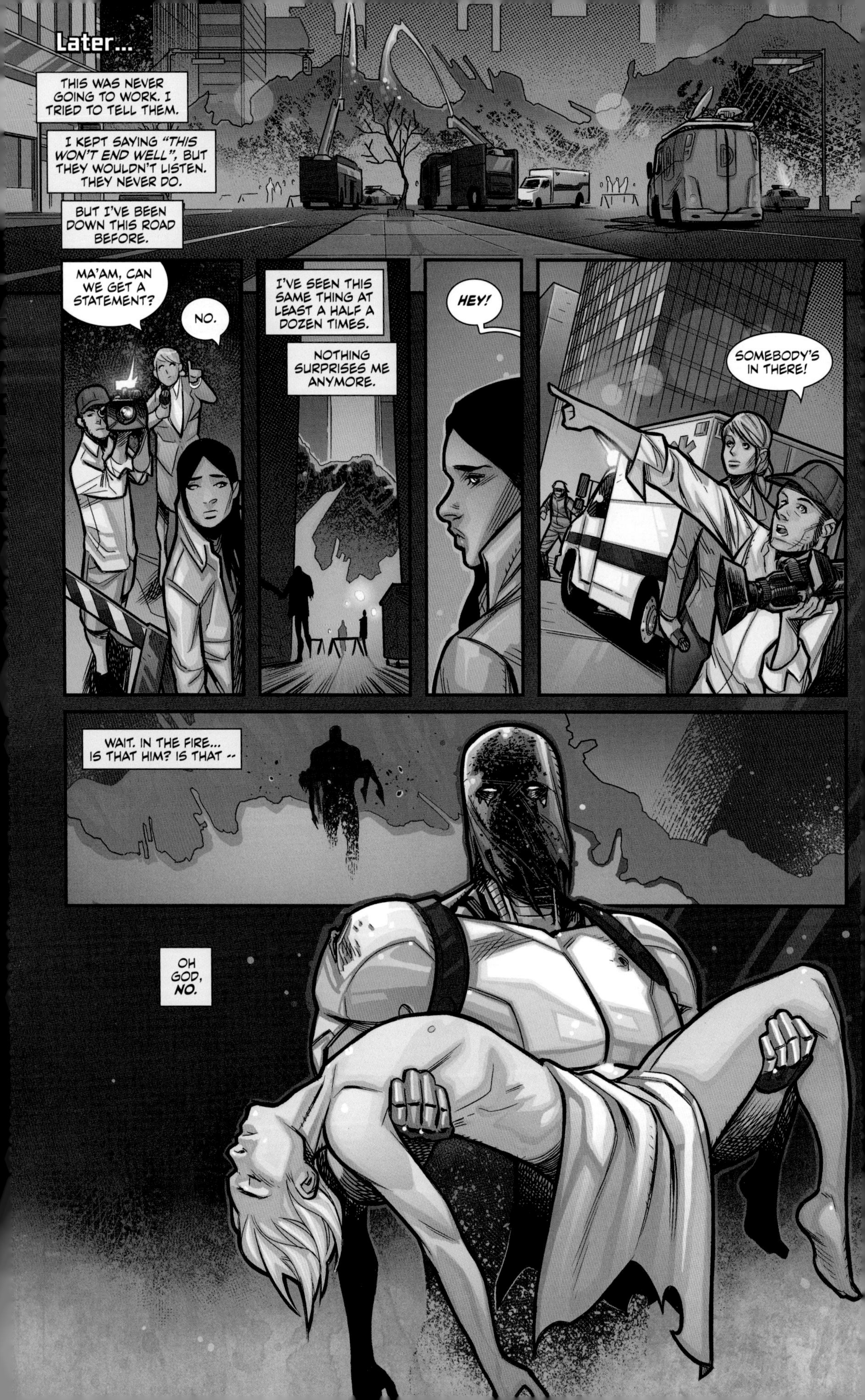
Later...
THIS WAS NEVER GOING TO WORK. I TRIED TO TELL THEM.
I KEPT SAYING "THIS WON'T END WELL", BUT THEY WOULDN'T LISTEN. THEY NEVER DO.
BUT I'VE BEEN DOWN THIS ROAD BEFORE.
MA'AM, CAN WE GET A STATEMENT?
NO.
I'VE SEEN THIS SAME THING AT LEAST A HALF A DOZEN TIMES.
NOTHING SURPRISES ME ANYMORE.
HEY!
SOMEBODY'S IN THERE!
WAIT. IN THE FIRE... IS THAT HIM? IS THAT --
OH GOD, NO.

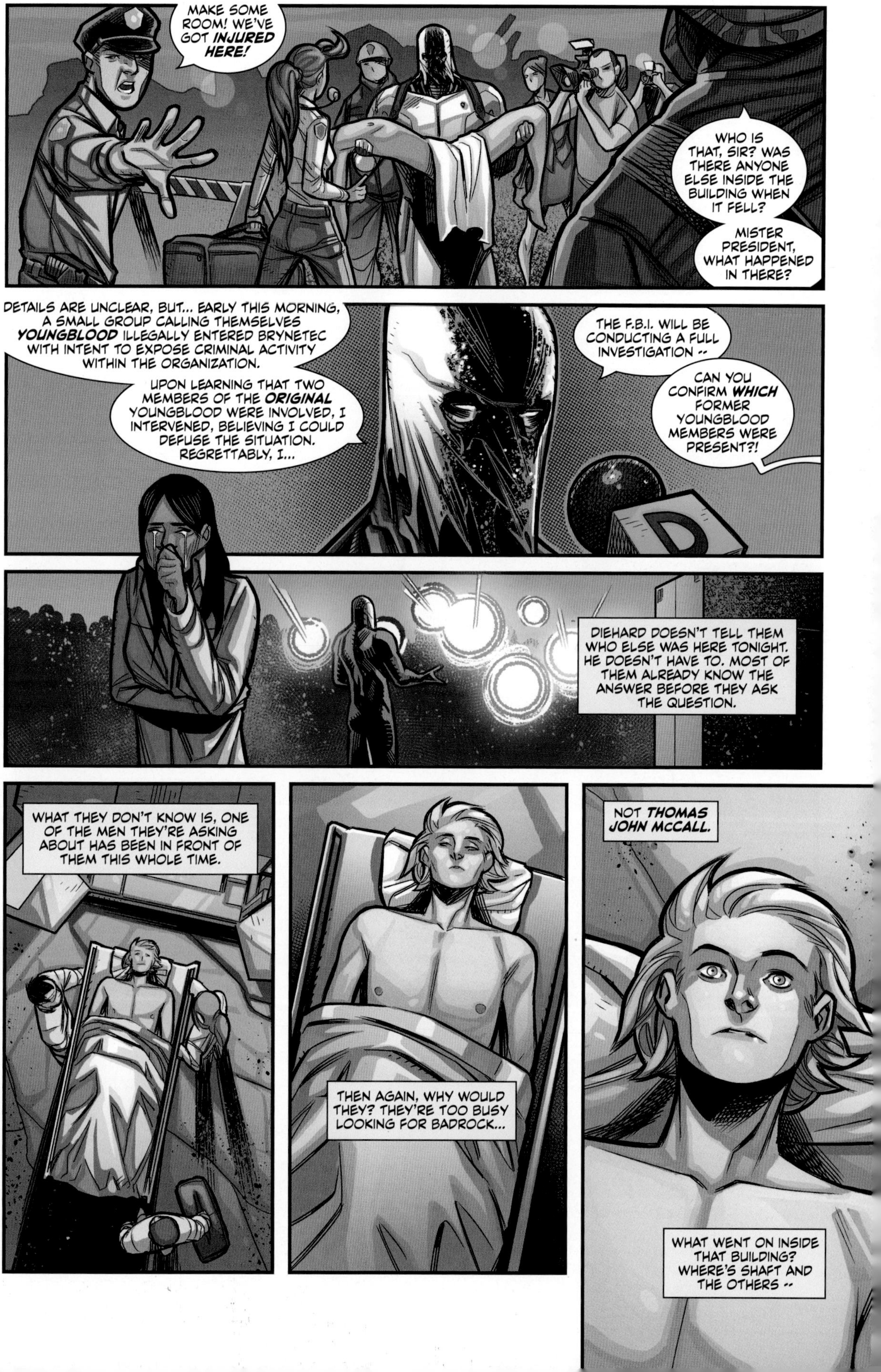
MAKE SOME ROOM! WE'VE GOT *INJURED HERE!*
WHO IS THAT, SIR? WAS THERE ANYONE ELSE INSIDE THE BUILDING WHEN IT FELL?
MISTER PRESIDENT, WHAT HAPPENED IN THERE?
DETAILS ARE UNCLEAR, BUT... EARLY THIS MORNING, A SMALL GROUP CALLING THEMSELVES *YOUNGBLOOD* ILLEGALLY ENTERED BRYNETEC WITH INTENT TO EXPOSE CRIMINAL ACTIVITY WITHIN THE ORGANIZATION.
UPON LEARNING THAT TWO MEMBERS OF THE *ORIGINAL* YOUNGBLOOD WERE INVOLVED, I INTERVENED, BELIEVING I COULD DEFUSE THE SITUATION. REGRETTABLY, I...
THE F.B.I. WILL BE CONDUCTING A FULL INVESTIGATION --
CAN YOU CONFIRM *WHICH* FORMER YOUNGBLOOD MEMBERS WERE PRESENT?!
DIEHARD DOESN'T TELL THEM WHO ELSE WAS HERE TONIGHT. HE DOESN'T HAVE TO. MOST OF THEM ALREADY KNOW THE ANSWER BEFORE THEY ASK THE QUESTION.
WHAT THEY DON'T KNOW IS, ONE OF THE MEN THEY'RE ASKING ABOUT HAS BEEN IN FRONT OF THEM THIS WHOLE TIME.
THEN AGAIN, WHY WOULD THEY? THEY'RE TOO BUSY LOOKING FOR BADROCK...
NOT *THOMAS JOHN McCALL.*
WHAT WENT ON INSIDE THAT BUILDING? WHERE'S SHAFT AND THE OTHERS --

Marrakesh, Kingdom of Morocco.
Nine days later.

DID VOGUE FIND HER FRIEND?

YO, CASIMIR --

YOUR DOG'S BACK. AND HE'S BROUGHT YOU A *PRESENT!*

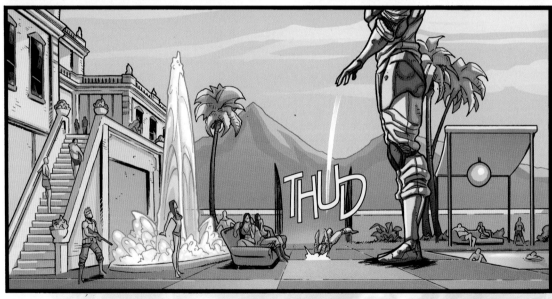

THUD

HMPH.

WHAT ABOUT THE REST OF HIS UNIT? DID YOU BURY THEM ALIVE LIKE I TOLD YOU TO?

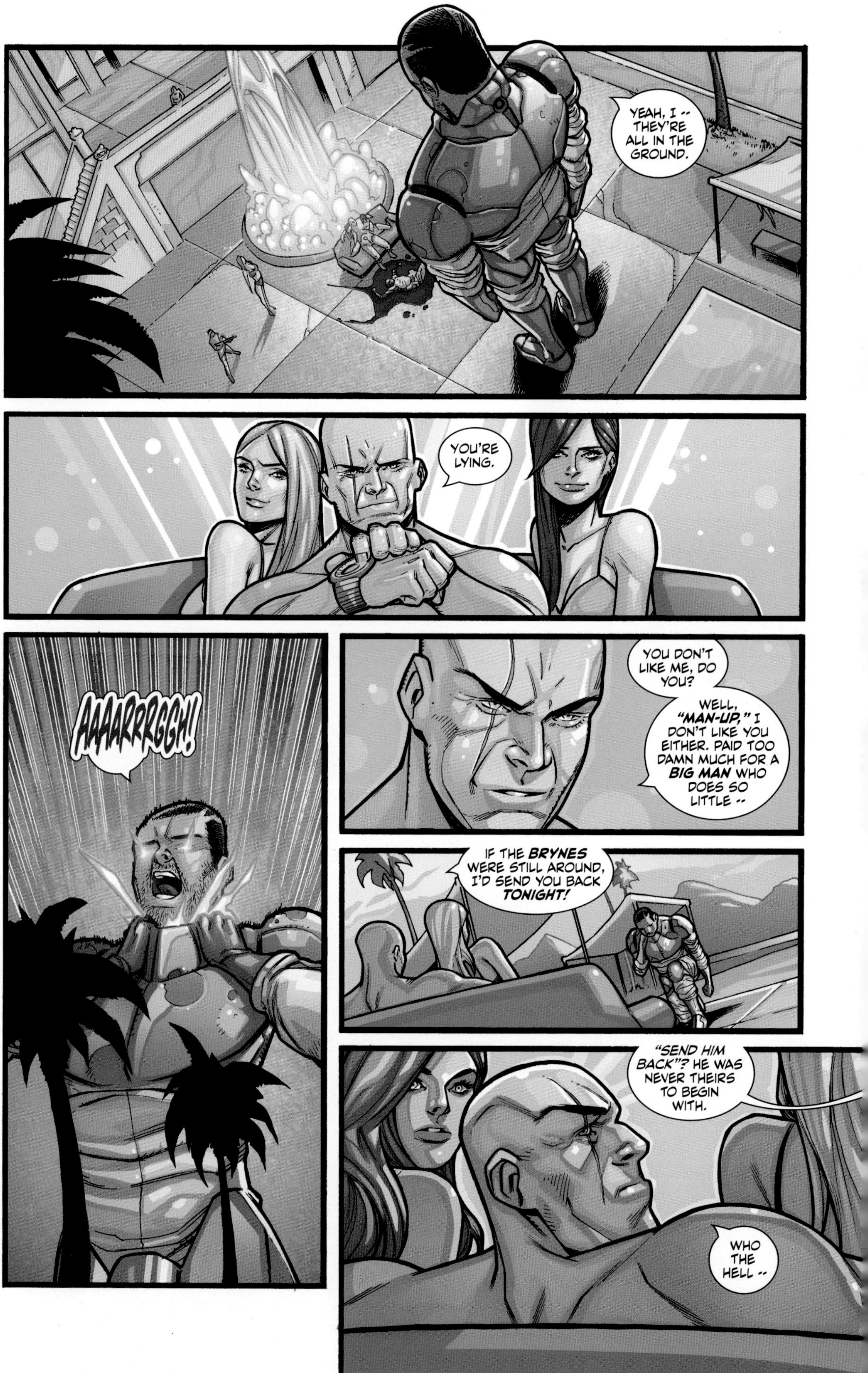
YEAH, I -- THEY'RE ALL IN THE GROUND.
YOU'RE LYING.
AAAARRRGGH!
YOU DON'T LIKE ME, DO YOU?
WELL, "MAN-UP," I DON'T LIKE YOU EITHER. PAID TOO DAMN MUCH FOR A BIG MAN WHO DOES SO LITTLE --
IF THE BRYNES WERE STILL AROUND, I'D SEND YOU BACK TONIGHT!
"SEND HIM BACK"? HE WAS NEVER THEIRS TO BEGIN WITH.
WHO THE HELL --

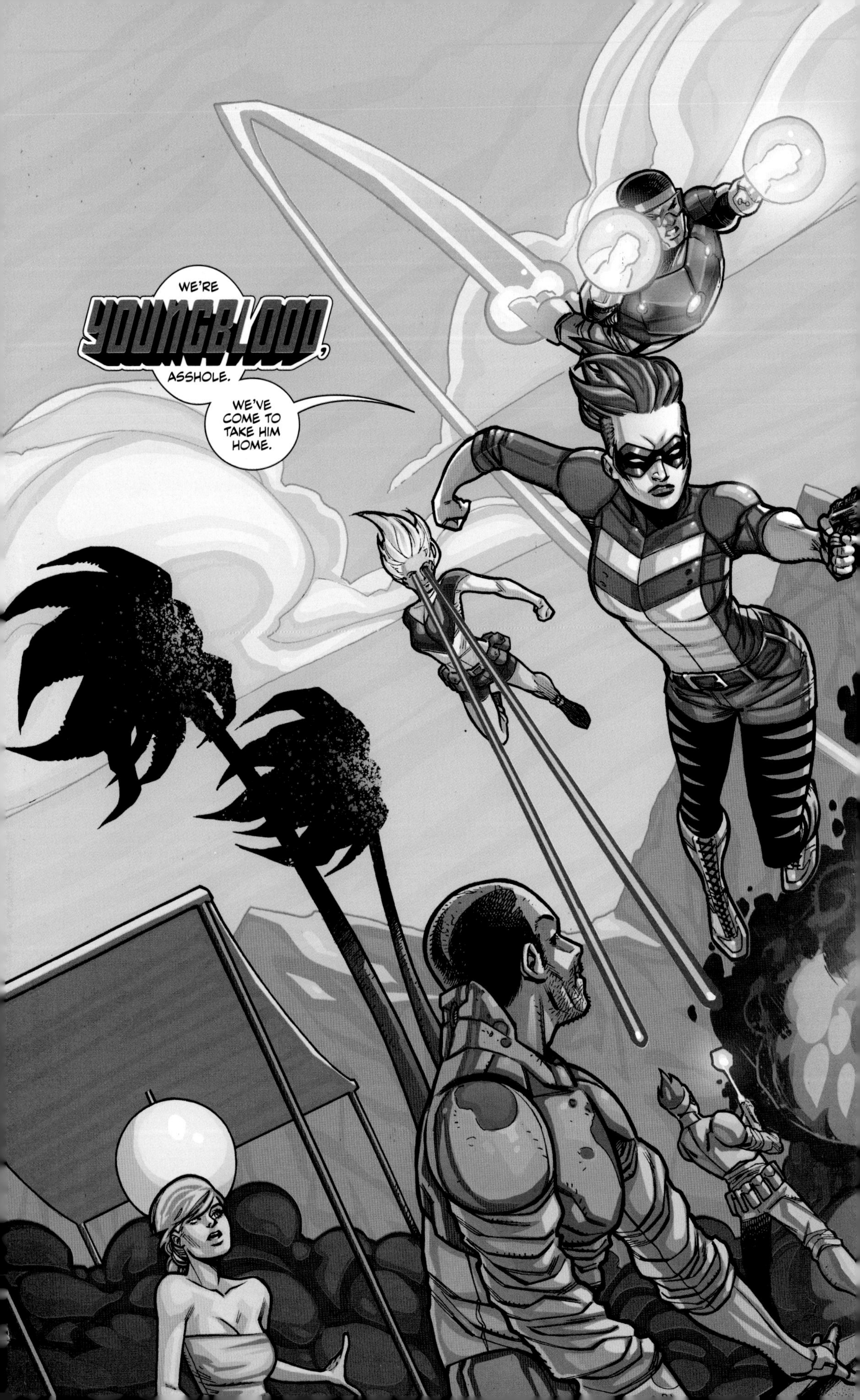
WE'RE
YOUNGBLOOD,
ASSHOLE.
WE'VE COME TO TAKE HIM HOME.

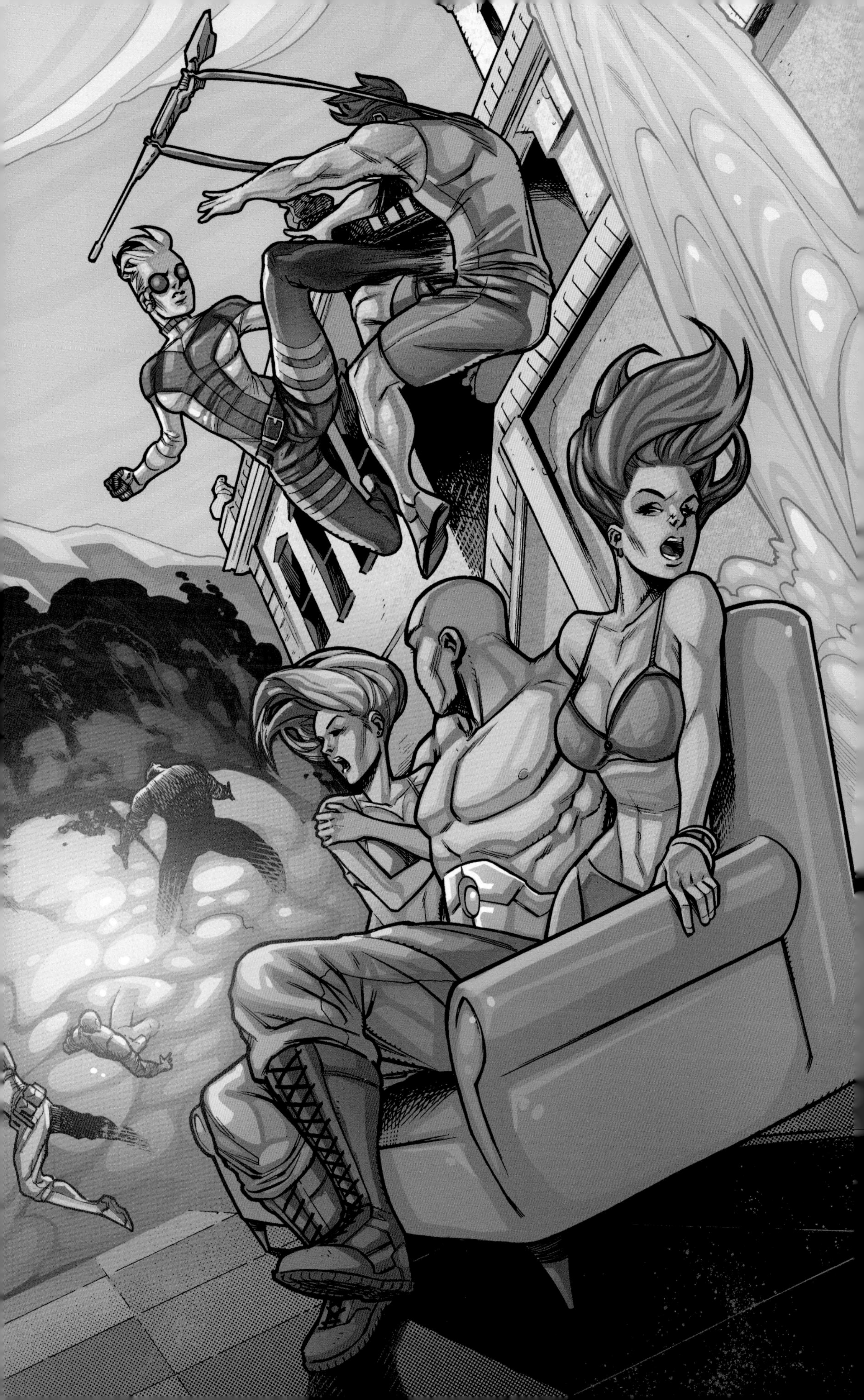

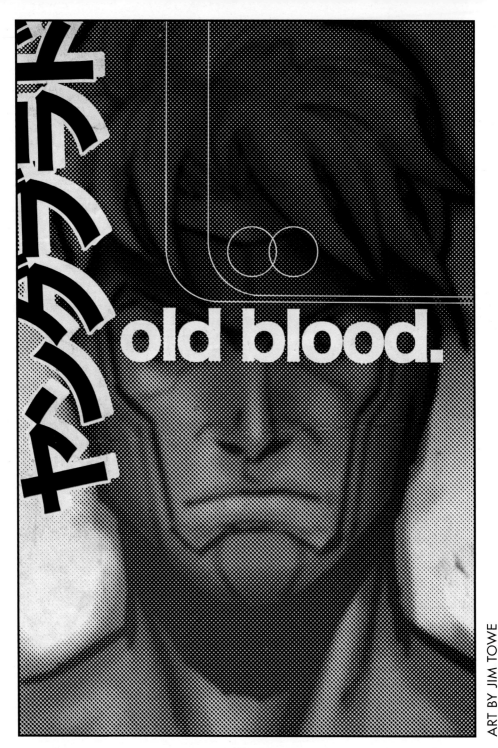

old blood.

ART BY JIM TOWE

IMAGE COMICS, INC. — Robert Kirkman: Chief Operating Officer / Erik Larsen: Chief Financial Officer / Todd McFarlane: President / Marc Silvestri: Chief Executive Officer / Jim Valentino: Vice President / Eric Stephenson: Publisher / Corey Murphy: Director of Sales / Jeff Boison: Director of Publishing Planning & Book Trade Sales / Chris Ross: Director of Digital Sales / Jeff Stang: Director of Specialty Sales / Kat Salazar: Director of PR & Marketing / Branwyn Bigglestone: Controller / Kali Dugan: Senior Accounting Manager / Sue Korpela: Accounting & HR Manager / Drew Gill: Art Director / Heather Doornink: Production Director / Leigh Thomas: Print Manager / Tricia Ramos: Traffic Manager / Briah Skelly: Publicist / Aly Hoffman: Events & Conventions Coordinator / Sasha Head: Sales & Marketing Production Designer / David Brothers: Branding Manager / Melissa Gifford: Content Manager / Drew Fitzgerald: Publicity Assistant / Vincent Kukua: Production Artist / Erika Schnatz: Production Artist / Ryan Brewer: Production Artist / Shanna Matuszak: Production Artist / Carey Hall: Production Artist / Esther Kim: Direct Market Sales Representative / Emilio Bautista: Digital Sales Representative / Leanna Caunter: Accounting Analyst / Chloe Ramos-Peterson: Library Market Sales Representative / Marla Eizik: Administrative Assistant — IMAGECOMICS.COM